BEHIND ENEMY LINES

Behind
Enemy Lines

An Advanced Guide to Spiritual Warfare

edited by

Charles H. Kraft
with Mark White

VINE
BOOKS

Servant Publications
Ann Arbor, Michigan

Vine Books is an imprint of Servant Publications especially designed to serve evangelical Christians.

Published by Servant Publications
P.O. Box 8617
Ann Arbor, Michigan 48107

Cover design by Patrick J. Powers

94 95 96 97 98 10 9 8 7 6 5 4 3 2 1

Printed in the United States of America
ISBN 0-89283-884-1

Library of Congress Cataloging-in-Publication Data

Behind enemy lines : an advanced guide to spiritual warfare
/ edited by Charles H. Kraft with Mark White.
    p.   cm.
   Includes bibliographical references and index.
   ISBN 0-89283-884-1 : $8.99
   1. Spiritual warfare.   I. Kraft, Charles H.
II. White, Mark H.
BV4509.5.B445   1994
235'.4—dc20   94-32956
                                        CIP

Contents

Introduction

As we Christians serve our Lord and Master in this world, we are living and working behind enemy lines. The New Testament indicates that in spite of Jesus' great victory, "the whole world is [still] under the rule of the evil one" (1 Jn 5:19, GNB) because it "has been handed over to [Satan]" (Lk 4:6, GNB). Consequently, we who follow Jesus find ourselves in constant conflict with this Evil One, the enemy of our God and his Son Jesus.

Most of the time it seems that we are in contention with the people of this world more than with unseen forces. This is not surprising, since the human beings around us have been blinded by our enemy (2 Cor 4:4) and recruited for the cause of the one Jesus calls "the god of this world" (Jn 14:30, GNB). These people, under satanic influence, hate and persecute us just as they did our King (Jn 15:18-21). With both visible and invisible forces arrayed against us, then, we need all the help we can get from God himself and from other believers. For we are engaged in a lifelong battle in Jesus' name, fighting both on the human level and "against the wicked spiritual forces in the heavenly world, the rulers, authorities, and cosmic powers of this dark age" (Eph 6:12, GNB).

This book is about what it means to be living and fighting behind enemy lines. The idea sprang out of discussions that followed the Lausanne II meetings in Manila in 1989. At those meetings, the three "tracks" (sets of workshops) that attracted the greatest amount of attention all had to do with spiritual warfare. This fact is especially significant since this was a congress sponsored by an evangelical, non-charismatic agency. Though Lausanne I (1974) had had no workshops on spiritual warfare, this topic had become one of such great concern to non-charismatic evangelicals that these workshops plus several other presentations were devoted to it.

Four of the following chapters were delivered in Manila as papers. The two chapters by Tom White (chapters six and eight) are a division of his very fine (and long) paper delivered on that occasion. My introductory chapter (chapter one) was also presented there, as was a much shorter version of Silvoso's case study (chapter eleven). To these I have added seven additional chapters, three of them completely new chapters by participants in that congress (chapters three, four, and five). These and the remaining chapters were specially written for this volume.

All of us who have written here come from conservative evangelical (non-charismatic) backgrounds. We have, therefore, both a strong commitment to and a deep grounding in the Scriptures. So we come to this subject cautiously. Though we feel we have discovered what for us is new biblical truth, we are unwilling to let this overbalance the foundational understandings we have lived with for most of our lives. We have, however, seen the power of God work in the ways we discuss here. So we are not about to return to the powerless evangelicalism of our earlier years.

We are not, however, in complete agreement at several points. We, along with the whole spiritual warfare "movement," are exploring, experimenting, and seeking to grow and mature in our understandings and practice. Each of us comes with our own background and experience. With our strong commitment to the authority of Scripture, then, we find common ground on nearly every issue where the Bible is explicit. Unfortunately, there are topics concerning which the Bible does not give us much guidance. In these areas, the reader will find a difference between certain of our authors, especially those who write on cosmic-level warfare.

A disturbing thing about all communication is that people do not ordinarily talk about what everyone assumes. In dealing with the Scriptures, written long ago by people who lived in cultures radically different from our own, we do not always have a clear understanding of what the authors assumed. For example, the Pauline epistles seldom allude to miraculous events such as the casting out of demons. Is this because they weren't happening? Or did Paul simply not refer to such events because they were commonplace or for some other reason not noteworthy? With regard to territorial spirits, then, both the Old Testament and extrabiblical sources seem to indicate that people believed in them. But we get virtually no help in trying to figure out biblically what to do about them. So, some of us are willing to experiment with approaches that seem reasonable but for which we have little, if any, biblical support. Others are not so daring.

We think we are gaining insight and growing in our experience. But major questions remain and are evident in several of the chapters of this book. For example, how much can we know about the organization of the satanic kingdom and of the good angels through whom God confronts it? Do or do we not go looking for demonic confrontation? Do we or do we not have biblical permission to confront high ranking territorial spirits? If so, who is to do it and how? Can we with confidence identify the demonic strongholds within a city (pornography, greed, prostitution, occult infestation), or are our attempts simply guessing games? And what do we do when the Bible is completely silent on many of these matters?

Be encouraged as you read to think long and hard about some of these issues. But don't expect easy answers. We attempt to be biblical, reasonable, and creative. But none of us claim to have all the answers (even when we seem most sure of ourselves). We would like to have these issues discussed and prayed over, however, and invite you to join us in seeking better answers and approaches than we now have.

THE CONTRIBUTORS

The chapters of this book are written by eight different authors. They are:

Ed Murphy (chapter three) earned his doctorate in Missiology at Fuller Seminary after serving as a missionary in Mexico. He is a vice-president of OC International (formerly Overseas Crusades) and has traveled worldwide, training and counseling on topics related to deliverance and spiritual warfare. He formerly taught at Biola University and now teaches at San Jose Christian College. He has recently published an extensive volume entitled *The Handbook for Spiritual Warfare* (Nelson, 1992).

C. Peter Wagner (chapter five) has been Professor of Church Growth in Fuller Seminary's School of World Mission since 1971, where he came after serving for sixteen years as a missionary in Bolivia. Since 1982 when he and I went through our "paradigm shift" together into believing and practicing healing, Peter has authored numerous very helpful books on prayer and spiritual warfare (see bibliography). In addition to his teaching and writing, he runs an organization dedicated to extending God's kingdom through prayer and spiritual warfare, Global Harvest. This organization coordinates the A.D. 2000 United Prayer Track.

Tom White (chapters six and eight) was converted out of an occult background and presently directs Frontline Ministries of Corvallis, Oregon, under which he travels extensively doing seminars and workshops dealing with spiritual warfare and deliverance. Tom has written two very helpful books, both published by Servant (see bibliography).

John Robb (chapter seven) directs the Unreached Peoples Program of World Vision International. John travels worldwide conducting seminars and doing research on the relationship between spiritual warfare and the reaching of peoples who have not yet heard or responded to the truth of Christ.

Mark White (chapter nine) is a student at Fuller Seminary who has recently discovered that he is gifted both in ministering to the spiritually oppressed and in editing. He has been my right-hand man in getting this volume together and has well earned the right to have his name on its title page of this and on a previous book of mine.

Lora Elizabeth (chapter ten) is a mother and housewife with a New Age past. Her contribution here is the marvelous story of how in response to prayer God was able to break through to her to bring her to himself.

Edgardo Silvoso (chapter eleven) was born and brought up in Argentina. After receiving a degree in Missiology from Fuller Seminary and being healed by God from a terminal illness, he has become prominent in strategizing what I am calling "warfare evangelism" in Argentina and around the world through his organization, Harvest Evangelism, based in San Jose, California. His first book, *That None Should Perish* (Regal, 1994), detailing his approach to evangelism, is expected to be published about the same time as this one is released.

Charles Kraft (chapters one, two, and four): My own background includes a term as a missionary in Nigeria, ten years of teaching in secular universities, and twenty-five years teaching anthropology, communication and, lately, spiritual warfare in the School of World Mission, Fuller Seminary. This is my fourth book in the spiritual warfare area.

THE ORGANIZATION OF THE BOOK

The book is organized into four parts. Part I contains foundational, perspective-building material. Chapter one starts as the Bible starts, with the recognition that there are two kingdoms, one the legitimate kingdom of God, the other that of the pretender, Satan. In chapter two, I try to point to some of the patterns we observe and experience.

Part II is made up of two chapters on what we call "ground-level" spiritual warfare. In the first of them, Ed Murphy alerts us to some of the pitfalls to watch out for in dealing with spiritual warfare at this level. The following chapter delineates the approach to deliverance from demons that my colleagues and I have been developing.

In part III we turn to what I call "cosmic-level" spiritual warfare (see below for a discussion of this terminology). Peter Wagner leads off the section by answering what he has found to be the most frequently asked questions concerning the conduct of spiritual warfare at this level. Next, in chapter six, Tom White raises and deals with the biblical issues relating to whether or not direct confrontation of higher level spiritual entities is valid. John Robb, in chapter seven, raises some of the same issues but goes on to illustrate from his worldwide experience the kinds of approaches that are effective. Then, in chapter eight, Tom White provides us with a three-year model for conducting an attack designed to rout cosmic-level satanic spirits.

Finally, in part IV we present three case studies, each of which embodies several of the facets of spiritual warfare discussed in the first eight chapters of the book. In chapter nine, Mark White tells the story of a deliverance that resulted in the conversion of the one delivered. This is ground-level warfare with an evangelistic outcome. Lora Elizabeth, in relating her own story in chapter ten, highlights the effectiveness of prayer in breaking through the blindness incurred by her allegiance to Satan. Then, in chapter eleven, Ed Silvoso discusses some of the insights gained from his experience in Argentina concerning how to do warfare evangelism on a city-wide basis.

A NOTE ON TERMINOLOGY

The term "ground-level spiritual warfare" is used here to refer to the strategies and activities we are to employ in resisting the activities of demons among and within human beings. Demons are Satan's foot soldiers, specializing in all aspects of assault on people, from the inside and from the outside. Such activity includes temptation to sin, demonic harassment, spiritual oppression, and demonization (demons dwelling in individuals).

You will note as you read that there are several ways of designating the levels of spiritual warfare above ground-level warfare. Sometimes it's referred to as "higher-level," sometimes as "cosmic-level." However, in a meeting of the Spiritual Warfare Network, to which most of our authors belong, it was objected that the term "cosmic" sounded too New Age-ish. We, therefore, looked for another term and some came up with the term "strategic-level" to label this higher level focus.

Though Peter Wagner, the most prolific writer in this area, has consistently used the term "strategic-level," I find it very unsatisfactory. The word "strategy" seems to me to be a broad term that involves the thinking through and planning of any course of action. I feel we should be able to talk of strategic ground-level activity as well as strategic higher-level activity and certainly of strategies that involve both levels.

However, since terminology is largely a matter of taste, the only important issue here is that the reader understand that when the terms cosmic-level and strategic-level are used here, they mean exactly the same thing.

Credits. I want to express my deepest gratitude to Mark H. White, who virtually coedited this book with me. I greatly appreciate his commitment both to the overall project and to the nitty-gritty of working over each chapter to adjust them to each other. Thanks also to Betsy Runkle-Edens who worked with some of the chapters in their very earliest stages.

I especially thank each of the authors for their contributions and their cooperation when they had to make adjustments in their personal schedules to meet the deadlines. Thanks also to Beth Feia, Ann Spangler, Dave Came, and the staff at Servant for the time and energy they have put into this project.

Finally, thanks to Meg, my wife, for sharing me with the computer, the telephone, and the UPS office for the sake of another contribution to the kingdom of God.

Translations. Rather than forcing a single Bible translation on the authors, we have allowed them to follow their own preferences. Thus, some of the Scripture quotations are from one version, some from another.

May God bless this volume to enable you, the reader, to contend more knowledgeably and effectively—behind enemy lines.

South Pasadena, California
July 1994

PART I

The Perspective

ONE

Two Kingdoms in Conflict

Charles H. Kraft

"'I will give you all this power and all this wealth,' the Devil told [Jesus]. 'It has been handed over to me, and I can give it to anyone I choose. All this will be yours, then, if you worship me'" (Lk 4:6-7, GNB). Knowing he was working "behind enemy lines," Jesus did not dispute the validity of this offer by his archenemy, Satan. Our enemy does not always lie. In this case he was using the sad truth that Jesus was operating in his territory to try to entice our Lord into submitting to him.

Jesus had indeed come to regain the authority over the universe that God had once given to humans. But this was not the way he would go about it. Jesus had come as the "second Adam" (1 Cor 15:47). And he remembered clearly the tragedy of the day the first Adam faced this same tempter and, through obeying him instead of God, gave over his rights to be in charge of the created universe (Gn 3).

Jesus would resist the temptation to take an easy route to regaining humanity's rights to the universe. Instead, he would do it God's way—through obedience to the Father. He would gain back those rights by entering the enemy's territory and defeating the powers of darkness on their own turf, atoning for human disobedience and crushing the principalities and powers under his feet. He would ascend by conquest, not by compromise. There are no shortcuts to spiritual dominion.

DOMINION BY DECEIT

God created the earth and created it well. When finished, he filled it with all kinds of living creatures. Last of all he formed his masterpiece, mankind. God's desire was not only to live in fellowship with his creatures, but that they, under him, would rule and reign over earth. "Have many children," he told them, "so that your descendants will live all over the earth and bring it under their control" (Gn 1:28, GNB).

There was only one thing he required of them as the condition of their authority—obedience. Meet this requirement and all would go well. Disobey and the result would be death (Gn 2:17). And this death, as we find out later, would involve both the breaking of the perfect fellowship with God for which we are made and the loss of authority over the creation.

But there came a tempter, a powerful and deceptive fallen archangel. Very skillfully, he questioned God's motives in requiring such specific obedience. "If you follow my advice and eat the fruit," he said, "you will be like God and know what is good and what is bad" (Gn 3:5, GNB).

So God's cherished creatures, his highest creation, the ones he walked with in the cool of the evening, broke the one rule God had made for them. They were tempted and disobeyed God. So they fell from their place of privilege and authority, and all creation fell with them.

What had been created very good now became cursed by God and dominated by the enemy. They now lived behind enemy lines. In their obedience they had had dominion, and every tree and plant that grew had been beneficial to them. But in a cursed and fallen world nothing would come easily.

They would only survive through hard, sweaty work. And even then the ground would produce weeds and thorns as abundantly as it once produced fruit. The world, the cosmos, and the created order all fell under a curse. Satan was free to roam the earth, corrupting God's creation, for humans had given him their authority over the universe.

It was this one act of disobedience that gave Satan the right to say to Jesus, "It has all been handed over to me" (Lk 4:6, GNB). In exchange for Jesus' obedience, Satan could legitimately offer to Jesus the power and authority he gained in the Garden.

FROM THEN ON CONFLICT

From the Fall on, we see in Scripture continuous conflict between the kingdom of Satan and the kingdom of God. This conflict takes place both on earth and in the heavenlies. Though the battles on earth are often obvious, only occasionally is the veil thrown back to allow us to see what is going on behind the scenes.

In the first two chapters of the Book of Job, we get to eavesdrop on a conversation between God and Satan. In it, God brags about his servant Job and Satan requests permission to test him. In response, God gives Satan permission to take away from Job all that he has except his life (Jb 1:12; 2:6). Job remains steadfast, though not without complaint. In the end, then, the victory is God's and Job is both vindicated and blessed by God with a tenfold return of what he lost.

In Daniel chapter ten we get another glimpse of the conflict between the two spiritual kingdoms. Daniel had apparently prayed and requested God's assistance. It took, however, a full three weeks for help to reach him because the angel sent by God was delayed by "the angel prince of the kingdom of Persia" (Dn 10:13, GNB). Not until the archangel Michael was sent to help was the first angel able to get through to Daniel.

A further glimpse of heavenly conflict occurs when Jesus announces that he "saw Satan fall like lightning from heaven" (Lk 10:18, GNB) in response to the authoritative ministry of Jesus' disciples. Later, we are told of Satan's desire to sift the disciples "as a farmer separates the wheat from the chaff" (Lk 22:31, GNB). But Jesus prayed for Peter that he would be strengthened in his faith and that, in turn, he would strengthen the rest.

Given these and other scriptural indications of spiritual conflict in the cosmos, we can assume that it continues to our day. As God's kingdom people, then, we live behind enemy lines and, whether we like it or not, are involved in the war in two ways. As those attacked by Satan, we ourselves are a battlefield. And as those commissioned to join with Jesus in taking territory from Satan, we are soldiers in Jesus' army.

SATAN'S KINGDOM

If Satan is "the evil god of this world" (2 Cor 4:4, GNB) and the "ruler of this world" (Jn 14:30, GNB) and if "the whole world is under the rule of the Evil One" (1 Jn 5:19, GNB), then we all live our lives in enemy territory. It is not, therefore, mere idle boasting when Satan claims that "all this power and all this wealth... has been handed over to me, and I can give it to anyone I choose" (Lk 4:5-6, GNB).

We live as aliens amid the forces of Satan's kingdom. No one, especially Christians, can avoid contact and conflict. But Satan's authority is both delegated and limited. Satan is not in ultimate control even of what he rules.

If, as most Bible students believe, the passage in Isaiah 14 is applied to Satan, we see that his desire was to "climb up to heaven and to place [his] throne above the highest stars. [He] thought [he] would sit like a king.... [He] said [he] would... be like the Almighty" (Is 14:13, 14, GNB).

Having been cast out of heaven for rivaling God, Satan attempted to be lord over the earth and lord of all mankind. Though he gained that position by deceit, he knew the promise that one day the Messiah would come and crush his head (Gn 3:15). For centuries he tried to destroy the righteous line of descendants through whom his great opponent would come. He tried desperately to destroy Jesus soon after his birth by inspiring Herod to slaughter all male children under three years old in Bethlehem (Mt 2:13-18).

After Jesus was empowered by receiving the Holy Spirit, he became an even greater threat to Satan's kingdom, and the battle was on in earnest. During the wilderness temptations, Satan sought to defeat Jesus by inducing him to bow down to him (Lk 4:1-13). In Gethsemane the enemy may well have attempted to kill him through his own anguish and the unfaithfulness of his disciples (Lk 22:39-46). Satan's big play, though, was made at the crucifixion, and he thought he had won at last. But on the third day the Father raised his Son and freed him "from the power of the spiritual rulers and authorities" (Col 2:15).

Thus thwarted in his ultimate aim, Satan seems to have purposed himself to ruin as much of God's creation as possible, and especially to destroy mankind. If Satan cannot attack God himself or ascend to his throne, his uncontrollable jealousy and hatred drive him to attack and destroy those on whom God has fixed his love.

Satan envies God and humans with their creative abilities that enable them to produce good things. For Satan is unable to create. He can only pervert and ruin things made by someone else. So in jealousy, envy, and hate born of frustration and pride, he goes about counterfeiting and destroying things produced by God and those made in God's image.

His kingdom appears to be well-organized and populated by a large number of fallen angels. In Ephesians 6:12 we read of several types of wicked spiritual forces inhabiting the heavenly world. Among them are "rulers, authorities, and cosmic powers" (Eph 6:12, GNB).

Though we don't know exactly how much authority and power Satan has, there is plenty of evidence that it is great. He seems to be on a long tether. Apparently he has been allowed to retain the authority and power he once had as an archangel. *He must, however, work within the limits set for him by God. For God's kingdom and Satan's kingdom are not equal kingdoms. Indeed, the only power Satan has to fight against God is that delegated to him by God. He is dependent on God even for the power to rebel and deceive.*

THE KINGDOM OF GOD IS AT HAND

Into this world controlled by the Evil One, God has planted his own kingdom. This kingdom of God was the constant theme of Jesus' ministry. He spoke of it, he demonstrated it, he illustrated it, and he commanded his disciples to put it first in their lives (Mt 6:33). After his resurrection, then, he turned the kingdom over to his followers to extend it to the ends of the earth under the guidance and power of the Holy Spirit. For this task he left them (and us) in the world, behind enemy lines as it were. And he armed us with his authority, and commanded us to take as much territory as possible for his kingdom before he returns.

This is a kingdom populated by those who are redeemed and thus freed to attempt to fulfill the mandate God gave to Adam—to obey and depend on him. Its basis is the conscious allegiance, faithfulness, and obedience to God for which humans were designed. Its characteristics are righteousness, truth, light, peace (well-being), joy, and the like.

The characteristics of God's kingdom are just the opposite of those that characterize Satan's. God brings freedom in place of the bondage imposed by the enemy (Lk 4:18-19), freedom in obedience to a loving God. Whether it is from spiritual, emotional, or physical problems, God seeks to bring freedom from satanic captivity. And each time a person comes to Christ and receives physical or emotional healing or is released from a demon's influence, territory is recaptured from Satan's kingdom and claimed for God's.

God's kingdom is even more good than Satan's is evil. It is even more truthful than Satan's is deceitful. It is a kingdom of light in place of the enemy's kingdom of darkness, a kingdom of well-being, of meaningfulness, of joyfulness, of fulfillment of what humans were intended to be.

GOD'S STRATEGY

There are three primary aspects to God's strategy to counter enemy schemes: God restricts, God protects, and God attacks.

1. God restricts the enemy by setting limits on his activity and his influence. Though Satan has great power, we know that "the Spirit who is in [us] is more powerful than the spirit in those who belong to the world" (1 Jn 4:4, GNB). In the discussion concerning Job, Satan pointed to the restrictions God had placed upon his activity when he said:

> "You have always protected him and his family and everything he owns. You bless everything he does, and you have given him enough cattle to fill the whole country. But now suppose you take away everything he has—he will curse you to your face!" Job 1:10-11, GNB

In response to Satan's complaint, God relaxed the restrictions so that everything Job had authority over—goods, family, and, eventually, even his health—was placed under Satan's power. God said, "All right, he is in your power, but you are not to kill him" (Jb 2:6, GNB).

In the New Testament, we find Jesus restricting the enemy when he demanded permission to "sift" the disciples (Lk 22:31). We also see God restricting and releasing Satan for various purposes throughout the Book of Revelation. It was only by God's permission that the enemy was allowed by God to inflict on the apostle Paul a "thorn in the flesh" (2 Cor 12:7-10).

If Satan were allowed to work unchecked, the result would be total destruction of the human race (Jn 10:10). But our merciful God does not allow this (Lam 3:22). Instead, whenever we are attacked by the enemy, God restrains and restricts him. Satan is only allowed what God permits.

2. God's restrictions on Satan's power result in our protection. God knows we are weak (Ps 103:4) and need protection from a multitude of harmful things we never know are there. Think of the many germs that don't make us sick or the many accidents that never quite happen to us. We are even protected from bearing the full consequences of many of our mistakes and bad judgments. It is God's protective activity that keeps such things from troubling and destroying us.

Why God doesn't protect people from more of the horrible things that go on, we don't know. Though a certain amount of protection is automatic, God has allowed both satanic beings and humans enough autonomy that they can hurt others. But we are assured that God "will not allow [us] to be tested beyond [our] power to remain firm; at the time [we] are put to the test, he will give [us] the strength to endure it, and so provide [us] with a way out" (1 Cor 10:13, GNB). We have a loving God who protects and cares for us as a shepherd protects and cares for his sheep (Jn 10:11-15). We are, however, instructed by Jesus to pray to the Father to "keep us safe from the Evil One" (Mt 6:13, GNB), suggesting that we gain more protection when we ask God for it.

3. On occasion, God's strategy is to attack. When he called Moses to go before Pharaoh, God went on the offensive; likewise, when Elijah was commanded to challenge the prophets of Baal. The coming of Jesus was, of course, God's most obvious and successful attack on Satan and his kingdom. We are told in 1 John 3:8 that "the Son of God appeared... to destroy what the Devil had done" (GNB). But Jesus did not launch his attack right away. During his early years, he did no miracles and apparently made little impression even on the people of his hometown. They were astounded when he began to teach with authority and to do mighty works (Mt 13:53-58).

The enemy must have been puzzled during this time, wondering when Jesus would make his move. That didn't happen, however, until Jesus received the empowerment of the Holy Spirit at his baptism (Lk 3:21-22). At that point, he aggressively challenged the kingdom of darkness, declaring war on Satan in the power of the Holy Spirit (Lk 4:14), healing, casting out demons, teaching concerning God's kingdom, and recruiting warriors to assist in the cause.

Each time Jesus healed a person or freed him or her from demons, he was attacking and taking territory from the Evil One. Even his teaching ministry was a part of his offensive against the enemy. When Satan connived to get him killed, then, thinking he had won the victory over Jesus, the Father took the offensive and raised Jesus victorious once and for all over the worst the enemy could throw at him.

THE HUMAN PART OF GOD'S STRATEGY

It is God's strategy for humans to play a major part in the defeat of Satan and his hosts. God chose to defeat the enemy in and through the Man, Christ Jesus. It was not in the form of deity that Jesus warred with Satan, it was as the second Adam, as a man.

Jesus limited himself to the empowerment he received from the Holy Spirit, accepting the same limitations as the rest of the human race. It was as a man that Jesus lived under the authority of the Father (Jn 5:30) in absolute allegiance, obedience, and dependence. He refused to do anything on his own (Jn 5:19), choosing to teach only what came from the Father (Jn 7:16, 46; 8:26-28, 38). He worked the Father's works (Jn 5:17), doing only what he saw the Father doing (Jn 5:19-20), demonstrating the Father through his deeds (Jn 10:37-38; 14:11), and in everything pleasing the Father (Jn 8:29). It was as a man that he declared his intention to release people from Satan in what has been called "the Nazareth Manifesto":

> The Spirit of the Lord is upon me, because he has chosen me to bring good news to the poor. He has sent me to proclaim liberty to the captives and recovery of sight to the blind, to set free the oppressed and announce that the time has come when the Lord will save his people.
>
> Luke 4:18-19, GNB

On earth, Jesus committed himself to training and equipping his followers to continue the war. He set an example that his disciples could follow, saying both "As the Father sent me, so I send you" (Jn 20:21, GNB) and "Whoever believes in Me will do what I do—yes, he will do even greater things" (Jn 14:12, GNB). And he gave his followers "power and authority to drive out all demons and to cure diseases" (Lk 9:1, GNB), and commanded them to teach their own followers "to obey everything I have commanded you" (Mt 28:20, GNB). At the very end of his ministry, Jesus told his disciples to wait in Jerusalem until they received the same gift of the Holy Spirit that had launched him on his ministry. (Compare Acts 1:4 with Luke 3:21-22.) Then they would be empowered to "be witnesses... to the ends of the earth" (Acts 1:8, GNB). And this is where we come in.

Our part in this war is first to receive the Holy Spirit's empowerment. Then we must imitate Jesus' obedience and intimate relationship with the Father. This enables us to follow his example in warfare against the kingdom of Satan. We are to put on the armor God makes available to us (Eph 6:10-18) and to fight in the power of the Holy Spirit "against the wicked spiritual forces in the heavenly world" (Eph 6:12, GNB).

We are not to run or to hide or to act as if there is no war going on. Whether or not we are carrying out our responsibility, our enemy, the devil, is continually active, roaming around "like a roaring lion, looking for someone to devour" (1 Pt 5:8, GNB). He does not stop his activity and we are not to stop or avoid the task God has given us.

One part of our activity is *defensive*. We are to claim the protection God offers us from the enemy's forces. Our armor is useless unless we put it on (see Eph 6:11-17). Defensively we can claim protection for ourselves, our families, and our property. We are given authority to defend people, places, and affairs from the attacks of the enemy by declaring in Jesus' name that they belong to God's kingdom. How to exercise such authority will be discussed in several of the following chapters.

Another part of our activity is *offensive*. We are to witness to the lost to rescue them from the Evil One and to bring them into "the glorious freedom of the children of God" (Rom 8:21, GNB). To be effective evangelists we must witness in God's power (Acts 1:8), not simply according to our own abilities. We must take authority over the places and circumstances in which we witness. It is amazing how freely the gospel can be shared when the place has been "cleaned out" of evil spirits beforehand by commanding them to leave in the name of Jesus Christ.

Bringing people to salvation is, however, only a part of the offensive activity to which we have been called as soldiers of God's kingdom. Even after salvation, many remain in considerable bondage to the Evil One in other areas of their lives. Jesus' victory is intended to bring them to freedom emotionally and physically, as well as spiritually.

Whether we are fighting to bring wholeness in physical, emotional, or spiritual areas, we are involved in the battle in which Jesus enlisted us—taking territory away from the Evil One. This fight is waged on several levels: individually, relationally, socially, organizationally, geographically, and perhaps in other transindividual areas.

Defeating Satan through ground-level warfare at the individual level is basic to the rest. To defeat the enemy in the relational area, then, there needs to be confession, forgiveness, and the development of mutual love and concern under the headship of God. This ordinarily takes place during seasons of prayer focused on getting right with God and with each other. Dealing with such relationship-destroyers as envy and competitiveness in a spirit of mutual commitment to God and to each other is usually important as well. The aims of such activities are to take from Satan the grip he has on a group, freeing that group to develop Christlike attitudes toward each other and to function organically as a truly Christian body.

Groups that have worked together to become as invulnerable as possible to the attacks of the enemy can, when so led by God, challenge the Evil One's control of geographical entities larger than rooms or buildings. In chapter eight, Tom White shows us both the possibilities for this kind of cosmic-level warfare and the dangers.

CONCLUSION

I will end my overview of the two kingdoms here. There is, of course, much more to say on this subject. Some of it is said in the chapters that follow. Much of it is said in other books and articles (see the bibliography). Much we have still to learn. I pray, however, that God will bless you and help you through reading this to take your proper place in his army to fight for his kingdom in whatever ways he leads you.

TWO

Spiritual Power: Principles and Observations

Charles H. Kraft

As Westerners, we have learned to assume what our society assumes concerning spiritual beings and powers. Our worldview assumptions barely allow a majority of our people to believe in God. Any other "spiritual beings and powers" are considered to be figments of overactive imaginations and therefore belong in the category of fairy tales or science fiction. It makes for nice stories if witches can wield supernatural power to hurt people but get bested by good fairies so that the hero can escape. But we all know that such beings and their exploits are not a part of the real world.

Influenced by this naturalistic worldview, even we Christians tend, whether consciously or unconsciously, to regard both biblical and contemporary miracle stories in the same way. Since most of us have not seen the kinds of supernatural things we read about in the Bible, we tend to think of such occurrences as things Jesus could do because he was God but mere humans like us cannot. To believe that the biblical characters who did spectacular things were just like us and that Jesus gave us power to do those same things (Lk 9:1; Jn 14:12) presses us beyond our limits.

Such conditioning is so deeply embedded that it is very hard for us to change our perspective. We still ask, "Who's to say that a given healing wasn't simply psychosomatic?" Or, "Why resort to a supernaturalistic explanation when there's a reasonably good naturalistic one?"

Meanwhile, some of us get to spend time in other parts of the world where even non-Christians seem to understand the spirit world more like biblical peoples did than like we do. "Do you believe in spirits?" I was asked soon after I arrived in Nigeria to serve as a missionary. I had been through seminary and, prior to that, had attended a Christian college. Since the age of twelve I had been a committed Bible student and a member of a solid, evangelical church. I knew that Jesus dealt with evil spirits in his day, but I had never encountered any myself and really didn't know how to answer the question.

I knew from my anthropological training that these people, like most of the peoples of the non-Western world, were quite focused on spiritual power. I also knew that cultural perceptions could be mistaken, both theirs and mine. But could it be that they knew more than I did in this area?

I knew we could trust the biblical accounts. But the experiences of biblical peoples seemed so different from my experiences in these areas that I doubted my ability to interpret accurately. I knew enough about the limitations of Western interpretations based on a skeptical, naturalistic worldview to not trust either mine or those of Western commentators. But could I go all the way with the perceptions of the Nigerian church leaders I was working with?

I never was able to solve these problems during my time in Nigeria in the late 1950s, but in the early 1980s God led me through a number of experiences that enabled me to make better sense of scriptural accounts of the interaction between God's power and that of the enemy. Reflection on my experiences in relation to the Scriptures and a good bit of reading has brought about major changes in my understandings and behavior with respect to the spiritual realm. Some of the fruit of these changes is apparent in chapter one above. Other fruit appears below.

SPIRITUAL PRINCIPLES AND OBSERVATIONS

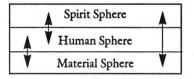

The Bible assumes power in spiritual, human, and material spheres. But in the Scriptures all three are closely interconnected (note the arrows on the diagram). The Bible does not support our Western tendency to compartmentalize reality. We dare not, therefore, assume three quite separate spheres or entities that have little relationship with each other.

We Westerners are, of course, really focused in on the material sphere and, to a lesser extent, on the human sphere. We have, however, been virtually blind to the influence of spiritual beings and power on human life in the material world. But, in spite of our Western blindness to spiritual reality, we are not the only beings in the universe. There are angelic beings who carry out God's plans (Heb 1:14). And there are others, evil spiritual beings who serve Satan, fighting against God and his purposes. The Scriptures are clear on this when they point out that we Christians "are not fighting against human beings but against the wicked spiritual forces in the heavenly world" (Eph 6:12, GNB).

The original hearers and readers of the Bible were quite

aware of the spiritual world and the beings that populate it. They were so conscious of the continuous interaction between spiritual beings and humans that the apostle Paul saw no need to elaborate on their activities. He simply notes that his hearers "are not unaware of [Satan's] schemes" (2 Cor 2:11, NIV). But, unfortunately, we twentieth-century Euro-Americans are, as a rule, quite ignorant both of the enemy's devices and of the principles governing the interactions between human and spiritual worlds. There is surely as much regularity there as there is in the interactions between human and material worlds. But, though Westerners have devoted centuries of research and study to ferreting out the principles that govern the material world and human interaction with it, we are centuries behind in our attempts to understand how the spiritual and the human worlds interact.

This chapter is a very preliminary attempt to figure out some of the principles of spirit world/human world interaction. Though dealing with all of the principles would be impossible even if we knew them, I will attempt here to list some of the things we think we have learned.

The overall assumption from which the following flows is that *God has built regularities into the ways in which the spiritual and human spheres interact.* Since science is the study of regularities, I conclude that a science can be built that focuses on this area. In such a science, theories can be advanced, tested, and modified by those who have gone beyond the "ABCs" in their thinking and experiencing of spiritual warfare. I welcome such interaction with the following principles and observations.

Here is a listing of the principles and observations discussed in the pages that follow:

Principle 1 *There are two dispensers of suprahuman spiritual power: God and Satan.*

Observations:

1.1 These "dispensers," God and Satan, are unequal.

1.2 Satan can gain permission from God to go beyond his limits.

1.3 Satan can hinder God's workings.

1.4 Angels, including Satan, are below humans in the created order.

1.5 Satan gained authority over creation from Adam.

1.6 There are spirit beings serving God and Satan.

1.7 Spirit beings are very active and influential in the human arena.

Principle 2 *There is a very close relationship between the spiritual and the human realms.*

Observations:

2.1 We must analyze cause at both levels.

2.2 The principles governing human-spirit world relationships seem to be essentially the same for both kingdoms.

2.3 Commitments entered into in one generation can be carried down to a person's descendants.

2.4 Rights given to spirit powers extend to property and territory.

Principle 3 *There are certain major differences between how God and Satan operate.*

Observations:

3.1 God works openly; Satan by deception.

3.2 God gives his followers freedom; Satan gives his followers captivity.

3.3 God inhabits his people with the Holy Spirit; Satan can only inhabit with an angel (demon).

3.4 Those committed to God adopt God's character; those committed to Satan adopt his character.

3.5 God can be trusted; Satan cannot.

3.6 God offers the genuine; Satan can only counterfeit.

Principle 4 *The obtaining and exercising of spiritual power and authority by humans flows from allegiance, relationship, and obedience to either God or Satan.*

Observations:

4.1 God and Satan can invest people, places, and things with power.

4.2 There are certain limitations to what God and Satan can do in the human realm related to the cooperation they receive from humans.

4.3 Through human allegiance and obedience, God and Satan gain greater rights than otherwise to work in human affairs.

4.4 Rituals such as sacrifice, worship, and prayer seem to especially enable God or Satan.

4.5 The spirit world works within the human world according to authority relationships.

4.6 Humans can be inhabited either by God's Spirit or by demons.

4.7 Both God and Satan are able to provide protection for their followers.

4.8 There is often a relationship between the amount of human support God or Satan has and his ability to attack the opposing kingdom and win.

4.9 Those related to God or Satan can use a variety of methods to transmit spiritual power.

4.10 People have the right to switch from one allegiance to the other.

Principle 5 *Cultural forms can be empowered.*
Observations:

   5.1 Material objects can be dedicated to spirit beings.

   5.2 Words used on the authority of God or Satan are empowered.

   5.3 Other non-material cultural forms can also be empowered.

   5.4 Buildings can be invested with spiritual power.

Principle 6 *Territories and organizations can be subject to spirit power.*
Observations:

   6.1 Cosmic-level spirits seem to exert what might be referred to as a "force field" influence over territories, buildings, and organizations, including nations.

   6.2 In order for spirit beings to have authority over territories and organizations, they must have legal rights.

   6.3 The rules for breaking the power of dedications over territories are parallel to those for breaking such power over individuals.

   6.4 Cosmic-level spirits seem to wield their authority over territories as defined by humans.

   6.5 There seems to be cosmic-level spirits that are in charge of organizations, institutions, and activities.

   6.6 There are rules that can be followed to launch attacks upon evil spirits assigned to territories and organizations.

Principle 1: There are two dispensers of suprahuman spiritual power: God and Satan. Though all power and authority in heaven and on earth come ultimately from God, Satan has his own kingdom and dispenses power within it. Satan seems to have been one of the highest, perhaps the highest, archangel before his rebellion (Is 14:12-15). As such, God would have delegated to him a large amount of power and authority. We observe that he still possesses great power and theorize that it is the same amount he was given before he rebelled.

Observation 1.1: The two dispensers of spiritual powers, God and Satan, are unequal. Christianity does not allow for a duality of equal powers, as do certain other philosophies and religions. Though we talk of two kingdoms headed by two kings, there is no chance that the satanic kingdom will emerge victorious overall—though Satan does win some battles. The power of God is infinitely greater than that of Satan. Furthermore, Satan has been miserably defeated at the cross and the grave. This defeat is indicated, according to Paul, by the fact that Satan and his followers have been "made a public spectacle" and led "as captives in [Jesus'] victory procession" (Col 2:15, GNB).

The power of Satan continues only as long as God allows it to continue and is only as great as God, working in terms of the rules he has built into the universe, allows it to be. Satan has no power that exists or functions apart from God's permission.

Observation 1.2: Satan can gain permission from God to go beyond his prescribed limits. We know from the Book of Job that Satan can request more authority and power and that, at least in that case, God responded to his request by giving him the right to afflict Job (Jb 1:9-12). Whatever power Satan had before this permission was granted, it did not extend to harming Job. After receiving permission, though, Satan had the power to destroy Job's possessions, kill his family, and eventually to harm his body—anything short of killing him (Jb 1:13-2:7).

Observation 1.3: Satan can hinder God's workings. In Daniel 10, we have the amazing story of the Lord answering Daniel's prayer immediately by sending an angel to deliver the answer. The angel was, however, blocked by a high-level demonic spirit called the "Prince of Persia." Michael, the archangel, was sent to the aid of the angel, enabling him to get through to deliver his message to Daniel. Though the struggle took three weeks, the angel, with Michael's help, prevailed (Dn 10:12-13). We don't know how often such hindering takes place, but I suspect it happens often. If God always got his way, as some theologies contend, everyone would be saved (2 Pt 3:9) and Jesus would not have instructed us to pray "may your Kingdom come; may your will be done on earth as it is in heaven" (Mt 6:10, GNB).

Observation 1.4: Angels, including Satan, are below humans in the created order. In Psalm 8:5 (properly translated by GNB) we read, "You made [humans] inferior only to yourself (*Elohim*)." It is clear from this verse and the characteristics of humans that we are second only to God himself in the universe. Only humans, no other beings in the universe, are in God's image. Only humans can reproduce others in God's image. Only humanity is adequate for God to unite with in Jesus. When Adam fell, however, humans descended to a place lower than Satan and his angels. Consequently, it is said of Jesus that he came to live "for a little while lower than the angels" (Heb 2:7, GNB). From this position Jesus as the second Adam (1 Cor 15:45-47) won back our right to be in second place again.

Observation 1.5: Satan gained authority over creation from Adam. In Luke 4:6, Satan offered to give Jesus all the power and wealth of the world, for, he said, "It has all been handed over to me, and I can give it to anyone I choose" (GNB). In the beginning, God gave Adam dominion over the earth and all that was in it. When Adam fell, however, that dominion passed to Satan. Though it has been won back by the second Adam, we have not yet seen that victory consummated.

Observation 1.6: There are spirit beings, arranged hierarchically, serving God and serving Satan. These beings have different ranks and, therefore, different powers and functions. They have names that relate to their ranks, such as archangels, princes (Dn 10:13), principalities (rulers), powers (authorities), rulers (cosmic powers) (Eph 6:12), and demons.

Among the characteristics of angels (whether God's or Satan's) is the fact that they simply take orders from their master. They are not creative like God and humans and cannot reproduce (Mt 22:30). Though they know the past, their knowledge of the future and of God's plans is limited (1 Pt 1:12). They are, however, very interested in what humans are doing (see Mt 24:36; Lk 15:10; 1 Tm 5:21).

Observation 1.7: It is clear from Scripture that spiritual beings are very active and influential in the human arena. The primary rule is that both God's and Satan's angels act on behalf of whichever master they serve. To do so, they need God's permission and, frequently, either a conscious or an unconscious invitation from human beings. For demons to live within a person, for example, they need a legal right granted by that person or someone in authority over that person.

Satan's angels are assigned to tempt, disrupt, harass, destroy, and kill (Jn 10:10). God's angels, on the other hand, are assigned to such things as protecting (Mt 18:10), perhaps governing (Rv 1-3), and conveying messages (Gn 22:11-12; Nm 22:31-35; Dn 10:13).

Principle 2: There is a very close relationship between the spiritual and the human realms. Throughout Scripture we see clear indication of this fact. When Adam sinned, his action affected his relationship with both the spirit realm and the earth. When Cain killed his brother, Abel's blood "[cried] out to [God] from the ground, like a voice calling for revenge" (Gn 4:10, GNB). Israel's wars were fought both at the human level and between Yahweh and the gods of Israel's enemies. And Israel won them whenever they obeyed Yahweh but lost whenever they disobeyed.

An example of this close relationship at the individual level is the fact that when King Saul gave in to human jealousy, he became demonized (1 Kgs 18:6-10). Dark angels are always ready and willing to take advantage of any opportunity to invade those who give them rights. At the national level, the story of the war between Israel and Moab recorded in 2 Kings 3 comes to mind. Israel was defeating Moab in spectacular fashion, even to the extent that they had driven the Moabite army back into their walled capital city. After an unsuccessful attempt by the king of Moab to escape with seven hundred swordsmen, "he took his oldest son, who was to succeed him as king, and offered him on the city wall as a sacrifice to the god of Moab" (2 Kgs 3:27, GNB). This act produced so much spiritual power against Israel that they were routed and "returned to their own country," without consulting God and exercising the superior spiritual power that their good relationship with him would have given them.

A different kind of example of this close relationship is seen in the names of the satanic princes mentioned in Daniel 10. Their authority was over Persia and Greece, human geographical entities. Whether on God's side or on Satan's, what humans do seems to affect what happens in the spirit world, and vice versa.

Observation 2.1: Any analysis of the cause of a given event in the human sphere needs to take account of both the human and spiritual dimensions. When negative things such as arguments, accidents, and wars are analyzed only on the human level, the analysis is incomplete. The same is true for good things that happen: revivals, healings, and healthy relationships. Though an understanding of the human motivations, decisions, and actions is crucial to analyzing the event, so is an understanding of the activities of spirit beings that relate to it. No analysis is complete that doesn't deal with both sets of factors.

Observation 2.2: The principles governing human-spirit world relationships seem to be essentially the same for both kingdoms. God has made rules for the interaction between spirit and human realms, rules that both he and Satan obey. These are largely based on allegiance and obedience. See Principle 4 for a detailing of how some of them work. There are, however, significant differences in the ways in which God and Satan carry out their interactions with humans. See Principle 3 for an elaboration of some of these.

Observation 2.3: A commitment, dedication, curse, or blessing entered into by a person in one generation can be carried down through generations to that person's descendants. On the satanic side, many people either in non-Christian religions or in occult organizations consciously dedicate themselves to false gods or spirits. Many others who belong to organizations such as Freemasonry or Scientology unconsciously commit themselves to the enemy. Satanic power that enters through such commitments or through cursing thus enters the family line and, if not broken, gets passed on to the following generations. In this way many children come into the world already demonized.

I have frequently found demons that claim to have been in a family for several generations, stemming from such commitments or curses. There is a mystical relationship between members of the same family that means that children participate in commitments made by their parents.

In God's kingdom, we see God keeping his commitments to Abraham for many generations even after Israel ceased to be faithful to God. In a specific case, we see the blessing of

God on David extending to Solomon and one after another of his descendants (1 Kgs 11:34-36), in spite of the fact that first Solomon, then many of his descendants were unfaithful to the Lord. In 2 Kings 8:19 we learn that "the Lord was not willing to destroy Judah, because he had promised his servant David that his descendants would always continue to rule." This they did until the fall of Jerusalem (2 Kgs 25). When God curses, then, as he did in the Garden of Eden, the effects also go on from generation to generation.

Observation 2.4: The rights given by people to spirit powers extend to their property and territory. When Adam sinned, he gave away his right to the land and its productivity (Gn 3:17-19). Satan could then claim ownership of the whole world (Lk 4:6). Pagan temples, the meeting places of false religions and cults, shrines, occult bookstores, and even the homes of those committed to Satan often show tangible evidence of the enemy's property rights. Those sensitive to spiritual things often feel the enemy's presence in such places.

On occasion I have been asked to spiritually "clean out" homes and rooms that have been dedicated to Satan or have come under his power due to people's sin and rebellion against God. A demon I once cast out of a woman claimed the right to inhabit her because she lived in a house in which a previous occupant had committed adultery. Only when we claimed her authority as the new owner of the property to break the power granted the demon by the previous owner were we able to cast him out. I have dealt with other demons who seemed to have rights to homes through occult activity, a death that occurred in the home and, on one occasion, a claim to a church through adultery that had been committed in the church.

On the positive side, when people serve God, their possessions are blessed and the houses and lands in which they live participate in that blessing. In 2 Chronicles 7:14, one of the blessings specified if God's people repent is that their land will be made prosperous again. God, of course, has rights to churches that are dedicated to him and used regularly in obedience to him.

Principle 3: There are certain major differences between how God and Satan operate. Having discussed some of the spiritual principles that govern similarities in the ways in which God and Satan operate, we need to recognize the differences. Note, however, that these are differences of operation *within* the same framework. The same principles apply to both, but they are used differently.

Observation 3.1: God works openly; Satan works by deception. God is a God of truth. Therefore, he presents his case to people in a straightforward manner, with love and concern. He doesn't attempt to mislead with promises he doesn't plan to keep. He offers such things as salvation (Jn 5:24), a place in his family (Jn 1:12), peace and rest (Mt 11:28), and carries through on his promises if we meet the conditions. But he also states honestly that following his way will result in disfavor with and persecution from nonbelievers (Jn 15:18-21).

Satan, on the other hand, usually gains allegiance through deceit. He ropes people in either through a promise, as with Eve (Gn 3:5), or through such devices as occult-oriented games, occult groups that mask as service groups (Freemasonry) or as religions (Mormonism, Islam, Buddhism), and the like. Though he can disguise himself as an angel of light (2 Cor 11:14), his real intention is to steal, kill, and destroy (Jn 10:10).

In dealing with demons, we frequently come across those who have appealed to a person's desire for greater power, comfort, or other blessings. They then usually provide these things for a little while, then go about destroying the person. In addition, one of the major ways in which demons exert their influence on people is through getting them to believe lies such as, "I'm no good," "I'm ugly," "Nobody could like me," "I'm too sinful for even God to accept me," and the like. The power the enemy has over people through such lies is incredible.

Observation 3.2: God gives his followers freedom; Satan gives his followers captivity. As Paul points out in Romans 6:16-18, 22, obedience to Satan is enslavement to sin, whereas obedience to God brings freedom from sin and, with it, eternal life (vs 22). Each spirit power can only give what he owns. Thus, Satan can only give the fruits of sin—such things as rebellion, deceit, anger, lust—perversions of potentially good qualities that God has built into humans. God, however, can give us freedom from such hindrances to becoming all we were created by him to be.

Observation 3.3: God inhabits his people with his Holy Spirit. The best Satan can do is to give his people an angel (demon). This is an incredible difference. Satan can only assign servant-level beings to indwell his people. And this would be true even if, on occasion, Satan himself inhabited a person. God gives us his very self. He comes into us with all the love, power, gifts, and fruits of the Holy Spirit. He puts his kingdom right inside of us (Lk 17:21) in the Person of the Holy Spirit, God himself. This gives us an incredible advantage over the servants of Satan.

Observation 3.4: Those committed to God adopt the character of God; those committed to Satan adopt his character. The character of the king goes with the kingdom. Those who commit themselves to God move into righteousness, peace, and love in the freedom of God's kingdom. Those who, either intentionally or by default, commit themselves to Satan's kingdom, move into the kind of pride, envy, deceit, and evil that characterize their leader.

Observation 3.5: God can be trusted; Satan cannot. The righteous, true, and honest character of God makes him trustworthy. The dishonest, deceitful character of Satan means that you cannot trust anything he says or does.

Observation 3.6: God offers the genuine; Satan can only counterfeit. Satan, by masquerading as one of God's angels (2 Cor 11:14), is able to counterfeit much of what only God can give. He can offer such things as happiness, comfort, and power, but always temporarily, with the aim of ensnaring, deceiving, and enslaving. Satan even has enough delegated power to do certain signs and wonders (remember Pharaoh's magicians). These are called lying signs and wonders (2 Thes 2:9-10). Only God can give genuine peace, joy, power, and the ability to do freeing signs and wonders.

Satan's whole kingdom is a counterfeit kingdom, buttressed by deceit in place of truth, the delegated power of a rebellious archangel in place of the power that comes from the true source, God himself, promises that he cannot keep, blessings that turn into curses, darkness in place of light, death in place of life.

Principle 4: The obtaining and exercising of spiritual power and authority by humans flows from allegiance, relationship, and obedience to either God or Satan. Spiritual empowerment in the human world can be granted either by God or by Satan. Jesus gave his disciples authority and power over all demons and diseases (Lk 9:1) while he was on earth. After his ascension, he sent the Holy Spirit to empower his followers (Acts 1:4-8) to do the works he did, and even more (Jn 14:12). Satan can also empower people to do miraculous things.

A basic requirement for humans to legitimately receive and exercise the authority and power of their leader is a relationship with that leader based on allegiance and obedience. Though the apostles regularly cast out demons in Jesus' name, the sons of Sceva attempted to exercise that same authority without the proper relationship to Jesus and were made to pay for it (Acts 19:13-16).

Observation 4.1: God and Satan can invest people, places, and things with power. Dedication and obedience to God or Satan give people delegated authority under the control of that power. With the Holy Spirit within us, Christians carry the authority and power of God himself. The amount of authority and power available to persons on Satan's side depends on the rank of the inhabiting demons. Higher ranking demons can give a person power to do signs and wonders, as with Elymas (Acts 13:8-10) and the demonized girl of Acts 16:16, even to move around out of body as in astral projection.

Places and things can be spiritually empowered through being dedicated to God or Satan or through frequent use in the service of that power. They can also be empowered through being blessed with the power of God or cursed with the power of Satan.

Scriptural illustrations of empowerment by God include the Ark of the Covenant (1 Sm 4-7), the Temple, Jesus' garment (Mt 9:20), and Paul's handkerchiefs and aprons (Acts 19:11-12). The power of Satan is invested in idols, cups, and tables of demons (1 Cor 10:21), even doctrines (1 Tm 4:1).

Observation 4.2: There are certain limitations to what God and Satan can do in the human realm related to the cooperation they receive from humans. Neither God nor Satan get his way all of the time. Satan's working is frequently frustrated by God's. But even God does not get his way all the time. For example, God does not want anyone to go to hell (2 Pt 3:9). But apparently many will. God desires for great things to be done in the areas of evangelism, healing, deliverance, and church planting. Much of it doesn't happen, however, because God's people do not cooperate adequately.

One of Satan's primary tactics to thwart God's plans is to get God's people to disobey him or to neglect their relationship with him. This the enemy does most effectively through either keeping people ignorant of what God desires (2 Cor 4:4), or by deceiving them into disobeying (Gn 3:1-7).

God, of course, frequently frustrates the enemy's plans through gaining the obedience of people who convert to Christ and serve him faithfully in ministry. I have encountered many frustrated demons whose major problem was that they could not get the persons in whom they lived to do their will because these persons were busy obeying God. Though the obedience to God did not succeed in getting rid of the demons, it did weaken them seriously and hinder them greatly in carrying out their plans.

Observation 4.3: Through human allegiance and obedience God and Satan gain greater rights than otherwise to work in human affairs. God or Satan gain rights they didn't have through the choices made by humans. When people obey one or the other, that one seems to gain more ability to do what he wants in the human context than was otherwise true. On God's side, obedience to his rules, including such things as committing ourselves to Christ, praying, worshiping, doing righteousness, loving others, confessing sin, and the like enable God to do what he seeks to do both within and through us. On the enemy side, disobeying God by sinning, not forgiving, hating, committing oneself to Satan, seeking help from him, worshiping him, doing unrighteousness, or the like enable Satan to do his work in and through us.

As long as Adam was obedient, God could work his will in Adam's life without hindrance. When Adam disobeyed God by obeying Satan, however, Satan gained the right to infect Adam and all his descendants with sin. He also was able to take dominion over the world that had been given to Adam (Lk 4:6).

The obedience of Noah enabled God to reach down into the human world and rescue a remnant at the time of the Flood. The obedience of Abraham enabled the Lord to raise up a people that would (hopefully) be faithful to him. Abraham had a choice between following the gods of his father or obeying the true God. On the basis of his choice to obey Yahweh followed by continual choices to obey (including the willingness to sacrifice Isaac), then, God could do great things through him. When Abraham's descendants obeyed, God was able to do mighty things through them. When they disobeyed (that is, obeyed Satan), however, God's plans were thwarted, at least at the time.

This principle affects God's and Satan's strategies. God's plan for the people to enter the Promised Land had to be revised when the people refused to obey him at Kadesh (Nm 13-14). On the enemy's side, it took some time for Satan to get a Pharaoh who would obey him by harassing Israel. When, however, a Pharaoh came to the throne who did not honor the agreement made with Joseph (Ex 1:8), he was able to get that king to carry out his plan. Through a family who were faithful to him, plus an Egyptian princess who disobeyed both Pharaoh and the gods of Egypt and unconsciously obeyed God, however, God was able to raise up and train Moses to rescue his people. A similar thing occurred shortly after Jesus' birth when Satan was able to get Herod to work with him to kill the boy babies in hopes of killing Jesus (Mt 2:16). Through listening to God and obeying him, however, Joseph and Mary were able to save Jesus (Mt 2:13-15).

When a person is tempted but refuses to go along with Satan, what the latter tries to accomplish does not happen. If a person is tempted by a demon to commit suicide but does not carry out the act, it cannot happen. A spirit cannot bring about suicide without the person's agreement. Likewise, when God seeks to enter a person's life, it won't happen until the person invites him to come in. When people don't obey God by praying and witnessing, people are lost, in spite of the fact that it is not God's will that any should be lost (2 Pt 3:9). When God's people obey by praying, repenting, and turning away from evil, God has promised to forgive and bring revival (2 Chr 7:14).

When a person is disobedient either to God or to Satan, the rights are weakened, though not necessarily broken. If a

Christian sins but obediently repents quickly, the relationship with God is maintained. When those who have committed themselves to Satan in occult organizations such as New Age or Freemasonry convert to Christ, their relationship to Satan is damaged but not broken. The demons they have let in while active in such organizations still live within them and exercise considerable influence. Complete freedom in Christ does not come until they are cast out.

On the positive side, the more the followers of God or Satan practice obedience, the closer their relationships to their masters grow. As Jesus said, "If you love me, you will obey my commands" (Jn 14:15), and, "If you obey my commands, you will remain in my love" (Jn 15:10). Obedience brings and maintains closeness.

Observation 4.4: Rituals such as sacrifice, worship, and prayer seem to especially enable God or Satan. When God is honored via such rituals, enemy forces have to stand back and cannot carry out their purposes. When Satan is honored in these same ways the forces of God may be pushed back. Again, obedience seems to be the key ingredient. When we obey God by praying, worshiping, fasting, living faithfully by his commands, and the like, he is enabled to do what he wants to do in and through us. The same seems to be true on the other side.

There seems to be a hierarchy of rituals, with blood sacrifice the most powerful. In Old Testament times, of course, the sacrificial system provided for this. The sacrifice of Jesus, then, being the most powerful of all sacrifices, has had cosmic consequences. The clearest scriptural example of the enemy's use of this principle is recorded in 2 Kings 3:21-27 (cited under Principle 3), where the King of Moab sacrificed his oldest son to his god on the city wall.

The importance and power of prayer need to be emphasized. Prayer is the most easily utilized ritual and the one most frequently practiced throughout Scripture. Jesus regularly prayed and commanded his followers to do the same. The most noticeable types of prayer in Jesus' ministry were what we may call "intimacy prayer" and "authority prayer." Jesus regularly spent time alone with the Father in his practice of intimacy. On the basis of the authority and empowerment received in those quiet moments, then, he was able to authoritatively teach, heal, and cast out demons. When Jesus chose his apostles, he commissioned them first for intimacy and then for authoritative ministry (Mk 3:14).

Observation 4.5: The spirit world works within the human world according to authority relationships. When, for example, a parent dedicates a child to God or Satan, that parent gives authority to his or her master to work in and through that child's life. Likewise, when adults put themselves under the authority of a demon, a cult leader, or a false religion, many of God's limitations on Satan's activities are removed.

The Scriptures point to the authority of a husband over his wife (Eph 5:23; 1 Tm 2:11-14), of parents over children (Eph 6:1-3; Col 3:20), of pastors and other leaders over the people in their churches (Eph 4:11-12; 1 Tm 3), of rulers over their people (1 Tm 2:2; Rom 13:1-2) and, I believe, of older people over younger ones. An additional authority seems to be implied in 1 Corinthians 7:14 of a believing parent to make the unbelieving spouse and their children acceptable to God. In dealing with demons, we have found that they take these authority relationships very seriously.

Those in authority over others need to be careful not to take their authority lightly. We see in Scripture that disobedience on the part of those in spiritual or civic authority over others affects the whole group over which they have authority (e.g., Israel's kings). In the case of Achan (Jos 7), the sin of one apparently not in leadership affected the relationship of the whole nation to the Lord. Many evangelical churches in our day are spiritually hindered by the fact that some of their leaders are under satanic authority through immorality or occult involvements with such practices as horoscopes, fortune-telling, Eastern mysticism, New Age, or Freemasonry.

Observation 4.6: Humans can be inhabited either by God's Spirit or by demons. God and Satan can indwell their followers. Though, as pointed out above in 3.3, there is a major difference between how God and Satan indwell, the fact that this principle exists needs to be noted. When people or those in authority over them invite either God or Satan to enter, they get what they ask for.

When Satan is invited in or people wallow in sinful attitudes or behavior, satanic beings are permitted to land (Prv 26:2). Obedience to God, repentance, and righteousness, however, bring cleansing to those committed to God so that with us, as with Jesus, the enemy can find nothing in us (Jn 14:30).

Observation 4.7: Both God and Satan are able to provide protection for their followers. Though the amounts of protection provided by God and Satan are not equal, nor are their motives the same, each shows concern to protect his interests. Satan blinds people to keep them from defecting (2 Cor 4:4). He also produces strongholds, arguments, and obstacles "raised against the knowledge of God" (2 Cor 10:4-5, GNB) as means of providing protection for his people.

God provides a certain amount of protection automatically to everyone. If he didn't protect, Satan would destroy all life. Though this protection is automatic, more seems to be available to those who ask or claim it. Unlike God, who protects for the good of his creatures, Satan's motives are selfish. He only protects as long as it serves his purposes to protect; then he destroys even those who have faithfully served him.

Superseding all claims to protection, however, seems to be the will of the one served. Job and Paul (2 Cor 12:7-9), for example, by God's choice had a certain amount of protection withdrawn from them. In the case of Gideon, however, God protected the whole nation of Israel until his death, even though he himself had become apostate (Jgs 8:28).

Observation 4.8: There is often a relationship between the amount of human support God or Satan has and his ability to attack the opposing kingdom and win. When there are large numbers of people obeying God, the Lord is in a position to order an attack with the possibility of winning. Under Joshua's leadership, the people of Israel in general, and their leaders in particular, usually listened for and followed God's orders, attacked, and won. Earlier in Israel's history, Moses gained great authority with God through his obedience. In spite of the fact that the people were not necessarily with him at first, he was used by God to attack and win. The prophets of Baal were defeated when God used Elijah in the authoritative position of the Prophet of Israel (1 Kgs 18).

On the satanic side, as long as the Pharaoh was favorable toward Israel, Satan could not get them. But when a Pharaoh came to power who gave out no favors to Israel (Ex 1:8), Satan could work with him to attack God's people. Likewise, when Satan had the cooperation of Herod, he could attempt to kill the baby Jesus (Mt 2:16). Later, when he had the cooperation of the Jewish and Roman leaders, he was successful in his attempt to kill Jesus as an adult (Mt 26-27).

With Moses and with Gideon, prior obedience set the stage and continuing obedience resulted in an effective attack. On the other hand, note what happened in the case of Joshua's army attempting to take the city of Ai (Jos 7). Through the disobedience of Achan the power of God was compromised and the battle to take Ai lost. When Israel obeyed, they were able to take the city (Jos 8:1-29).

Observation 4.9: Those related to God or Satan can use a variety of methods to transmit spiritual power. Spiritual power can be transmitted in a variety of ways. Some of the vehicles most frequently used are words (such as prayer, blessing, cursing, dedication), touch (such as laying on of hands, 2 Tm 1:6), being in sacred places (such as temples, churches, shrines), and possession of empowered objects (such as objects that have been dedicated, blessed, or cursed). God usually uses words to transmit his power to humans and empowers us to do the same.

Those working under the authority of God or Satan can bless or curse with the power of their leader. Through human words, spiritual power is thus transmitted. In addition, dedicated people, buildings, or objects can carry the power of the spirit being in whose name they were dedicated. The experience of the sons of Sceva in Acts 19:13-16 warns us, though, that those who attempt to transmit the power of God without the authority to do so are in danger. On the other hand, even the possessions of Paul, who had Jesus' authority, were effective in transmitting God's power (Acts 19:12).

Observation 4.10: People have the right to switch from one allegiance to the other. People who have pledged their allegiance to God or Satan have the authority to take it back and give it to the other. Those who have been dedicated to God (as in baptism) by people in authority over them can, by neglecting that commitment and living as members of Satan's kingdom, change their allegiance. God allows them to leave freely. Those dedicated by authority figures to Satan can change their allegiance, but usually then need help from others to get rid of the demons that have been working within them. Those who have themselves made a conscious commitment to Satan sometime during their lives usually need special, sometimes long-term help.

Though allegiance to Christ redeems us, reuniting our human spirits with God's Spirit, Satan can still interfere in the Christian's life under certain circumstances. When we sin, we give him permission to harm our fellowship with God until we repent. If we wallow in sin, we open ourselves up to demonization and usually need help to get free again. Much of the rest of this book details the specifics of breaking Satan's power.

Principle 5: Cultural forms can be empowered. In addition to the empowerment of humans, we have to deal with the empowerment of cultural forms such as words, material objects, places, and buildings. Blessings and curses, talismans and shrines, rituals and music all fit under this principle. The empowerment of words is basic to this whole section. Words usually serve as the vehicles through which other items are empowered.

Observation 5.1: Objects can be dedicated to spirit beings. In many societies it is customary for those who make implements used for worship, work, decoration, or other functions to dedicate them to their gods or spirits. Many groups of Christians dedicate articles used in worship, including sanctuary furnishings, anointing oil, the communion elements, and holy water. Once dedicated, such objects carry the power of God, as did the Ark of the Covenant and other sacred objects in Old Testament times.

As with the Ark (1 Sm 5) and cursed items retained by the Israelites in Joshua's day (Jos 7), empowered items in the hands of the other side can cause great disruption. Often it has been found that when missionaries or Christian travelers bring home objects from other societies and keep them in their homes, there is disruption by demons until the objects are either spiritually cleansed or gotten rid of. My colleague, C. Peter Wagner, had such disruption in his home several years ago until he got rid of a group of items he and his wife had brought back with them from Bolivia. Unknown to them, these items had been dedicated to evil spirits.

In the New Testament, objects such as Paul's handkerchiefs and aprons conveyed God's power for healing and deliverance (Acts 19:12). In ministry, we often (but not always) find blessed oil to be effective in healing (Jas 5:14) or lessening the power of demons. Some people have found it helpful to bless such things as water, salt, a cross, a Bible, or the communion elements and to use them for similar purposes. Lest we take a magical attitude toward such items, though, we need to recognize that the power is not in the object itself. The power comes from God and is merely conveyed through the blessed item.

Observation 5.2: Words used on the authority of God or Satan are empowered. Blessings and curses are ordinarily empowered by the one to whom the speaker is committed, with the exception noted below. Words used to dedicate, and for other purposes (such as sermonizing or witnessing), may also be empowered by God or Satan, whichever one the speaker serves. Christians can bless persons specifically with such things as peace and joy. We can also bless such things as cars, homes, offices, and other things with protection from enemy interference.

The exception is when a servant of God speaks words that serve Satan's purposes rather than God's. Negative words spoken against God's people or activities even by Christians can be empowered by Satan, since they are in obedience to his temptations. This means we have to be careful how we use our words. Through negative statements, for example, I find that many people have cursed themselves or those close to them.

Blessings and curses are the "property" of those who utter them. In Luke 9 and 10, Jesus sent his disciples out to witness, commanding them to bless a home first, then to retract the blessing if they were not welcomed there. The fact that the disciples had given the blessings meant that they could also retract them; the power of their own words was under their own authority. If, then, we have cursed ourselves, we can renounce such curses and be freed from them. These and other curses empowered by Satan can usually be broken fairly easily by the power of Jesus once they are discovered.

Observation 5.3: Other non-material cultural forms can also be empowered. Music is frequently empowered through dedication to either God or Satan. So are rituals, dances, and other worship activities. The blessing we feel in Christian worship is likely due to a combination of the pleasantness felt at the human level and the blessing of God flowing from the spiritual level.

There are musical groups active in America and Europe who openly dedicate their music to Satan, and probably some who do so unconsciously. Such music conveys satanic power to its devotees. Christian worship music may also be consciously or unconsciously blessed and is, I believe, effective in conveying God's power to those who listen to it. Blessed music played in our homes and cars is also effective in suppressing enemy activity and protecting against satanic attacks in those places.

Observation 5.4: Buildings can likewise be invested with spiritual power. Both Christians and non-Christians dedicate buildings to their divinities. Church buildings, homes, shrines, and other places can become spiritually "clean" by being dedicated to God. On the other hand, buildings can also be dedicated to Satan. They can also become satanically empowered through regular use for evil purposes such as prostitution, gambling, pornography, homosexual activity, financial swindling, abortions, and occult meetings. It has been my experience that Masonic lodges, pagan shrines, temples, occult bookstores, some establishments dealing with health food, environmental concerns and martial arts, abortion clinics, offices of occult and sin-enhancing organizations, and other buildings used for satanic purposes can be dangerous for Christians to enter without claiming God's protection.

I was once consulted by a mission leader concerning one of his colleagues who became disruptive during mission meetings. I asked this leader if he had spiritually cleansed the meeting place before each meeting. He had not, but started to do so after our conversation. The disruptive person's behavior changed dramatically when he was in that meeting place. Several teachers have told me they have found their students' behavior to change after they started blessing their classrooms.

Principle 6: Territories and organizations can be subject to spirit power. From references to high-level satanic spirits called the "Prince of Persia" and the "Prince of Greece" (Dn

10:13, 20), plus references to God's archangels, Michael and Gabriel, many of us conclude that some of God's and Satan's spirit beings serve on more of a cosmic level than others. These seem to be more powerful than ordinary angels and demons and to deal with groupings of people rather than individuals. We often refer to them as "territorial spirits," even though it is the people, not the land, within a territory that are their primary focus.

Observation 6.1: Cosmic-level spirits seem to exert what might be referred to as a "force field" influence over territories, buildings, and organizations, including nations. In Daniel 10, reference is made to high-level satanic princes who ruled over Persia and Greece. On God's side, each of the churches of Revelation 1–3 seems to have had an angel in charge.

Sinful activities and business such as prostitution, gambling, abortion, pornography, homosexuality, and occult bookstores are often clustered in certain sections of cities, suggesting that there might be ruling spirits in charge of those areas. Those involved in spying out the enemy's activities by mapping geographical areas to detect such activity speak of discernible patterns of this kind (see Wagner, *Breaking Strongholds* and Dawson, *Taking Our Cities for God*). Churches and other Christian organizations and their properties are perhaps superintended by God's angelic messengers in the same way.

Such "force field" influence also extends to individuals. As pointed out in 2 Corinthians 4:4, our enemy is able to keep the minds of unbelievers in the dark, blinding them to the truth. Indeed, the verse goes on to indicate that Satan is able to counter the force field activity of God, saying, "[Satan] keeps them from seeing the light shining on them, the light that comes from the Good News about the glory of Christ, who is the exact likeness of God" (1 Cor 4:5, GNB).

It is this blinding activity of the enemy that Ed Silvoso (see chapter eleven) and others are now learning to nullify through cosmic-level spiritual warfare, leading to impressive conversion and church growth statistics.

Observation 6.2: In order for spirit beings to have authority over territories and organizations, they must have legal rights. Such rights are given them through the allegiances, dedications, and behavior of the humans who now use and have used the territories and organizations in the past. Territories and organizations can be consciously dedicated to the kingdom of God or to the kingdom of Satan. They also seem to be dedicated by the purposes for which they are used, whether to God or Satan. Such dedications appear to continue from generation to generation until broken by the current authority figures. When a place or organization has been dedicated, that dedication can be weakened, sometimes broken, by subsequent opposite usage.

In Papua, New Guinea, I learned that a whole mission compound has been built on territory formerly used for tribal warfare. In an American community I was told that a church and a high school are built on an ancient Indian burial ground. In neither case does it appear that the power has been broken simply by opposite usage. Until the power given to the enemy over those territories by evil activities is broken by the power of God, Satan will continue to have great ability to interfere with God's activities in those places.

Observation 6.3: The rules for breaking the power of dedication over territories are parallel to those for breaking such power over individuals. The dedication to God or Satan of a territory can be weakened, sometimes broken, either through the opposite dedication or through usage for the opposite purpose. This is parallel to the way dedications or commitments of individuals can be broken.

With individuals committed to Satan, we need to look for and clean out the "garbage" that gives satanic spirits rights in the individual. For territories, it is crucial to find and break the power of commitments, dedications, curses, and sins that have been committed on the land, as well as agreements made consciously or unconsciously by those in authority over the land that gave legal rights to the enemy.

Examples of such territory would be cities known to have been dedicated by Freemasons (e.g., Washington, D.C., and several Argentine cities), places where blood has been shed unjustly (e.g., Wounded Knee, South Dakota), and sections of cities given to violence, prostitution, and homosexuality. Just as with individuals, being cleansed from sin is an important step in breaking the enemy's power and is crucial to the attainment of lasting freedom.

The power of the enemy over areas infected by sinful usage can be weakened, perhaps broken, through repentance on the part of those now in authority over them. We call this "identificational repentance." It consists of contemporary representatives of groups who sinned against other groups taking responsibility for the sins of their ancestors and repenting (preferably in public) to contemporary representatives of the groups wronged. Such ground-level human activity prepares the way for more aggressive offensives against evil powers.

Observation 6.4: Cosmic-level spirits seem to wield their authority over territories as defined by humans. The fact that the guardian angel over Persia (Dn 10:13, 20) and the one over Greece (Dn 10:21) are labeled by human territorial names would point in that direction. So would the impression gained by those who study and deal with territorial spirits that there are national spirits, regional spirits, spirits over cities, and spirits over sections of cities.

A missionary distributing tracts in a small border town along a street that divided Brazil from Uruguay found that people accepted the tracts on the Brazil side but refused them on the Uruguay side. Furthermore, some who had refused them on the Uruguay side received them gladly after they had crossed over to the Brazil side. The missionary's interpretation was that the prayer of Christians on the Brazil side was what made the difference. There was a difference in the enemy's ability to control the response of the people on either side of the human political border between these two countries.[1]

Observation 6.5: There seem to be cosmic-level spirits that are in charge of organizations, institutions, and activities. Probably there are cosmic-level spirits whose job it is to promote pornography, abortion, homosexuality, prostitution, and occult organizations.

In the kingdom of God we know of angels that are assigned to children (Mt 18:10) and to churches (Rv 1–3). Why not also to Christian activities such as missionary and other para-church organizations? Institutions such as churches, seminaries, and Bible schools probably all have high-level angelic spirits assigned to them. So, possibly, do social institutions such as marriages, governments, educational institutions, and the like.

Observation 6.6: There are rules that can be followed to launch attacks upon evil spirits assigned to territories and organizations. Both for servants of God attacking evil spiritual beings and for servants of Satan attacking God's kingdom, the most important weapon is prayer (especially intercession). Both God's and Satan's servants regularly attack through prayer, worship, and fasting, both as individuals and groups. God's servants need to add repentance, both individual and group, by people committed to God, to each other, and to battling the enemy through the use of such weapons. Those praying need to have rid themselves of as much internal "garbage" as possible so that the enemy can find nothing in them on which to get a grip (Jn 14:30).

In prayer, they need to give attention to breaking all historical and contemporary commitments, curses, and dedications holding the territory or organization in Satan's grip. They need to repent of any sins committed in that territory (see Observation 6.3 above). Next, in authoritative praying, they may speak to "the spiritual powers in space" (Eph 2:2), laying claim to the territory or organization in the name of Jesus.

Steve Nicholson, former pastor of Vineyard Christian Fellowship in Evanston, Illinois, did this in claiming a certain territory for his church. Over a period of time, in prayer, he proclaimed to the satanic spirits that he was taking a specified territory for God. After some time a powerful spirit appeared to him refusing to give him as much territory as he was claiming. At this, he again asserted his claim and succeeded in breaking the power of that spirit (a spirit of witchcraft). He saw his church double in size soon after.[2] See the chapters by John Robb (chapter seven) and Tom White (chapters six and eight) later in this volume for details on such an approach.

CONCLUSION

There is much that we don't know in the area I have tried to examine above. In attempting to discover the principles that govern the spiritual realm, we are probably about at the level where people were in their attempts to figure out physical laws a thousand years ago. Nevertheless, it is worth noting what we think we understand, if for no other reason than that others can react to it and advance our understandings by making additions and corrections. In the chapters that follow, the reader will see many if not all of these principles discussed and illustrated.

PART II

Spiritual Warfare: Ground-Level

~ ❋ ~

THREE

Spiritual Warfare Pitfalls

Ed Murphy

History cannot be interpreted accurately without being examined through the lens of spiritual warfare. Furthermore, the history and expansion as well as the failures of the Christian church cannot be understood apart from the battle with spiritual principalities and powers.

The entire biblical account is written in the context of spiritual warfare. From Genesis 3, where it all began for the human race, to Revelation 20, where it all ends even for Satan and his kingdom of evil, all of human history and all human-divine encounters have taken place in the context of spiritual warfare.[1] Spiritual warfare as I define it refers to both the believer's multidimensional war against personal sin, and to warfare with Satan and his fallen angels.[2]

TWO LEVELS OF SPIRITUAL WARFARE

Spiritual warfare is seen in this volume as consisting of two distinguishable but closely related levels: "ground-level" and "cosmic-level" (also called "strategic-level"). In this chapter of the book I will concentrate primarily on ground-level warfare.

On this level, we deal with most of the direct effects of demonic beings on humans, such as temptation to sin, demonic harassment, oppression, and demonization (demons inhabiting people). I will mention some of the conditions under which such demonic activity occurs and how the situation can be remedied. In this chapter, I will raise certain concerns, stated as pitfalls, related to this type of spiritual warfare.

Pitfall one: Not dealing adequately with sin. The sin problem has three major dimensions (diagrammed below). First of all, sin is *personal;* it comes from within as we engage in warfare with the flesh. Secondly, sin is *social;* it comes from without as we engage in warfare with the world around us. And thirdly, sin is *supernatural;* it comes from above as we engage in warfare with Satan's invisible cosmic kingdom of evil made up of Satan himself and all the demonic hierarchy under his command (Eph 6:10-20). I call this third area "evil supernaturalism." It is the main focus of ground-level spiritual warfare and of this chapter.

One of the greatest dangers and pitfalls in spiritual warfare teaching and counseling is the tendency to consider only one of these three sin areas to be the major cause of human sin while neglecting the other two. Since the Fall, all three work together in promoting human evil. In any particular case, one sin area may be the primary cause. That area would require special attention, but all three areas should be *carefully dealt with* in spiritual warfare counseling and deliverance ministry.

The televangelist scandals that rocked the Protestant Christian world in the late 1980s were certainly due as much to the sin of these highly visible Christian leaders loving "the world" and "the things in the world" (1 Jn 2:15, NAS) as to the lusts of the flesh. To adequately counsel and restore such persons they would have to be taught to crucify the flesh and the lusts that come from within. They would need to deal with the world's fourfold lust system: the lust for power, position, pleasure, and possessions (1 Jn 2:15-17).

But was it only the lusts of the flesh and the lusts of the world that led to their downfall, or did the devil and his demons have any part? Of course they did! That is why the first pitfall warns against failing to recognize the interaction between the personal, social, and supernatural aspects of sin. Our spiritual warfare ministry and counseling are too often ineffective because of our limited understanding of the complexity of human evil. Regardless of where the sin originated, from the flesh, the world, or evil supernaturalism, it must be dealt with on all three levels because all three are *always* involved.

Pitfall two: Inadequate pre-deliverance counseling. Failure to do adequate counseling before attempting deliverance (if deliverance is needed) is the second pitfall. The purpose of pre-deliverance counseling is to discover what is truly occurring in the counselee's life. If there is demonic activity, the purpose is to help the individual understand the "sin handles" to which demons have possibly attached themselves in the lives of their victims. While demonic powers can afflict anyone, including believers, they can only gain entrance through attachment to sin areas in a person's life. Hence the term "sin handles" is appropriate. Other teachers consider sin handles to be part of what they call "the grounds" in a person's life. The apostle Paul calls them "footholds" for the devil in the believer's life (Eph 4:27, PHILLIPS).

It does not matter how these "footholds" first originated. They may have originated in generational or familial sin (Ex 20:5; 34:6-7; Dt 5:5-10), willful sin on the part of the individual, or victimization by the sin of another person or persons. Such victimization can be physical, sexual, psychological, religious, or any combination of the four.

In generational or familial sin, satanic influence or control passes down through a family's line from one generation to the next. The enemy may have gained entrance into the family by one of several ways: 1) through dedication of one's self or family to an occult organization, a non-Christian religion, a god (which Paul calls a "no god" in Gal 4:7), or evil spirits; 2) through curses put on a family or its members (including self-curses); 3) through the commitment of a family head to sinful business (crime, prostitution, or pornography) or to an occult business (palmistry, New Age practices, conducting séances, reading tarot cards, ancestral veneration, or producing and selling occult literature); 4) through violence and bloodshed; 5) through abuse; or 6) through deceit of various kinds and similar sinful activities. Generational demonization will usually continue until someone in that family line finally takes responsibility for the ancestral sins, repents, and claims the cleansing blood of Christ to break the demonic power. After this occurs all curses can be broken, and the demons cast out. Such acceptance of responsibility for generational sin, repentance, and cleansing needs to precede deliverance.

We must *never forget* that people often come into bondage to sin as the result of becoming the victim of the sins of others. This can happen even if the person is too young to sin personally or to remember the abuse itself. Such reactions produce sins such as anger, rage, hatred (including self-hate), shame, rejection (including self-rejection), and even attempts at suicide. It can also lead to a myriad of sexual problems such as excessive masturbation, promiscuity, sexual addictions, and frigidity. Often victimized people are continually drawn into these types of sinful behavior without knowing the hidden causes of their bondage.

Only as such sin areas are recognized by the person and dealt with through confession, repentance, and forgiveness through the cleansing power of Christ can total freedom from demonic attachment truly occur.

Unfortunately, many who practice spiritual warfare ministry and deliverance counseling often fall short at this point. Too often the counselor or deliverance minister goes directly after the demons, battles them sometimes for hours until finally the demon's suffering becomes so extreme that it leaves or is "cast out" of the victim—but for how long?

If effective pre-deliverance counseling is short-circuited, the deliverance will usually only be temporary. If the sin handles still remain, the original demons can easily return or others like them can come (Mt 12:42-45). If the original demons are forbidden to return, there are millions of other "free-floating" demons like them ready to latch on to the still existing sin handles in the believer's life. Truly, "the last state of that man becomes worse than the first" (Mt 12:45, NAS).

Pitfall three: Inadequate post-deliverance counseling. The third pitfall in spiritual warfare ministry is the failure to do adequate post-deliverance counseling. Why is such counseling so important? I will briefly mention ten reasons.

1. Post-deliverance counseling over a course of time may be required to discover all of the sin handles that have allowed the demons to remain attached to the victim's life.

2. The newly delivered believer is only beginning to learn how to walk in full victory. Like the rest of us, he or she is still susceptible to demonic deceptions.

3. The newly delivered believer will be assaulted by the enemy who will attempt to regain control and even to extend his previous influence if the person does not guard against it. The person must be taught how to discern and overcome these counterattacks.

4. The newly delivered believer may have to return to live or work in a hostile environment or to a place where demonic forces are active.

5. The person may not be fully aware of the extent to which evil forces have attached themselves to his life through past sinful contact and/or that of other persons against him. This will be revealed by the Holy Spirit over a period of time and usually through ongoing counseling.

6. The person may need deep and painful humbling to break a prideful and rebellious spirit. Often it is not until a person has been freed from demonization that God is really able to fully deal with such character flaws (Jas 4:1-10).

7. Frequently, all the demons attached to the life of the victim are not exposed and expelled in the initial deliverance sessions. This may be true even when the gifting of the deliverance team was spectacular and the freeing power of the Holy Spirit very obvious in the early deliverance sessions.

8. The biblically prescribed manner of overcoming the adversary given in such key passages as Ephesians 6:10-20, James 4:1-8, 1 Peter 5:8-11, and Revelation 12:11 demands time to be learned and practiced in one's daily life.

9. Where extreme sexual abuse, physical harm, religious deception, or emotional damage have occurred, a victimized person will usually need ongoing spiritual and professional counseling and healing. Where necessary we must be willing to refer such counselees to professionals better skilled than ourselves in such delicate areas of counseling and emotional health.

10. Finally, deliverance is more of a process than a single crisis event, or even a series of crisis events. Newly delivered persons, like new believers, must be encouraged to identify with a support group of persons whom I call "James 5:16 prayer-share-healing partners." As they do so, ongoing deliverance will usually occur over a period of time. This serves to build their faith in the power of God operating in their *own* lives and in the lives of their James 5:16 partners.

When I do ongoing deliverance counseling I follow what I call a "45-10-45" spiritual warfare counseling ministry. Forty-five percent of my time is given to pre-deliverance counseling, 45 percent to post-deliverance counseling, and only about 10 percent of the time is needed for actual deliverance.

Pitfall four: Correct diagnosis. The fourth pitfall in spiritual warfare ministry is the problem of correct diagnosis. The most important question the counselor must ask God, himself, and his ministry team is, "What is truly occurring within the counselee's life?" How do we know if the problem is directly demonic? How do we know what aspects of the person's condition are biological, physiological, psychological, or the result of human tendencies and the world around us? At times the problem is a combination of physiological malfunctions (such as hormonal imbalances and/or brain malfunctions), emotional bruising, and the complications of mild to severe demonization.

The importance of correct diagnosis cannot be overestimated. Generally speaking, there are two extremes. One is trying to handle all serious human personality malfunctions exclusively through medication and/or counseling. If demonization exists, the demons, of course, delight in this approach because their presence remains undiscovered. Though the counselee may receive a certain amount of help with the emotional or physiological aspects of his problem, the demons remain, and total freedom eludes the client.

At the other extreme, people often try to cast out non-existent demons. This is the practice of many deliverance ministers who do not believe in the validity of any form of psychological counseling, or if they do, they are not able to recognize the difference between personality malfunctions that are physiological or psychological and those that are demonic. Some spiritual warfare counselors assume that all serious human personality and sin problems are directly demonic. The result is that they are actually trying to cast out not-existent demons, as in the case of a person suffering from personality disassociations such as multiple personality disorder (MPD).[3]

Either position does damage, sometimes great damage, to the counselee. As a spiritual warfare counselor, I need to be able to deal with both human and spirit causation. I need to learn to discern between that which is demonic and that which springs from the human level. Severe physiological and psychological malfunctions often take on some of the same symptoms and appearances that occur when demons are present. At the same time, demons can "mimic" symptoms, causing further potential for confusion on the part of the counselor. In most cases of serious personality malfunction it is not a case of either/or, but of both/and. The counselee's problems are often a combination of physiological and psychological damage that are dealt with not by deliverance, but through effective medical treatment or counseling or both. Demonic activity, though it can sometimes be partially and temporarily suppressed through counseling therapy, cannot thereby be eliminated. Both the victim and the counselor end up deceived.

In one case I tried for years to cast demons out of a very wonderful young Christian man. This young man had all the symptoms of schizophrenia. At that time, through the influence of well-meaning but erroneous Christian literature, I was taught that all schizophrenia was demonic. My presuppositions precluded the existence of such a brain dysfunction (especially for Christians).

In session after session, both I and other counselors whom I invited to help me minister to him tried to set this youth free from demonic activity. I must add that some of my helpers were internationally recognized deliverance ministers. Not one of us was capable of truly helping him through deliverance alone. The interesting thing is that demons were present. A very large number were expelled. The demons would leave through a combination of our prayers, the young victim's prayers, and the power and grace of God. But because his main problem was true biological schizophrenia, there was little or no change in his erratic behavior and lifestyle.

Finally, through renewed study and consultation with experienced Christian psychologists who knew the spirit world, I came to the conclusion that the young man suffered from the severe brain malfunction called schizophrenia. In time, we were able to encourage his family to take him to a trained psychiatrist who could put him on medication for his schizophrenia. The change was remarkable. In time he became almost normal.*

Demons are totally evil. They "love" to take advantage of debilitating human weaknesses. When people do not have full control over their brains or mental and emotional faculties, demons are sometimes able to secretly attach themselves to wounded areas of their lives. If the person goes off necessary medications, the condition can become worse even after the demons are expelled. They or other demons may again attach themselves to areas of the unguarded life. If, however, the person continues on useful medications and there is noticeable improvement, this may be because the primary cause of his problem was not spiritual but biological.

Pitfall five: Simplistic strategies to break demonic strongholds. The question of territorial spirits, that is, powerful high-level demonic personages who rule given geographical or socio-cultural groups of human beings (often called people groups), will be dealt with later in this volume. The fact that we treat these levels separately for analytic reasons should not

---

*I say "almost normal" because he is one of those individuals whose schizophrenia evidently until now cannot be totally controlled with even the most powerful medications. Also, the side effects of some of the medications are so debilitating to his life that while he goes through long periods of being almost normal, he will often go into phases of deep depression, especially if he goes off his medications. He is a very godly, Christian man. He loves the Lord with all his heart. It's possible that every time he slips back into a bad schizophrenic phase more demons come into his life.

lead us to neglect the influence of higher-level spirits as we work at ground-level.

In our day we are seeing certain high-visibility Christian leaders directing believers en masse to seek to identify and dethrone the principalities and powers who govern communities, cities, and even nations. That such powers exist is clear from the Old and New Testaments. The Jews understood that the gods of the pagan nations were territorial demonic majesties (Lv 17:19; Dt 18:9-14; Dn 9-10). The New Testament confirms this position (1 Cor 10:20-21; Acts 8; Eph 6:12; Rv 2-3; 9-20) but also warns of carelessness in reviling angelic majesties (Jude 8).

While it is not my purpose to deal with the pros and cons of this ministry, I believe this dimension of spiritual warfare presents grave dangers for believers who, without much experience in dealing with ground-level "worker" demons, are led to feel they are capable of challenging and dethroning ruling principalities who are the most powerful demonic forces in Satan's kingdom. As a result, many believers, even Christian leaders, are coming under unnecessarily severe demonic attack. Believers who have not even been through spiritual warfare boot camp, that is, trained in ground-level spiritual warfare, are certainly not ready to handle such an advanced dimension of encounter with the spirit world.

What is even more alarming is that some high-visibility teachers are giving the impression or even directly declaring that after one or two highly charged brief deliverance conferences, the ruling spirits over the city or area in question have been removed or dethroned perhaps once and for all.

The history of the expansion of Christianity reveals that this type of battle is not won in a few short conferences led by charismatic power persons. What happens when the power people leave the community? While they may have, in the words of one insightful sister, "beat up a bit" on the demonic strongholds, they have by no means dethroned them. And they have certainly not broken their complex deceptive hold over the community in question.

As we learn from the later chapters in this book, it is important to strategize our approach. I see the need for at least four steps in this process: 1) to neutralize and defeat these types of evil forces we need to start with a long-range, united intercessory ministry, accompanied by widespread repentance and the practice of a godly kingdom lifestyle by the believers of the area. Often it takes years of crying to God day and night for him to establish his kingdom; 2) next comes spiritual boot camp training, learning to put on and use spiritual weapons of God; 3) then they must join with other more experienced believers and learn what I will call limited warfare counseling and limited warfare praying; 4) then when the older, more mature warriors believe they are ready, they may move on to greater spiritual encounters and warfare praying (Eph 6:10-20) that directly challenge the territorial spirits.

Pitfall six: Overestimating Satan's power. The sixth major pitfall in spiritual warfare counseling is the potential of overestimating the power and authority of Satan and his kingdom. What follows is a summary of the biblical teaching on the absolute defeat of evil supernaturalism by the Lord Jesus. I will state each biblical truth with no commentary:

1. The Lord Jesus has already bound the strong man (Mt 12:22-29).
2. The Lord Jesus has already proclaimed release to the captives and recovery of sight to the blind and has set free the oppressed (Lk 4:14-19; Acts 10:38; Eph 4:8; 2 Cor 4:3-6).
3. God has already taken all of us as his children out of the kingdom of darkness and placed us exclusively in the kingdom of his Son (Col 1:12-14).
4. The Lord Jesus has rendered the devil powerless against his elect and has delivered all of his children from slavery to him (Heb 2:14-18).
5. The Lord Jesus has already totally destroyed the works of the devil in the lives of all the children of God (1 Jn 3:1-10a).

6. All this was accomplished in his redemptive event by the Lord Jesus on our behalf as the Representative Man, the Last Adam, and the Second Adam (Phil 2:5-11; 1 Cor 15:45-47; Heb 2:9-18).

7. God's Word declares Jesus' lordship over Satan and his kingdom (Mt 28:18; Mk 16:19; Eph 1:19-23; Phil 2:9-11; 1 Pt 3:22).

8. Jesus totally defeated the entire kingdom of evil supernaturalism on our behalf (Col 2:13-15).

9. God promises all obedient believers victory in spiritual warfare over Satan and his entire kingdom of evil (Rom 16:20; 2 Cor 2:11 cf. 10:3-5; Eph 2:6 cf. Col 2:8-15; Eph 3:10; 6:10-20; Jas 4:7-8; 1 Pt 5:8-11; 1 Jn 2:12-14; 5:18-19; Rv 12:11).

I have only dealt with half a dozen pitfalls of spiritual warfare. Dozens more could be mentioned. We are at war. The Captain of our salvation has delegated to us, his church, authority over "all the powers of the evil one" (Lk 10:17-19). Yet Satan and his demons, though defeated by the Lord on our behalf, are not dead. It is an "already but not yet" defeat. They remain active, deceiving the nations and the children of God when and wherever they are able. Thus we are commanded not to be "ignorant of Satan's schemes" (2 Cor 2:11, NAS).

Spiritual warfare is the very context in which we live and minister as God's sons and daughters—his soldiers. We would do well to master the Christian soldier's instruction manual given us in the Word of God. We would do well to know the schemes of the enemy so that he will not be able to take advantage of us.

Finally, we would do well to judge and evaluate all our spiritual warfare teaching and practice by the Word of God and the experience of the church. We must avoid nonbiblical and questionable methodology, critiquing all "prophetic pronouncements." Finally, we should be accountable to mature and godly men and women for all aspects of our spiritual warfare counseling and ministry. The goal of our ministry should be to present "every person mature—full grown, fully initiated, complete and perfect—in Christ, the Anointed One" (Col 1:28, AMPLIFIED).

FOUR

Dealing with Demonization

Charles H. Kraft

This chapter attempts to summarize insights the Lord has led me into over the last decade or so concerning how to regard and handle Satan's "ground-level" troops, the beings we usually refer to as demons. More detail on this topic is presented in two of my recent books, *Defeating Dark Angels* and *Deep Wounds, Deep Healing*, as well as in a number of the other books listed in the bibliography at the end of this volume.

THE BIBLE TAKES SATAN AND DEMONS VERY SERIOUSLY

As we have seen, our enemy and his forces are taken very seriously throughout Scripture. Throughout the Old Testament, we see an awareness that the evil kingdom is always lurking in the background and affecting what goes on in the human realm. But Satan is not omnipresent. He has to depend on his principalities, powers, rulers, and ground-level demons (dark angels) to carry out his plans. Whether in the Garden of Eden or in afflicting Job, whether in his activities during Israel's wars or in influencing the pagan nations, these messengers of evil have been the agents of Satan's working.

In the New Testament, it would have been ground-level demonic spirits that pushed those who killed the babies when Jesus was a child (Mt 2:16-18). Though Satan himself confronted Jesus in the wilderness (Lk 4:1-13), he was undoubtedly accompanied by a host of demonic spirits. Dark angels were especially active during Jesus' ministry. Indeed, we frequently see him exposing and casting them out. Satan must have assigned some of his choicest ground-level spirits to work with the Pharisees and the other Jewish leaders to build up the opposition to Jesus. Demonic beings were very active in many of the events recorded in the Book of Acts (e.g., Ananias and Sapphira, Acts 5:1-11; the demonized slave-girl, Acts 16:16-18) and in activities recorded throughout the epistles and Revelation (e.g., the table of demons, 1 Cor 10:21; blinding those who don't believe, 2 Cor 4:4; teachings of demons, 1 Tm 4:1; many of the activities throughout the Book of Revelation).

> For our struggle is not against flesh and blood, but against the rulers, against the authorities, against the powers of this dark world and against the spiritual forces of evil in the heavenly realms. Ephesians 6:12, NIV

In spite of this, neither Jesus nor the other New Testament personages seemed alarmed by the satanic kingdom or its activities. They didn't seem to be impressed by them at all. When confronted, they dealt with them matter-of-factly, knowing that God's kingdom and power are infinitely greater. But they took the satanic kingdom seriously. While they were never afraid of evil spirits, they certainly acknowledged their existence and used the power of the Holy Spirit to fight them.

Over and over again references to demons and Satan's king-dom appear in the Gospels. In the Gospel of Mark, for exam-ple, over half of Jesus' ministry is devoted to delivering the demonized.

The biblical writers never questioned the existence of demons or of the supernatural realm. Jesus' critics questioned where he got his power from (Lk 11:14-22), but, unlike those infected by contemporary Western worldviews, they never questioned that demons existed and that they indwelt and harmed people.

The Bible is clear that Satan has a powerful kingdom that Christians must reckon with at every turn. And we are living in the midst of it—in enemy territory. To understand demon-ization, it is critical that we understand Satan's kingdom and how it operates. In Paul's day, he could state, "We know what [Satan's] plans are" (2 Cor 2:11, GNB). In our day, we need to be taught. Learning as much as possible of the enemy's strategy will better equip us for battle.

OUR POWER AND AUTHORITY

One of the satanic realm's major tactics is to keep us from knowing the power and authority we have been given by our Lord. Satan and his kingdom are jealous of us. For we, not they, are in second place in the universe. Only we (not Satan or any other creature) are created in God's image. And, though both Satan and humans rebelled, only we have been redeemed from our rebellion. This makes our enemy anxious to do all he can to keep us from discovering who we really are. He, of course, doesn't want us to discover who God is. But *he is equally afraid we'll discover who we are*. He envies us the attention God showers on us and the position he gives us.

The enemy has a wide range of tactics to keep us from dis-covering our identity. For if we learn to enter into our inheritance, he's in trouble. He knows that *with the Holy Spirit within us we carry infinitely more power than he does.* The question is: Do we know who we are and how much God has endowed us with as we consider the battle he has called us into?

A friend of mine was chatting one day with a woman who had recently been converted to Christianity out of the occult. While serving Satan, she had the ability to "see" the amount of spiritual power different people carry with them. She stated that each non-Christian carries a certain amount of power, some more than others. But Christians carry an enormous amount. Indeed, she could spot a Christian immediately in any group or even at a great distance, by noting the amount of spiritual power he or she carried. This is due, she now knows, to the presence of the Holy Spirit in Christians.

She and the fellow members of her occult group, however, felt no threat from the vast majority of Christians, even though they well knew that Christians carried more power than they did. For the Christians usually had no idea what to do with the (Holy Spirit) power they carried. Though this Holy Spirit power provided them with a good bit of protection from evil power, they did not know how to use the Holy Spirit's power to go on the offensive in spiritual warfare.

When these occultists ran into Christians who did know how to use this power, they steered clear of them. Fortune tellers, occultic healers, and others working under the power of Satan discover, for example, that when there are Christians around, they cannot function smoothly. A missionary friend of mine once went into a Mexican cathedral where several traditional healers were functioning. He simply sat down and prayed against one of them. As he sat there praying, the woman looked up at him several times, then packed up her paraphernalia and left with her client. The missionary's prayer ruined her attempts to carry out her functions. *How different things would be for a lot of Christians if only we realized how much power we carry.*

The satanic kingdom wants us to fear it. When one realizes how little power that kingdom has when compared to the power of God, however, there should be very little fear left. We should respect Satan and demons. Never take them lightly. But most of what looks like power on their part is either deceit or bluff, or both. *They really have little more than the power given them by the person they are in.* If, then, that person's will is engaged against the demons, it is only a matter of time until the demons have to go. There may be a struggle at first, if the person's will is not yet on God's side. But as soon as God has the person's will, the tough part is over. And most people who come for deliverance prayer have already chosen to turn to God for help.

A study of the Gospels reveals that Jesus did two things: he spoke about the kingdom of God and demonstrated that it was already present on earth. As he states, the fact that he drove out demons "proves that the kingdom of God has already come to you" (Lk 11:20, GNB). Repeatedly, Jesus did things that made clear the fact that he operated in God-anointed spiritual authority. He came to defeat Satan both during his life and through the Cross and Resurrection. Time and time again in Scripture, we see him exercise his spiritual authority over the enemy. Over half of the Gospel of Mark is devoted to Jesus' demonstrations of this fact through healing and deliverance.

Jesus made it plain, however, that he didn't limit this authority to himself. During his earthly ministry, we see him conferring on his apostles (Lk 9) and the seventy-two (Lk 10) the "power and authority to drive out all demons and to cure diseases" (Lk 9:1, GNB). With this authority and power, then, they were to go about healing the sick and letting people know that "the kingdom of God has come near you" (Lk 10:9, GNB). Then he says to the disciples and to us, "As the Father sent me, so I send you" (Jn 20:21, GNB). It was Jesus' intent that his followers imitate his approach to witness, accompanying words with power (see Acts 1:8).

From Jesus' words in Matthew 28:20, then, we learn that he meant for his followers to teach their followers the things he had taught them. He states that they are to teach their followers "to *obey everything I have commanded you*" (GNB). That this teaching was to include how to operate in the authority of Jesus to perform signs and wonders seems clear from his promise in John 14:12 that "whoever has faith in me will do what I have been doing. He will do even greater things than these, because I am going to the Father" (NIV).

WHAT ARE DEMONS?

The fallen angels we call demons or evil spirits (I make no distinction between these terms) seem to be the "ground-level" troops, as opposed to the "cosmos-level" principalities, powers, and rulers of Ephesians 6:12. These are the ones we encounter most often during spiritual warfare. Scripture tells us that demons seek people to inhabit (Mt 12:43-45). They apparently envy us our bodies. They have different personalities, are destructive (Mk 9:17-29), and differ in power and wickedness (Mk 5:4; Mt 12:45).

Since Satan can only be in one place at a time, the other members of the hierarchy, including demons, carry out his schemes throughout the universe. In addition to their broader assignments, it is apparently the task of evil spirits to bother humans, especially Christians. Satan does not like anything that God likes. He, therefore, picks on God's favorite creatures—us. I believe he has at least one demon assigned to each person.

We can assume that they are especially interested in disrupting and, if possible, crippling anything or anyone that might be a threat to Satan's domination over the world. Therefore, they aim their guns at individuals, groups, and organizations of all kinds that in any way seek to serve God's purposes. They produce "strongholds" in people's minds (2 Cor 10:4) and, probably, in other places as well. They attack Christian ministries. They are agents of doctrinal aberrations (1 Tm 4:1). They affect health (Lk 13:11), perhaps affect weather (Lk 8:22-25), and even have "the power over death" (Heb 2:14), though they have no power except that allowed them by God.

Within the hierarchy, these evil beings, whatever their level, seem to respond only to those over them or to a greater Power. Therefore, they can only be released from whatever they are assigned to do by their supervisor or by a Power (i.e., God) greater than the one to which they are accountable.

Satanic beings are involved in every kind of disruptive activity in human life. They can hinder earthly activities, and even delay answers to prayer (Dn 10:13). They seem to have authority over places and territories (i.e., buildings, cities, temples). In addition, they appear to have authority over social groups (e.g., organizations, people groups) and influence sinful behavior such as homosexuality, drug addiction, lust, incest, rape, murder, and so forth.

HOW DEMONIZATION HAPPENS

In order for demons to live in a person, there need to be two conditions: First, they must discover an "entry point." This could be an outright invitation. Or it could be an emotional or spiritual weakness through which they can enter. Second, they must have a "legal right" to stay there, a right that accords with the principles of the spiritual universe (see chapter two). Both are provided in one or more of the following ways:

1. Demons can enter a person by invitation. *Conscious invitation* to demonization happens whenever there is deliberate involvement with or actual worship of gods or powers other than the true God. Few, if any, of those involved in satanism or witchcraft escape demonization since they consciously open themselves up to demonic invasion. Likewise, with those involved with such occult aspects of the New Age movement as seeking spirit guides and channeling. Other occult involvements that usually result in demonization include organizations such as Freemasonry and Christian Science. Attending séances, going to fortune-tellers, being involved in "table tilting" and levitation are also dangerous. Even more innocent-looking activities such as playing with occult-oriented games and using tarot cards put a person in great danger.

We classify such activities as *conscious* invitations in spite of the fact that persons in our society, given our worldview blindness to spirit world activities, often do not actually know that they are inviting demons in. Few involved in Freemasonry know, for example, the risk in which they are putting themselves and their families. Yet the decision to get involved in any of these activities would have been a conscious one, just as a decision to defy the law of gravity would be a conscious decision, whether or not one knew the law.

Unconscious invitation is more subtle than conscious invitation of demons. This type of invitation frequently happens when a person "wallows" in some negative attitude derived from a difficult past experience. For example, when people are physically or emotionally mistreated it is normal for them to react by getting angry. When, as a response to such victimization, however, this anger is clung to, resulting in permanent resentment, bitterness, and unforgiveness, a weakness is created that can give demons the opportunity to enter. Such attitudes create what I call emotional or spiritual "garbage" that demons can feed on.

Demons gain a legal right to inhabit people when they do not get rid of such normal reactions as anger. The anger itself is not a sin, for we read in Ephesians 4:26, "*If* you become angry..." (GNB). The implication is clearly that we will become angry. But when that happens, we are told to "not let your anger lead you into sin, and do not stay angry all day," so that we "don't give the Devil a chance" (Eph 4:27, GNB).

Wallowing in unforgiveness or other unconfessed sin (e.g., sexual sins, misuse of power) is a very common form of unconscious invitation to demons to enter. So is repeated giving in to potentially addictive behavior (e.g., pornography, alcohol, drugs, lustful thoughts, envy, worry, fear, self-hate). Demonized people are often holding on to one or more of such things and refusing to confess and deal with them as sins. Such behavior weakens one's spiritual defenses, providing what John Wimber has pictured as "a runway with lights showing the way for demons to enter."

To avoid such danger, we are to deal both with obvious sins and with any suspicious attitudes and behavior. We are responsible to God to work with him on the "garbage" in us, the works of our human nature. Such works as those listed in Galatians 5:19-21 cannot be cast out as if they were evil spirits.

Demons actively encourage all of these things and frequently find entrance through the weakening effect of increasing sinfulness. Scripture is clear that whether or not there is demonization, sins must be dealt with by repentance and self-discipline. And no demonization was suggested for some of the greatest sinners referred to in Scripture (e.g., the adulteresses of John 8 and Luke 7 or the sinful Corinthians of 1 Corinthians 5–6). Demons cannot enter simply because people commit sin. They can, however, enter if a person chooses *not* to repent but to continue in the sinful behavior or attitude.

2. Demons can enter a person through the invitation of someone in authority over the person. A woman I know who was brought up in a satanist family was dedicated by her mother to Satan. At that point one or more demons entered the girl, having been invited in by one in authority over her. Such dedication of children to spirits or gods is a common practice worldwide.

Adults who submit to the authority of others in cults can become demonized through dedication or satanically empowered "blessings" uttered by those in authority over them. Parents can demonize their children through cursing (see below). Cursing can also result in demonization of wives by husbands and vice versa.

3. A third source of demonization is through inheritance. I cannot understand why God allows this, but children may be born demonized (see Exs 20:5). We often refer to this condition as the passing on of *generational or "bloodline" spirits/power.*

Typically, family spirits have gained entrance through some commitment made by an ancestor or some curse put on an ancestor. I have frequently found inherited spirits in people whose parents or grandparents, or both, were involved in witchcraft or occult organizations such as Satanism, Freemasonry, Mormonism, Christian Science, and the like. Such generational spirits tend to cause similar emotional problems, sins, illnesses, or compulsions from generation to generation in the family. Generational demons are often (though not always) present if we see in several generations of a family such problems as alcoholism, depression, sexual perversion, hypercriticism, extreme fearfulness, cancer, diabetes, or almost any other emotional or physical problem or besetting sin.

4. A fourth way in which demons may enter is through cursing. We have mentioned cursing several times above. It is a very common phenomenon and I have frequently found a curse to be a major factor in the power a demon has attained over a person. Curses are often the result of hateful words aimed at a person. Sometimes, though, the curse is more formal, involving a ritual by someone practicing witchcraft.

But *cursing does not always result in demonization.* Indeed, demonization that occurs solely as the result of cursing is probably rare. Cursing and its siblings—oath making, the casting of spells, hexes, and the like–are more likely to bring about demonization when combined with other things than by themselves.

Some of the weaknesses, sins, or giving of authority spoken of in the above paragraphs would probably also need to be there for a curse to have the effect of enabling a demon to enter. As pointed out in Proverbs 26:2, without something in a person to "hook on to," a curse is like a bird that flutters around but can't find a place to land. Curses that do "land" probably carry demons with them. A prominent Jewish Christian leader once described for me the total newness that came into his life when he was delivered from a demon hooked to the curse the Jewish people put on themselves at the time of Jesus' crucifixion: "Let the responsibility for his death fall on us and on our children!" (Mt 27:25, GNB).

CAN DEMONS LIVE IN CHRISTIANS?

There has been considerable discussion as to whether or not Christians can have demons living within them. Much of the problem stems from two sources: the term "demon possession" and the lack of experience within the Christian community in delivering people from demons.

The use of the term "demon possession" complicates things greatly. This is the unfortunate rendering given by many translations of the two most frequently used Greek terms, each of which means no more than "have a demon." This rendering should be abandoned since it has absolutely *no* support in the Greek and it greatly overstates the influence wielded by the vast majority of demons. Most of us working in deliverance prefer the term "demonized" to refer to one or more demons living inside a person.

The lack of experience in dealing with demonization within our churches leads to the idealistic belief that Christians cannot be demonized. Though all of us wish that Christians were impervious to demonic inhabitation, experience contradicts such a belief. All of us who work in deliverance frequently have to cast demons out of Christians. C. Fred Dickason, whose book *Demon Possession and the Christian* (1987) treats the subject exhaustively, speaks for all of us when he states that

> I have encountered from 1974 to 1987 at least 400 cases of those who were genuine Christians who were also demonized....I would not claim infallible judgment, but I know the marks of a Christian and the marks of a demonized person. I might have been wrong in a case or so, but I cannot conceive that I would be wrong in more than 400 cases.[1]

With over three hundred such cases in my own experience, over four hundred in Dickason's experience to 1987, and the concurrence of every expert I know of who has actually worked with demonized people,[2] the evidence that Christians can be (and frequently are) demonized is so conclusive that we can be dogmatic about asserting it. So, as Dickason states,

> The burden of proof lies with those who deny that Christians can be demonized. They must adduce clinical evidence that clearly eliminates any possibility in any case, past or present, that a believer can have a demon.... We must note that those who deny that Christians can be demonized generally are those who have not had counseling experience with the demonized. Their stance is largely theoretical.[3]

One significant fact, often missed by those who write on demonization, is,

> Demons cannot indwell a Christian in the same sense that the Holy Spirit indwells. God's Spirit enters a believer at salvation, permanently, never to leave (Jn 14:16). A demon, by contrast, enters as a squatter and an intruder, and is sub-

ject to momentary eviction. A demon never rightfully or permanently indwells a saint, as the Holy Spirit does.[4]

The way the Holy Spirit enters is, I believe, by uniting with the spirit, the "heart" or innermost being of a person who gives him or herself to God. I have tested this scores of times by commanding the demons (under the power of the Holy Spirit, who forces them to tell the truth) to tell me if they live in the person's spirit. They consistently reply something like, "No, I can't get in there. Jesus lives there." Then, when they are commanded to tell when they had to leave the Christian's spirit, they give the date of the person's conversion.

I conclude, therefore, that demons cannot live in that innermost part of a Christian, the spirit, since it is filled with the Holy Spirit (see Rom 8:16). That part of us becomes alive with the life of Christ and is inviolable by the representatives of the enemy. *Demons can, however, live in a Christian's mind, emotions, body, and will.* We regularly have to evict them from those parts of Christians. I suspect that one reason a demon can have greater control of an unbeliever is because it can invade even the person's spirit.

THE KINDS OF THINGS DEMONS DO

Demons encourage several kinds of activity. They prefer to do these things from inside of people if possible, since they can do more damage that way. If they cannot get in, however, they work from outside as best they can, attempting to do the same sorts of things. If possible, they try to fool people into believing they are inside.

1. A major activity of demons is to disrupt. Though they cannot create problems out of nothing, they can work on things that already exist. They push, prod, tempt, and entice people to make bad or at least unwise decisions. They work to make bad things worse and to get people to overdo good things so that they are no longer positive. If God was not actively protecting us (Christians and non-Christians alike), the kinds and extent of accidents, disruption of relationships, physical, mental, and sexual abuse, and all other kinds of disruption we would experience defies imagination.

Christians are special targets of the enemy. A psychologist friend of mine discovered this fact right from a demon's mouth. Her session with a demonized Christian lady was being observed by a non-Christian psychologist who asked the demon why he lived in the Christian lady rather than in him, the non-Christian. The reply (through the woman's voice) was, "You are of no interest to me. You already belong to the Evil One.... Evil is within you—deeply rooted." The demon even gave the names of four of the demons living within the man. But, pointing (with the lady's hand) to the demonized Christian and two other Christian women, the demon said, "I'm interested... in possessing *her and her and her.*" Earlier the demon had said, "I am interested in destroying, in tormenting her so she doesn't pray, doesn't seek God, so that she will fall away from him and be like the rest of them."[5]

2. We can assume that demons are the primary agents of temptation. They do Satan's bidding at his command (e.g., Gn 3:1-7; the Book of Job; Mt 16:22-23; 26:69-75; Acts 5:3; etc).

They can, apparently, put thoughts in people's minds, though we are responsible for what we do with those thoughts. Since demons know what each of us is susceptible to, they will tailor-make the particular thoughts they put in any given person's mind so they will be appropriate for that person. For example, demons seldom tempt a person in sexual areas who is not already vulnerable in those areas. Nor are they likely to tempt a nonreligious person to go overboard in the religious area, or one unconcerned about money to become a miser.

They constantly hammer away, however, and will do whatever it takes to tempt, in hopes that they can contribute to the person's failure. That is their job.

3. Demons do their best to keep people ignorant of their presence and activity. This is a particularly successful strategy in Western societies. They love it when people don't believe they exist. Demons have repeatedly told us this during ministry sessions. During a recent session observed by a psychologist who was learning about demonization, a demon became so angry during the ministry it yelled (through its host), "I hate it that she [the psychologist] is learning about us. For years, we've been hiding and making them think we are psychological problems!"

The fact that demons piggyback on problems already there, rather than originating problems that were not there, enables them to hide quite effectively from many people. People reason that if they can explain the problem as resulting from "natural" causes, there is no need to look further. Thus the demon wins, since his function is to reinforce the problem in such a way that the person gets discouraged, stops fighting it, and blames himself or herself for it. Many have given up hope, thinking they were crazy or that nothing could be done about it.

4. Demons often resort to getting people to fear them. The way they work in this area takes a variety of forms. I've had people come who feared they had a demon and, if so, that there must be something very wrong with them spiritually. They didn't know that the presence or absence of a demon usually has little to do with their present spiritual condition, except to hinder it. They are often very mature spiritually in spite of the impeding spirits inside them. They usually have become demonized through inheritance, through some kind of abuse, or through pre-Christian involvements, rather than through spiritual failure and rebellion. But the demons have pushed them to fear the worst.

Then there are a certain number of people who come who are afraid they *don't* have a demon! Sometimes these are people who would like to avoid responsibility for their problems; they hope there are demons to blame them on. Some, however, have been hearing messages accusing them of being crazy or otherwise permanently disabled and are genuinely in hopes that a major part of the problem is demonic and, therefore, can be done away with. It usually can.

Many people fear the power of demons. They have heard stories, seen movies, or talked to people who got involved in fear-inspiring physical battles with demonized people. They haven't learned that most of the physical battles can be avoided through inner healing and by exercising the spiritual power we have through the use of empowered words, not the power of muscles.

5. In all that demons do, deceit is a major weapon. Demons lie to us about who we are, about who God is, about who they are and what they do. As in Eden, they deceive sometimes through direct contradiction, sometimes through indirect questioning of truth. Then, as mentioned above, one of their favorite tricks is to lead people to think the false concept or idea is their own thought.

6. By whatever means possible, the job of demons is to hinder anything good. They try to keep people from God or from doing anything God wants. They hinder unbelievers from believing (2 Cor 4:4). They also work over Christians in the belief area. Such things as worship, prayer, Bible study, acts of love and compassion, and the like are high on the demonic hit list. They specialize in discovering and attacking weaknesses. The greater the weakness, the more often a person is likely to be attacked in that area.

Notice how demons, often supported by cosmic spirits, attack Christians on Sundays, often from outside of them. They like to encourage conflict within families on Sunday mornings as they are getting ready for or traveling to church. Demons like to push people's minds to wander during worship or the sermon. Headaches, babies crying, or other means of breaking concentration in church are other demonic techniques. In addition, demons like to influence pastors to run churches as clubs rather than as hospitals, to focus on preaching and program rather than on ministering to people, to preach theoretically rather than practically, to perform rather than to communicate. They can push musicians to show off, those who give announcements to interrupt the flow of worship, ushers to be too obvious, and anyone else to weaken what God wants to do in church.

7. Demons specialize in accusing. The term "Satan" originally meant "accuser." Many such accusations are negative statements or thoughts, imagined or real, of others toward the person being attacked. One of the enemy's favorite devices is to get people to accuse themselves, others, and God of causing disruptions to truth, health, life, love, relationships, and anything else that comes from God.

The self-rejection engendered by Western societies provides especially fertile ground for this aspect of demonic activity. In addition to self-accusation, demons like to plant in our minds thoughts that get us to accuse others or God. Demons encourage such things as rumors, disrupted relationships based on misunderstandings and anger at God, and blame of God for things he allows to come our way. Among their devices are pushing people to retain guilt even after they have received forgiveness from God, convincing people that there is something incurably wrong with them, enticing people into blaming themselves for abuse they have received from others, and strongly suggesting that the troubles they experience are from God and are deserved because of their failures. They also like to push people to blame others or God for their difficulties.

8. Demons like to support compulsions. They delight in helping people to develop a compulsive approach to both good and bad behavior. They, of course, reinforce compulsions relating to lust, drugs, alcohol, tobacco, overeating, undereating, pornography, gambling, materialism, competitiveness, the need to be in control, and the like. They also encourage exaggerated attention to "good" things such as work, study, attractive dress, religion, doctrinal purity, family, achievement, success, and so forth. They delight in pushing people to build on weaknesses and exaggerate strengths. The roots of compulsions often lie in such attitudes as fear, insecurity, feelings of worthlessness, and the like. Demons, knowing this, are quick to exploit them to produce compulsiveness as fruit.

9. Demons are adept at harassment. Demons nip at our heels like angry dogs. Satan is referred to as "the ruler of this world" (Jn 14:30, GNB), and doesn't like it that those who belong to another King are wandering around in his territory. So he harasses us whenever and however he can. Demons can do whatever God allows to disrupt our lives through influencing such things as traffic, weather, health, stress, relationships, worship, sleep, diet, mechanical things (especially cars and computers), and anything else that affects us.

I suspect, for example, that harassment was the aim of Satan when he ordered demons to manifest themselves when Jesus was teaching in the synagogue (e.g., Lk 4:33-34) and to stir up a storm while Jesus was in a boat on Lake Galilee (Lk 8:23-24) and to influence the Pharisees to continually bother him. To counter such influences, I have gotten into the habit of saying when things go wrong, "If this is the enemy, stop it!" It is amazing to me how many things stop when I take that approach.

Demons don't seem to harass every Christian equally. They seem to pay more attention to those who are the greatest threat to them and to those who don't have enough prayer support. Many Christians are so passive about their Christianity that they are no threat to the enemy. They may get off with very little attention from him. Those who threaten the enemy but who do not have enough prayer support also tend to get regularly and effectively harassed. The fact that even Jesus was harassed, however, suggests that no strategy enables Christians to live completely free from demonic attention as long as we are in his territory.

RATS AND GARBAGE

Rats are attracted to places where trash and garbage pile up. If we find rats in our houses, we know we have to do something about what has attracted them. So it is with demons. Inside a human being, emotional or spiritual garbage provides just such a congenial setting for demonic rats. Wherever such emotional or spiritual garbage exists, demonic rats seek and often find entrance. If, however, the garbage is disposed of, the rats cannot stay or, at least, cannot remain strong. With people as with homes, the solution to the rat problem is not to chase away the rats but to dispose of the garbage. *The biggest problem is not the demons, it is the garbage.*

Demons are most frequently attached to damaged emotions or sin, or both. Because of this, demons usually have names appropriate to the emotion they are attached to. These names are what we call their "function" names (see below). They may also have personal names. In dealing with demons through inner healing as I do, it is more useful to know their function names than their personal names, since it is this name that indicates which emotion or attitude needs to be dealt with in getting the demon weakened and out.

Demons seldom come singly. They are most often in groups. They are, however, arranged hierarchically, with a leader demon in charge of a whole group. My practice, then, is to discover which is the head "rat" and to bind to him all others under his control, by the power of the Holy Spirit. This enables me to deal with the whole group at the same time. The head or controlling spirit, then, speaks for the whole group. There may, however, be more than one group of spirits in any given person, with a head spirit over each group of roughly equal power to the other head spirits. It is usually possible, once each group has been bound to its head spirit, to bind all the groups together as well.

FUNCTION NAMES OF DEMONS

As mentioned above, demons respond to names related to their functions. Thus, most demon names are the names of emotions. And they tend to come in clusters. A selection of the names we find in typical clusters is as follows. Note there is repetition and that I have used boldface for the names that often head the group.

Death, suicide, murder
Destruction, violence
Darkness, deceit
Rage, anger, hate
Hate, revenge, murder
Unforgiveness, anger, bitterness, resentment
Rebellion, stubbornness
Rejection, self-rejection, fear of rejection
Fear, terror, torment, fear of... (e.g., rejection, pain, dark, being alone, being outdoors, heights)
Self-rejection, inadequacy, unworthiness, perfectionism
Guilt, shame, embarrassment, sensitivity
Worry, anxiety, worry about... (e.g., future, impression one makes)
Deceit, lying
Confusion, frustration, forgetfulness
Criticism, condemnation, judgmentalism, faultfinding

Adultery, seduction
Rape, violence
Depression, anger, defeat
Nervousness
Sensitivity, fear
Doubt, unbelief, skepticism
Pride, arrogance, vanity
Perfection, insecurity
Competition, insecurity, pride
Infirmity, sickness (may be a specific disease such as
 cancer, diabetes, arthritis, or the like)
Blasphemy, cursing, mockery

In addition to such "emotion" demons, there are those that function to encourage compulsions and addictions. These may go by such names as:

Compulsiveness or **compulsion**
Control, domination, possessiveness
Performance, pleasing others
Intellectualism, need to understand, rationalization
Religiosity, ritualism, doctrinal obsession
Lust, sexual impurity, adultery
Pornography, sexual fantasy
Homosexuality, lesbianism
Masturbation (obsessive)
Alcohol
Drugs
Nicotine
Gluttony
Anorexia
Bulimia
Caffeine

Occult and cult spirits (including those of false religions) are another category to be dealt with. These can often be quite powerful. Some of those to look for are:

Freemasonry
Christian Science
Jehovah's Witness
New Age
Rosicrucianism
Unity
Mormonism
Occult-oriented games
Horoscope
Witchcraft
Astrology
Fortune Telling
Palmistry
Water Witching
Buddhism and various Buddhist spirits
Islam and various Islamic spirits
Hinduism and various Hindu spirits
Shintoism and various Shinto spirits

STRENGTH OF ATTACHMENT

A variety of factors contribute to the strength of the grip a demon has on the person in which he lives:

1. Demons have different strengths. Some kinds of demons seem to be inherently stronger than others. Occult demons, those coming through inheritance, and similar ones seem to be inherently stronger than those attached to emotions. Likewise, those invited consciously or empowered through dedication seem to have a stronger grip than those picked up unconsciously during life experience. Demons enforcing compulsions, furthermore, seem usually to be stronger than those attached to emotions.

2. In general, the more garbage, the stronger the attachment. The greater the amount of hurt a person has suffered and the stronger the negative emotional reaction, the tighter the demon's grip. Even if the garbage is dealt with and the demon weakened, however, it can only leave if permitted by its superior to do so. Several times I have been surprised to find a very weak demon hanging on to a person and asked it why it hasn't left, given the fact that it has so little grip on the person. Its reply is always, "I haven't been allowed to."

3. Demons seem seldom to work alone. They are usually organized in hierarchical groupings with one of them at the head. I have very seldom found only one or two demons in a person. In a typical ministry session we will first make contact with one of the lesser demons in a group, say, lust. Lust may have three or four demons under him (e.g., sexual perversion, fantasy, and deceit). But either by his admission or by word of knowledge we find that there is a spirit of anger over lust and a spirit of fear over anger. Fear may be toward the top of the group, with two or three others (e.g., rejection, abandonment, and pornography) between him and lust. Above fear, then, we may find demons with names like rage, destruction, darkness, and death, any of which could be the head of the group.

4. Among the non-occult demons, certain ones are more likely to be head demons than others. For example, if there is a spirit of death, he is likely to be in charge. Destruction or darkness will often be in charge also and sometimes rejection or fear, especially if there is no spirit of death. Any of these spirits can function under an occult demon. Frequently, however, I have found an occult demon to be parallel (i.e., approximately equal in power) to a spirit such as death or destruction and to have a separate group of demons functioning under him. For example, in one man I found an American Indian spirit to be in charge of one group while a spirit of rage was in charge of another.

5. The spirits inside a person seem to be under the authority of higher-level spirits outside the person. They have often been sent to the person by these higher-level spirits and, apparently, are not free to leave until those spirits allow or are forced to let them go. For this reason it is good to begin every ministry session where demons are challenged with the breaking of any authority or ability to help of the higher-level spirits outside the person.

6. Demons within a person can be suppressed or weakened by certain things that person does. As noted earlier, among the things that weaken the demons inside people is their spiritual growth. When demonized Christians make choices that enhance their closeness to Christ, the demons lose ground. I have asked several demons why they didn't have a stronger grip on the person they lived in. Their replies were always something like, "She's too close to God. I can't get her."

Activities such as worship, prayer, Bible reading, and Christian fellowship seem to suppress demons at least temporarily. When one deals with sin or emotional hurts in one's life the result is permanent weakness for those demons in charge of the areas that get healed.

A very important weakening technique is prayer by others. Demons often speak of how the amount of protection God gives a person limits their ability to influence that person. Sometimes they speak of the number of angels assigned to carry out that protection. Such protection is related both to the person's own spiritual condition and to the prayers of others for that person. It affects the influence of demons both inside and outside the person. Those of us in deliverance ministries, for example, require a good bit of prayer support as we plunder the enemy's camp. See chapter nine for a dramatic example.

7. On the other hand, there are things a person may do that result in the demons getting a stronger grip. The more a person gives in to temptations (e.g., lust, drinking, lying) or the emotions being reinforced by the demons (e.g., fear, anger, bitterness, worry), the stronger the demons get. Or, if during a deliverance session a person gives up fighting the demon because the pain or other discomfort is so great, that demon gains strength. He has won that battle. Likewise, if a person gets rid of a demon but later invites him back in, the demon comes in stronger than when he left, and perhaps with others (Lk 11:26).

WHAT DEMONIC STRENGTH MEANS

Demonic strength is a combination of the inherent strength of the demon and the amount of garbage it is given by the host person. As we have seen, occult and inherited spirits tend to be inherently stronger than those that attach themselves to emotional and spiritual problems during the course of a person's life.

One indication of a demon's strength is whether or not he can take control of the person and how much control he can take. At the weaker end of the scale, many demons don't seem to be able to exert anything that would be called control. So they have to be content with simply harassing the person. Three levels of harassment or control may be illustrated as follows (see my book, *Defeating Dark Angels*, for a more complete treatment).

1. Harassment by a weak spirit. Weak spirits are frequently present in people who have not allowed them much ground. A spirit of fear that invaded a woman when she was raped is unlikely to be strong if she, through counseling (without deliverance) and spiritual growth, has dealt with most of the emotional issues that such an experience brings with it. Though the demon may have once been strong, it may have been so weakened that it can only cause a weak surge of fear whenever she remembers the event, sees a man who reminds her of her attacker, or hears of someone else being raped. The demon is still there to harass but its ability to disrupt her life is severely reduced.

2. A measure of control by a stronger spirit. Another rape victim who may have contracted one or more demons (e.g., anger, fear, pain) during the rape but has not been able to work through her emotions may experience times when she is quite out of control. For example, she may find that while disciplining her children, she gets "carried away" by her anger and seriously overdisciplines them. She may find herself frequently (though perhaps not all the time) overcome with anger, fear, resentment, and a mixture of other unanticipated emotions when she and her husband make love. She may find herself compulsive about her need to bathe after each act of sexual intercourse.

In cases such as this, the demons are able to exert quite a bit of control over the person at certain times and in certain experiences. The out-of-controlness the person feels is frequently puzzling to the person, but usually not sufficient for that person to suspect external interference. She may think every young mother has this problem.

3. An even greater measure of control by an occult spirit or one that has come by inheritance. Occult spirits and either occult or "emotion" spirits that have come by inheritance tend to have a stronger grip than do emotion spirits picked up during life experiences. Occult spirits to whom persons have given themselves voluntarily are usually very strong. So are inherited family spirits of death, violence, destruction, rebellion, and the like, as well as inherited occult spirits. Such spirits often claim to "own" the person. It is usual when people come to us with occult or inherited spirits (or both) for them to report major interference with worship and general thinking patterns and often big problems with rage, suicidal thoughts, depression, fear, and their ability to respect and love themselves and others.

In one case after deliverance, an ecstatic husband exclaimed, "I have a brand new wife!" As is typical with inherited demons, the garbage in this woman's life was at least partly attracted under the influence of the inherited demon and those he invited in rather than simply developed during life experiences.

One factor that needs to be mentioned is that certain people seem to have a greater ability than others to resist demonic influence. That is, some people with a comparatively high level of infestation seem to be able to hide their symptoms quite well. Others, however, with a comparatively low level of interference seem to fall apart. This fact seems to be related to the strength of a person's will to fight.

GETTING DEMONS OUT

Discernment. There are several components to the kind of discernment needed in a deliverance ministry. Among them are supernatural things such as direct revelation (called words of knowledge or wisdom) and more "natural" things like experience, ability to interpret commonsense observations, and imagination.

Since the Holy Spirit is guiding (after we have asked him to come in a special way), we can expect the total process to go well beyond any mere human abilities. In that sense the whole is supernatural. But much of what God uses springs from "natural" capabilities. These are combined with supernatural leading to make up both the discernment component and all other components of the ministry process.

Many seem to have the impression that if God is really leading, lots of spectacular things will be happening. Not so. *God seldom does things in a spectacular way if he can do them in some other way.* So when we pray for God to lead in every part of the process, look for his leading, but don't expect a lot of fireworks. Many have missed a lot because they expected God to be more obvious in his leading than he usually chooses to be.

What I call "natural discernment" is by far the most frequent kind of discernment in any given ministry session. Therefore, keep your eyes open, literally, for whatever can be observed. Look for any overt manifestations. Often the mere presence of the Holy Spirit flushes demons out and causes them to make the person act strangely. This may happen as the result of simply inviting the Holy Spirit to take over in a ministry session. Or demons may manifest themselves in response to God's presence in worship or in personal devotions or when the person receives a blessing in Jesus' name. I have even seen clear demonic manifestations when I was simply teaching on this topic.

Visible manifestations of demonic presence may also happen in response to any challenge for the demon to manifest itself. They may also show themselves at other times when someone makes authoritative use of Jesus' name in, for example, speaking healing to an emotional, spiritual, or physical problem. I've frequently seen them become obvious in one person in response to challenges made to a demon in another person.

Not infrequently, in addition to overtly visible manifestations, persons inhabited by demons will experience inner interference that they are able to hide from others. Many demonized people regularly have headaches or other physical problems in church, intended by the demons to disrupt their concentration.

Though each of these symptoms can indicate other things and we need to be careful lest we jump too soon to the conclusion that there is a demon, the following may indicate demonic presence. Among the common indications (in no particular order) are: headaches or other pain in the body, lightheadedness, feeling sick or like one is about to throw up, stiffness or shaking of the body, unusual sleepiness, a strong desire to strike the counselor, and a strong desire to run from the session.

Less common manifestations (usually indicating more severe demonization) are: violent shaking; facial and/or body contortion; screaming; swearing; throwing up; eyes glazed, squinted, or rolled back; "acting out" (as with a homosexual spirit trying to seduce the counselor); and speaking with another voice.

These are some of the things that can be discerned naturally, either by observation or by asking questions. In addition, God does show things to people supernaturally, though usually in combination with the observation of natural phenomena. As you develop more experience, you will find your ability to discern sharpened. You will also notice that *demons make a lot of mistakes that give them away. Learning to spot these mistakes and to take advantage of them is an important part of the operation.*

Conducting a deliverance session.

1. First of all, every deliverance session should be *bathed in prayer*, both by oneself and by one's prayer partners. It is good to fast as well, especially if the session promises to be difficult. We should be spiritually ready at all times to minister in the power of the Spirit to any need.

2. It is best to *minister in teams* whenever possible. Include those with gifting that you may not have. Whether or not their gifting differs from yours, though, they can be praying and listening to the Lord for you during the session. I think a good number for a team would usually be between three and five.

3. At the start of a session, *take authority, claim protection, forbid help from other evil spirits, and forbid violence.* We often use words such as the following:

> We speak in Jesus' name against any emissaries of the Evil One who may be here. We command you to leave. We claim this place, this time, these people for the Lord Jesus Christ and forbid any activity by any satanic beings except what we specifically command.

We then claim protection using words such as:

> We claim protection in the name of Jesus Christ for each one of us, our families, our friends, our property, our finances, our health, and everything else that pertains to us from any revenge or other dirty tricks from the enemy.

Next, we cut off any spirits inside the person from help by other spirits outside or inside the person, saying something like,

> In the name of Jesus, we cut off any spirits inside this person from any help they might get from outside spirits or from any others inside the person.

We then forbid any violence, vomiting, or other spectacular behavior:

> We forbid any spirits inside this person to cause any violence, any throwing up, or any other showy behavior.

4. There are *certain things to remember concerning the person being ministered to:*

- Do everything in love.
- Maintain the person's dignity at all times.

- Strengthen the person's will at every opportunity.
- Continually encourage the person before, during, and after the session.
- It is best to deal with the person's inner garbage through deep-level healing[6] to weaken the hold of the demons before casting them out. Otherwise, there is more likely to be violence, because the demons will have more ability to resist.

Challenging demons. During the initial process of deep-level healing, we often come upon clues that lead us to suspect that there may be demons. The following symptoms often give such an impression: compulsive behavior, disturbing dreams, a strong urge toward suicide or murder, strong self-rejection, homosexuality, occult involvement, and the like. If there is serious dysfunction in the person's parental or grandparental family, we may suspect the possibility of a family (intergenerational) spirit or curse. We will also look for the possibility of any other curse, whether a self-curse or one put on by another person.

1. If we suspect a demon, we will typically *ask the person's permission* to test the possibility. It is good never to go beyond what a person is willing to do. If we ask this kind of permission, then, and the person refuses, we go no further at that time.

2. If permission is given, I usually first ask the person to either close his or her eyes or to look straight at me as I *challenge one demon* by name, if possible. I'm often not sure whether or not there are demons present, but I let the person know that I'm going to act as if there are to see if I can rouse one. The best way we've found to discover demons is to challenge them directly. I will usually challenge it by using the name of whatever emotional or spiritual problem we suspect may be reinforced by demons. I'll typically say something like:

Spirit of _____ , I challenge you in the name of Jesus Christ. I forbid you to hide and command you to come to attention.

We instruct the person to report whatever comes into his or her mind in case (as often happens) the spirit speaks to his or her mind. Or, if the spirit is strong enough to use the person's voice, we instruct the person to allow that to happen. When the interaction really gets underway, the person will feel like an observer, a third party, as a conversation goes on between the demon(s) and myself.

Usually I have to challenge a demon several times before I get it to respond. They like to remain hidden as long as possible. Not infrequently, it is necessary to challenge several demons before I get a response from any. I often try several names in succession. This requires patience and persistence. I'll frequently press hardest on those I feel may be weakest on the assumption that the weakest may be easier to make contact with than the stronger ones. Eventually, they have to respond to the power of God, so be persistent.

If I don't already have an idea of what the spirit's name might be, I command it to tell me what it is or simply address it as "spirit." Getting them to admit their names is often difficult. Expect words of knowledge at this point. Follow up on any "hunch." Sometimes the spirit has already done something by which it can be identified. For example, "Spirit that has caused that shaking, come to attention."

Keep control. If they try diversionary tactics such as causing pain, shaking the person, telling the person lies, bringing diversionary thoughts into his or her mind, forbid them. Though it may not work at first, continue to assert your authority. *Forbid them to exert any control at all.* But you don't need to shout or do strange things. Demons are neither hard of hearing nor impressed with our antics. Though this is a power game, they will try to bluff you and to discourage the client. Don't let this happen. Be in charge, even if you feel insecure inside.

3. At this point, I like to *ask Jesus to assign several large, powerful angels to assist in getting this person free*. When this is done, often the demons will admit that they see both the angels and Jesus. This intimidates them.

4. Next, I try to *discover what the hierarchy is within the person.* I'll try to get whatever demon I get contact with to tell me who is over him. This may be difficult, but sometimes it is possible to bluff them into "ratting" on the other demons by guessing that those demons that tend to often appear at the top are there. In this way, plus word of knowledge, we usually can find who is on top. *When I find who's on top, I bind all the underlings to the top spirit so I can work with all of them at once.* This saves a lot of work when, as usual, there are many demons to deal with.

As mentioned above, demons seem to cluster in groups with one at the head of each group. Sometimes there will be more than one group in a person, headed by demons of approximately equal authority. When I find this, I bind each group to its head thus:

> By the authority of the Holy Spirit, I bind you all together with... [name the head spirit].

I then make sure this binding together has actually happened by quizzing the head demon about whether or not all of them are bound to him. Often he will indicate that some are not bound with him. In this case, I command him to give me the reason. Often, then, either the head demon or one of those not bound will, when commanded, tell me what still needs to be dealt with. Dealing with whatever the issue is, then, usually weakens the wandering demons to the point where they join the bound ones.

Go for intergenerational spirits or curses first. Force the demon to tell you if he has any grip through inheritance. You may already suspect this. To be sure, however, I will often say:

> In the name of Jesus I command you to tell me if you have any grip through inheritance.

If there is something, ask, "Through mother or father?" and then, "How many generations back?" If there is an inter-generational root, I say something like the following:

> In the name of Jesus I take authority over that ancestor [six] generations back through [person's name] father/mother and break your power in the sixth, fifth, fourth, third, and second generations. Now I cut off any power you have over her/him through your involvement in this family at the point of [person's name] conception.

When this is done, we often see a noticeable change in the strength of the demon. If you suspect an intergenerational root but for some reason can't get confirmation either by word of knowledge or from the demon, guess that there may be one and say something like:

> In the name of Jesus, I take authority over you intergenerational spirit of [depression] coming through the father's bloodline and I break your power in Jesus' name. I forbid you to have any more power over [person's name].

Or:

> I break the power of the curse concerning [homosexuality] that has come through the mother's bloodline in the name of Jesus Christ.

In this area especially, we're not always sure what is happening. When in doubt, though, I feel it's better to go ahead and speak against a curse or intergenerational spirit anyway, since breaking any power operative at this level can have a major effect on the strength of the demons.

Getting rid of demons. By now, most of the demons' power should be gone through the effects of the inner healing and the breaking of intergenerational ties. Frequently, however, there are things that remain hidden. So don't be upset if the demons aren't quite ready to go.

I frequently ask the head demon if he and his underlings are ready to go or if the person has any remaining garbage to give them reason to stay. They will usually claim they have nothing left, even if there is still something. Sometimes, though, they will truthfully volunteer that there is more to deal with. If so, go back to the inner healing mode and deal with it.

Feel free to interrupt the process at any time to take care of whatever comes up, especially to get reports on what the person is experiencing. There is nothing magical about the continuity of any given part of the ministry. Frequently, it is advisable to take a break to discuss strategy with your team. If you do this, I suggest you say, "In the name of Jesus, I forbid the spirit world to hear what we are about to say." (It works!) Or take a break to stretch, to go to the bathroom, and to seek more guidance or power in prayer.

When you are ready, take authority and command the head spirit with all of its followers to leave. As at all other times, commands should be firm and forceful, but they don't have to be loud. Jesus did not coax out demons as did the Pharisees of his day. He treated them roughly. He *cast* (Greek *ekballo*) them out (Mk 1:25). Be forceful, authoritative, and determined, but be patient if it takes a while.

There are *several ways to get the demons out.* Sometimes you can simply say,

Spirit of _____, I command you to leave/come out in Jesus' name and to go to the feet of Jesus.

If they leave, well and good. Usually, however, this is not enough. If the head demon refuses, command it to tell you what right it still has to live in the person. Command it in the name of Jesus to tell the truth and to tell everything. You may find it useful to remind the demon again who he is and how he and his kingdom have been defeated. Colossians 2:15 is a good verse to quote. Remind him of the Cross and the empty Tomb. Demons don't like to hear about the blood shed on the Cross or the Tomb that Jesus escaped from.

What seems to work best for me, then, in sealing the deal is to ask Jesus if he will have the angels lower a "box" over the demons in their groupings and lock them in so they are all together and none can escape. I then check with the head demon to see if they are all in the box. When they are, I ask the angels to take the locked box to Jesus. Then I ask Jesus to dispose of the box and separate the demons from the person forever. The person usually sees a mental image of what Jesus does with the box.

When Jesus has disposed of the box, then, I say something like:

> I separate these demons from [name] as far as the East is from the West and place the Cross on which Jesus died and the Tomb from which he rose again between [name] and these demons forever. *I forbid any of these demons to ever return or to send any others.*

That usually does it. If not, look for more garbage and deal with it through inner healing. Then do this again.

Tactics—theirs and ours. There are certain tactics that demons regularly use to keep from having to leave. Among their ruses are:

1. Demons like to hide to make you think they are not there or that they have left. When you perceive that this is happening, simply forbid them to continue to do it. Command the demon you want to respond to you. If this doesn't work, deal with another one or go back to inner healing. As the more powerful ones get weakened, they have less ability to resist such orders.

Sometimes the spirit will disappear because he is *shared* with someone else. If so, he simply goes to that other person. Command all "shared spirits" to be here, forbidding them to go to any other person, and this will stop.

2. Sometimes demons will respond one after another in an attempt to keep you from being sure which one you're talking to. If this happens, you'll quickly discover it. Simply command the one you want by name and forbid him to allow another to talk until you address that other one. You are in charge. Don't let them take control over any part of the process.

3. They often talk big to try to get you to fear them. They seldom are as big or powerful as they contend, even if they cause weird facial expressions, pain, or bodily distortions. Sometimes they'll tell you, "I'm a principality," or even, "I'm Satan," to get you to fear them. Or they'll threaten to kill you or your family. Don't give in to them; you have more power than they do. Claim God's protection for anyone threatened and call their bluff by reminding them of who they are and who you are.

4. They will deceive and lie. Though the Holy Spirit forces them to give us important information, take everything they say with a grain of salt. Order them to tell the truth but still don't trust them. Always be on your guard against their attempts to mislead you and to get you to leave them alone. Often, a demon has said to me, "I'm leaving now," or, "I'm gone." Don't believe statements like those. Keep pressing until the deal is sealed.

5. They often give excuses and even plead to be allowed to stay. "This is my home. Where would I go?" they say, or, "I only help her," or, "If I promise not to hurt him, will you let me stay?" or simply, "I don't want to leave." Sometimes they ask to be allowed to enter someone else. Don't allow it. If they threaten, simply forbid that to happen and it cannot. Claim protection for the person in the name of Jesus and the person is safe. Or, remind the demon that the group is already protected (in the opening prayer) and that, therefore, he has no power to attack anyone.

Don't fall for any such excuses or bargaining. Demons are evil beings. They won't play fair. Nor will they keep any promises. No matter how sincere their pleas sound, or how much they try to play on your sympathies, don't weaken.

6. *Demons will try to wear you all down.* They will use fatigue in any way they can. So don't let sessions get too long. I find two to three hours about the maximum. Take breaks from time to time. They will also try to get the person to feel tired even if true fatigue is not really a factor. They will often try to put the person to sleep. Forbid it. All of these tactics are designed to discourage and weaken the will of both the demonized person and the counselor. Carefully watch and protect against this ploy.

If you have worked long enough but there is more to do, simply shut the demons down by commanding them not to cause the person any harm "until the next time they are challenged in the name of Jesus." It is good to state your condition this way so that if another person challenges them in Jesus' name he or she will have access to them.

If they simply won't come out no matter what you do, don't get discouraged. Schedule further sessions and arrange for more experienced people to be on the ministry team. Then get others praying for the sessions, pray and fast yourself before the next session, and patiently but persistently keep working to get the person free.

Though it may take time, most attempts to free a person will eventually be successful. If, whether consciously or unconsciously, the person does not want to be freed, however, it is very unlikely that it will happen. One important caution needs to be given here: even if you suspect that the person doesn't want to exercise his or her will to be freed, never accuse the person of this. Since we can't know for sure (unless the person states it), love requires that we do not accuse the person but, rather, that we do whatever we can to lead the person to want to be freed.

7. The person will usually know when the demons leave. There will usually be a sizable feeling of relief, as if a great weight has been removed. Sometimes the person will feel the demons leave through an orifice, usually the mouth. This happens most often when the demons are commanded to leave in this way. Often, though, they will try to deceive you into thinking they've left by causing yawning, burping, and so on. Sometimes there will be a shaking of the body, followed by release. Or, if the demon has a grip on some part of the body (e.g., head, throat), the person will feel the release of that grip.

When the demons are commanded to get into the locked box, the feeling they are leaving through an orifice doesn't occur. When the box is taken to Jesus, however, the person will usually feel some definite release within the body and know that he or she is free.

8. Fill the space left by the demons with blessings. We like to bless the person with freedom in the areas in which the demons held the person in bondage. That is, if the demon was a spirit of fear, bless with peace and hope; if a spirit of anger, bless with patience and forgiveness; if a spirit of self-rejection, bless with self-acceptance and love.

POST-DELIVERANCE COUNSELING

Before concluding the ministry session, don't forget to forbid the demons to return. If you forget, they may be able to come back. I like to use words such as the following:

In Jesus' name we forbid any of these spirits or any others to return or to send any others. We declare that this person belongs totally to Jesus Christ and forbid further trespassing by enemy agents. We place Jesus' Cross and empty Tomb between this person and the spirits.

I then like to "seal" all that the Holy Spirit has done by saying,

I seal in Jesus' name all that he has done here. We close all doors through which the demons gained entrance and remove all vulnerabilities in Jesus' name.

It is important to counsel the newly freed person concerning what is likely to happen. Demons will often try to come back to claim their former territory. They will try to get in, but if they have been forbidden to, they will be unable to. The person should know that they cannot come back if they have been forbidden to come back. But demons can try to fake it by working from outside the person if allowed to. The person should, therefore, be instructed concerning a Christian's authority in Christ and be told to use the power Christ gives us to forbid any more demon activity. The newly delivered person should point out that he or she has the same Holy Spirit as the one who ministered and, therefore, the same authority. James 4:7 says, "*Resist* the devil and he will flee from you." We are, therefore, to take authority over any demons that try to return and to send them away again. Eventually they will get tired of trying and go somewhere else. If the demons don't give up right away, neither should we.

We should strongly remind the person of his or her identity in Christ. Almost always, the enemy has been lying to the person about this, for he doesn't want us to know who we are. So now, purposefully, the freed person needs to make this truth personal. This person is Jesus' child (Rom 8:14-17; 1 Jn 3:1-3; Gal 4:5-7), set apart to become like Jesus (Rom 8:29), called by Jesus his "friend" (Jn 15:15). Jesus himself chose us (Jn 15:16) and empowered us (Lk 9:1). And any fear that we feel is to be banished since fear is not from God (2 Tm 1:7).

Complete healing requires a support group of some sort and, often, work with a professional Christian therapist. Often the best arrangement is for part or all of the ministry team to continue as a support group. Close relationships with other Christians, in a church or Sunday school class, can help ward off most of what the enemy brings to us. Such a group can also advise concerning the need for more therapy, if necessary.

It is very important for the person to keep clean of whatever the demon attached itself to. Habits, attitudes, and friends may need to be intentionally changed to keep and build on the healing and freedom God has given. Getting back into the old patterns can open the door for further infestation. (For example, a woman I was working with, out of whom we had cast a spirit of death, attempted suicide again. Another spirit of death entered her.) Lest demons find a way to reenter a person through related problem areas, the person should be advised to seek further deep-level healing.

Above all, encourage prayer, praise, worship, and development of the person's devotional life.

CONCLUSION

This is much of what I have learned concerning freeing people from ground-level satanic beings. This treatment needs, however, to be understood as closely related to the interaction between the spirit and the human realms (see chapter two) and in the overall context of the warfare between the kingdoms in which we live. As pointed out, higher-level spirits are involved in assisting the ground-level troops. So the kinds of strategy dealt with in the next section of this book need to be kept in mind. Furthermore, it is crucial to deal with the garbage in demonized people. Thus, books such as my *Deep Wounds, Deep Healing* need to be studied to fill in that part of the equation.

PART III

Spiritual Warfare: Cosmic-Level

~ ❊ ~

FIVE

Twenty-One Questions

C. Peter Wagner

The process of exploring strategic-level spiritual warfare, which some also call cosmic-level spiritual warfare, is four years old at this writing, although ministries such as Youth With a Mission, the International Fellowship of Intercessors, and others have been practicing it for a longer time. The seeds for the wider body of Christ were sown at Lausanne II in Manila in 1989. This new field, if it may be called that, was given form in February 1990 with the first meeting of the U.S. Spiritual Warfare Network.

Some outstanding literature has been produced since then such as John Dawson's *Taking Our Cities for God* (Creation House) and *Healing America's Wounds* (Regal Books), George Otis, Jr.'s *The Last of the Giants* (Chosen Books), Cindy Jacobs' *Possessing the Gates of the Enemy* (Chosen Books), Francis Frangipane's *The House of the Lord* (Creation House), and my *Engaging the Enemy* (Regal Books), *Warfare Prayer* (Regal Books), and *Breaking Strongholds in Your City* (Regal Books).

Interest in strategic-level spiritual warfare is spreading

rapidly. In fact, I cannot recall any other relatively new area of interest penetrating the body of Christ across geographical and theological boundaries with quite such a degree of excitement and acceptance. Charles Kraft and I have introduced courses dealing with these and related subjects into our curriculum at Fuller Seminary. Other seminaries have announced similar courses on aspects of spiritual warfare.

But not all agree on the direction in which we are heading. Of course, some question whether demonic personalities (as opposed to impersonal evil forces in individuals or societies) really exist at all. Some who do believe in real demons are not convinced that they are organized into some kind of dark hierarchy. Among those who think there might be a hierarchy are some who are uneasy with the notion that Satan has assigned principalities to oppress geographical territories, physical objects such as mountains or trees, and human social networks.

Even if demonic principalities are assigned territories, others argue, there is relatively little biblical evidence that we believers are given authority to confront them in a proactive, offensive mode. We may defend ourselves if they attack us, but we should not deal with demonic forces which have not attached themselves to human beings. According to this school of thought, such activity exceeds the limits of our authority and places us in unnecessary danger.

INNOVATIONS GENERATE HEAT

It is not surprising that Christian leaders are discussing these issues, at times heatedly. Diffusion of innovation theory, formulated by social scientists, tells us that when important new ideas (innovations) are introduced into social networks (in this case the body of Christ), a predictable process is set in motion. The process produces four types of responses to the innovators and their product or idea.[1] Following the innovators are:

- Early Adopters
- Middle Adopters
- Late Adopters
- Laggards

When the innovation first becomes known, it seems to meet existing needs of a limited number of individuals, and they almost immediately accept it and begin advocating it to others. This happened, for example, with the introduction of the horseless carriage, Sunday School, hybrid corn, Social Security, sliced bread, pantyhose, and thousands of other innovations that have now become part of our daily lives.

Invariably, these early adopters find themselves in a situation which invites controversy. The first ones to drive a Model T Ford through their towns often found their behavior quite unpopular with the majority. For a time, that is. The most intense controversy over an innovation is generated in the early adoption stage. And this is good, because it encourages valuable corrections and fine-tuning early on in the process.

The length of the early adopters stage will vary from innovation to innovation. Typically the number of those who adopt the innovation remains relatively small through this period. When it is over, however, and the middle adopters begin to come on board, the controversy usually cools off and the numbers increase rapidly. The rate of adoption slows down and often plateaus in the late adoption phase.

CONTROVERSY GENERATES UNDERSTANDING

I clearly recall the heated controversy over "signs and wonders" among evangelicals in the early- to mid-1980s when

John Wimber and I started teaching it in Fuller Seminary. That was the early adoption stage. We are now well into the middle adoption stage, however, and today it is rare to find those in evangelical churches who oppose overt prayers for divine healing and ministries of the miraculous. There are some laggards, of course, but they find themselves in a distinct minority compared to a decade or two ago.

Strategic-level spiritual warfare advocates aggressive spiritual confrontation with cosmic powers of darkness. It is, at this writing, in the early adoption stage. We are expressing different opinions, exposing weaknesses, introducing mid-course corrections, and reaching more consensus. As one of the innovators, I am grateful for the support of early adopters, but I am also grateful for the skeptics and cynics who force me to reexamine my presuppositions and refine my conclusions.

THE QUESTIONS

Over a period of time, I have compiled a list of the twenty-one questions I am most frequently asked about strategic-level spiritual warfare. I will answer these questions to the best of my ability, knowing full well that many of my answers will in turn provoke further questions that we will be required to answer.

1. How does "strategic-level spiritual warfare" differ from other types of spiritual warfare?

Recent studies in spiritual warfare have described three levels, one of which is strategic-level warfare. These levels seem to indicate a hierarchy of evil forces. The effects of successful spiritual warfare on any one of the levels can be seen on all three because the kingdom of darkness has its own internal system of communications and relationships. The three levels are:

- *Ground-level spiritual warfare.* This is what is commonly known as "deliverance," or casting demons out of individuals.
- *Occult-level spiritual warfare.* This deals with the demonic forces at work in witchcraft, Satanism, the New Age movement, shamanism, Eastern religions, spiritism, and any number of other such manifestations of the power of the devil and his dark angels.
- *Strategic-level spiritual warfare.* Also called "cosmic-level spiritual warfare," this deals with the higher ranking powers of darkness assigned to geographical territories or significant human social networks. The term "territorial spirits" is frequently used to describe these forces.

It is helpful to observe that in Ephesus the apostle Paul saw an impact of his ministry on all three levels, according to Acts 19. On the ground-level, demons were cast out through anointed handkerchiefs (Acts 19:12); on the occult-level, magicians burned their books and paraphernalia (Acts 19:19); and on the strategic-level, the power of Diana of the Ephesians, the territorial spirit of the region, was shaken (Acts 19:27). To show the interrelatedness of the three, Paul himself is reported to have operated only on ground- and occult-levels, but the impact was also felt on the strategic-level.

No wonder that when Paul later wrote back to the same believers in Ephesus he said, "We wrestle not against flesh and blood, but against principalities and powers... " (Eph 6:12, NKJV).

2. Since Scripture teaches that Jesus defeated the principalities and powers on the cross (see Col 2:14-15), is there really anything left for us to do except claim Jesus' victory?

This is a very important question. One of our significant critics says in part that the final answer to the question of who rules the city is that Jesus actually rules. He has disarmed the powers. The power over the city was defeated on the cross.

The size and number of cities may increase, the problems within them may be multiplied, but the powers cannot win. Jesus rules over the city.

We must understand that the sovereign God has so designed his world that much of what is truly his will he makes contingent on the attitudes and actions of human beings whom he created in his own image. We rarely question the fact that Jesus' death paid the penalty for all human sin and yet that he also assigns human beings the task of evangelization and soul-winning. Human inaction does not nullify the atonement, but it can make the atonement ineffective for individuals whom God loves.

Likewise, Jesus defeated the god of this age on the cross. Nevertheless, Satan and his principalities and powers persist in blinding the minds of millions who ultimately leave this life for a Christless eternity. Jesus gave his disciples authority to bind principalities which he also referred to as "strong men" (Mt 12:29). But human inaction can permit principalities to retain their human trophies and to keep whole people groups in spiritual captivity.

Just as God gave us a digestive system but expects us to take the initiative to eat in order to stay alive, he has also given us weapons of spiritual warfare, but he expects us to use them or they will not fulfill their intended purpose. Yes, I believe that even though Jesus secured the ultimate victory, there is much left for us to do in his power.

3. Do Christians have the authority to confront higher ranking satanic principalities as they do ordinary demons in individuals?

Francis Frangipane says it well: "I believe the Scriptures are clear: Not only do Christians have the authority to war against these powers of darkness, but we have the responsibility to as well. If we do not pray against our spiritual enemies, they will, indeed, prey upon us!"[2]

Luke 10 is one of the key biblical chapters describing Jesus' instructions to his disciples about dealing with the demonic. If Jesus were going to limit the authority of his disciples, one would expect that he might have done it there.

Jesus did take the opportunity at that time to lay out *ministry priorities* to the disciples. He said "Do not rejoice in this, that the spirits are subject to you, but rather rejoice that your names are written in heaven" (Lk 10:20). All spiritual warriors need to keep in mind that salvation is a higher priority and value than spiritual warfare. For one thing, salvation is eternal while spiritual warfare is, at best, a temporal activity.

At the same time, Jesus also bestowed what seems like *unlimited* authority over the forces of darkness. He says, "I give you the authority to trample on serpents and scorpions, and over *all the power of the enemy*" (Lk 10:19, NKJV, italics mine).

Although I realize some will disagree, I believe that the same authority Jesus gave to his disciples he gives to us today. Through the name of Jesus and the blood he shed on the cross, we can confront dark angels on any position in their hierarchy. This authority, however, must be exercised only in God's timing and in response to his specific direction.

4. Our ordinary concept of "prayer" is talking with God. How, then, can we say that we "pray against evil spirits" as, for example, Francis Frangipane did in his book *The House of the Lord*?

The notion of prayer signifies, in the broadest sense, communication between those of us in the natural world with personalities in the invisible world. Satanists pray to Satan. Hindus pray to a number of gods on their god shelf. Native American shamans pray to the Great Spirit. None of the above is praying to God, but there is little reason to deny it is prayer.

Christians should not attempt to pray *to* any person in the invisible world except to God. That is why we carefully use the phrase "pray *against* evil spirits," never "pray *to* evil spirits." For example, Paul once "prayed" or spoke directly to a demon whom he could not see and said, "I command you in the name of Jesus Christ to come out of her" (Acts 16:18, NKJV).

Verbally exercising the authority that Jesus has given us against dark angels is "praying against evil spirits." I believe that such communication gets through to the demonic beings and has some effect when done under the anointing of the Holy Spirit.

Having said that, I am also aware that some, like Tom White, do not recommend the use of the verb "pray" in these cases. He says, "We do not 'pray' at the devil. We resist him with the authority that comes out of the prayer closet."[3] Perhaps Tom is right.

5. Isn't there a danger that "command prayers," such as commanding a territorial spirit to leave a city, could lead us into unauthorized areas of ministry? Should we not call upon almighty God to do this?

Few dispute whether demons can and should be commanded to come out of individuals because the Scriptures are quite explicit on this issue. For example, Jesus said to a demon, "Be quiet, and come out of him!" (Mk 1:25, NKJV). Biblical scholar Wayne Grudem says that "the New Testament pattern seems to be that God ordinarily expects Christians themselves to speak directly to unclean spirits."[4]

As we move upward in what John Dawson calls the "limited hierarchy of evil spirits,"[5] the Scriptures do not give us clear directions one way or another. My personal conclusion is that we should do both, depending on the circumstances. Sometimes, in obedience to the prompting of God, we should directly command the principalities to leave or to release their hold or to stop some evil activity. We exercise our authority and bind the strongman. At other times we should beseech almighty God to release his sovereign power or to dispatch warring angels or to take any action he deems appropriate for the occasion.

6. Jude 9 says that even Michael the archangel would not bring a reviling accusation against Satan. Isn't this a biblical indication to us that we should steer away from strategic-level spiritual warfare?

There are five reasons why Jude 9 should not be regarded as an authoritative guide to what should or should not be done in strategic-level spiritual warfare:

1) The context of this Scripture is not a passage on how Christians do spiritual warfare, but on how to expose those who have a spirit of rebellion and who resist authority. Wayne Grudem says, "The lesson of the verse is simply, 'Don't try to go beyond the authority God has given you!' When Jude 9 is viewed in this way, the only question that arises for a Christian from this verse is, 'What authority has God given us over demonic forces?' And the rest of the New Testament speaks clearly to that in several places."[6] Grudem goes on to point out that both Peter and James encourage all Christians to resist the devil himself, and, "During Jesus' earthly ministry, when He sent the 12 disciples ahead of Him to preach the kingdom of God, He 'gave them power *over all demons*' (Lk 9:1, italics added)."[7]

2) If Jude 9 were to be made a principle of spiritual warfare, it would seem to apply to Satan himself, but it does not specifically reference the many lesser powers of darkness. As we have seen, the authority Jesus has given us applies to all demonic forces under Satan.

3) Jesus' incarnation, death on the cross, and resurrection permanently changed human history. His shed blood sealed the ultimate doom of principalities and powers. That is why Jesus said that the least in the kingdom of heaven is greater than John the Baptist, who represents the last of the Old Testament era (see Mt 12:11). In the

very next verse, Jesus says that the kingdom of heaven comes with violence "and the violent take it by force" (Mt 12:12, NKJV). The reference in Jude 9 to "the body of Moses" is set in Old Testament times before the cross and before believers were given the authority they have today. Circumstances changed radically when Jesus introduced the kingdom of God into the equation.

4) Human beings are the highest form of creation, being made in the image of God. Angels are not in the image of God, nor did Jesus die on the cross for angels. Peter tells us that salvation is something the angels can only "desire to look into" (1 Pt 1:9, 12). Therefore the authority derived from the blood of Christ may, indeed, not be available to angels, but only to disciples of Jesus. Michael was only an angel.

5) The text of Jude 9 itself gives problems to exegetes because it is a quotation from the apocalyptic Book of Enoch. This is strange because the Old Testament tells us nothing about a supposed "body of Moses." Whatever Jude 9 means, it is not the kind of text upon which careful Bible scholars would base a principle of Christian doctrine or practice.

7. In Matthew 18:15-20 "binding and loosing" are used in the context of exercising church discipline. Why do you associate them with spiritual warfare?

While "binding and loosing" are indeed applied to church discipline in Matthew 18, the terms are first introduced by Jesus in Matthew 16, in conjunction this time with world evangelization. Evidently, binding and loosing have a part in many different aspects of Christian ministry.

In Matthew 16, Jesus announces that he will build his church (Mt 16:18, NKJV) and then immediately adds, "And the gates of Hades shall not prevail against it" (16:18). This clearly implies that as the church of Jesus Christ spreads around the world, spiritual warfare, directed against "the gates of Hades," is inevitable.

Victory, however, is assured and the enemy will not prevail. Jesus gives his servants "the keys of the kingdom of heaven" (16:19) to come against these gates of Hades, and these keys are described as "whatever you bind on earth will be bound in heaven, and whatever you loose on earth will be loosed in heaven" (Mt 16:19, NKJV).

Jesus uses the same word "bind" when he refers to Satan's kingdom (Mt 12:26) and speaks of binding the strong man (Mt 12:29), namely Beelzebub, who is one of the highest ranking spirits under Satan. This is a clear biblical association of binding (and loosing) with strategic-level spiritual warfare.

8. Jesus commands us to cast demons out of people, but since we have no explicit command to cast demons out of cities or territories, should we not restrict our deliverance ministries to individuals?

When Jesus sent out his disciples and "gave them power over unclean spirits, to cast them out" (Mt 10:1, NKJV), he made no statement as to a limitation on the types of unclean spirits that should be dealt with. The subsequent examples relate only to ground-level spiritual warfare, but there is nothing in the teaching itself that would restrict it to casting demons only out of individuals.

I realize that my point is not particularly strong because I am arguing from silence. At the same time, those who say that there must be a limitation and that we have no power to bind or evict high-ranking territorial spirits should recognize that they are also arguing from silence. Arguments and counter-arguments from silence tend to neutralize each other.

With such an agreement, we then must go on and offer our best *interpretation* of explicit biblical teaching. My inclination is to take a literal interpretation of Jesus' clear statement that "I give you authority... over all the power of the enemy" (Lk 10:19, NKJV). Critics will point out that in biblical exegesis "all" does not always mean "all," and I concede this. The question then becomes: Does it mean literally "all" here? My opinion is that it does.

If I am correct, then, as I said in the answer to the last question, we have power to deal with the demonic through all levels of the hierarchy. Confronting Satan himself might be different, as we will see later on.

9. How do you know that the forces of evil are organized into some hierarchy? What are the different ranks in such a hierarchy?

The fact that some hierarchy or ranking of demonic spirits exists seems fairly clear. The positions on such a hierarchy are more problematic.

The Bible teaches that there are invisible personalities called "archangels." It speaks of "Michael the archangel" (1 Thes 4:16). "Michael and his angels" are mentioned in Revelation 12:7. Gabriel is also regarded as an archangel. These are obviously references to a hierarchy of some kind among good angels. Few dispute this.

We also read of Satan and his angels in Revelation 12:9. It seems logical, therefore, to conclude that a hierarchy exists among dark angels as well as among good angels.

It would be helpful if the Bible clearly stated the rankings and relative positions of the angelic sphere, but it does not. Some feel that Ephesians 6:12 comes close to this, however. Tom White, for instance, refers to "Hell's Corporate Headquarters," and argues that it is reasonable to assume that Ephesians 6:12 ranks the hierarchy in descending order. He sees the *archai* ("principalities") as "high-level satanic princes set over nations and regions of the earth"; the *exousias* ("powers") as cosmic beings who arbitrate human affairs; and the *kosmokratoras* ("rulers of the darkness of this age") as "the many types of evil spirits that commonly afflict people."[8]

On the other hand, biblical scholar Walter Wink disagrees. He says, "The language of power in the New Testament is imprecise, liquid, interchangeable, and unsystematic. An author uses the same word differently in different contexts, or several different words for the same idea." He points out how *archon*, *exousia*, *dynamis*, *kyriotes*, and other key Greek words for the powers should not be artificially arranged in hierarchical order.[9]

In my opinion, it is correct to say that a hierarchy of demonic forces of darkness exists, but that we cannot be dogmatic as to how it is ultimately arranged.

10. Is it essential to learn the names of the principalities over a city? How can such a thing be justified?

The Bible records proper names of spirits from time to time. Examples are Diana (Artemis) of the Ephesians (Acts 19:23-41), Beelzebub (Lk 11:15), Wormwood (Rv 8:11), Abaddon or Apollyon (Rv 9:11), and several others in the New Testament. A notable one is the spirit called Python mentioned in Acts 16:16, although most English translations obscure this by calling it a "spirit of divination."

In the Old Testament we see names of demonic principalities such as Baal (2 Kgs 21:3), Ashtoreth (1 Kgs 11:5), Milcom (1 Kgs 11:5), and many others. Extrabiblical sources reveal names of spiritual beings as those involved in deliverance ministries know well, but special discernment is needed before they can be accepted as fact.

Occasionally practitioners can cite cases where demonic forces have been removed without learning names, either proper or functional. At the same time, most will affirm that if the name is discovered, the subsequent deliverance is notably facilitated.

As I detail in my book *Warfare Prayer*, it was helpful to know that the names of the six spirits which dominated Resistencia, Argentina, were Pombero, Curupí, Reina del Cielo, Freemasonry, witchcraft, and San La Muerte when the intensive field experiment on prayer evangelism was conducted with Edgardo Silvoso.[10] John Dawson tells in his book *Taking*

Our Cities for God that only when he and his team discovered that the ruling principality of Cordoba, Argentina, was "the pride of life" could they come against it by ministering in the opposite spirit, which was humility.[11]

11. You mention the name of your book, *Warfare Prayer*. Since that is not a biblical term, why do you use it?

It is true that some have objected to the term "warfare prayer." While we do not find the term in the Bible, we do find that we are in warfare. Paul tells Timothy to "wage the good warfare" (1 Tm 1:18, NKJV). He uses the analogy of the Roman legion when he tells the Ephesians to "take up the whole armor of God" (Eph 6:13, NKJV).

The biblical weapons for waging this warfare are said to be spiritual, not carnal (see 2 Cor 10:4), and of all the weapons prayer is supreme. Clinton Arnold says, "If Paul were to summarize the primary way of gaining access to the power of God for waging successful spiritual warfare, he would unwaveringly affirm that it is through prayer."[12]

Taking these biblical concepts, we have coined the term "warfare prayer" to describe the type of prayer used for confronting the demonic forces of darkness. Using an extra-biblical term for biblical concepts is well accepted in Christian circles. We frequently use the word Trinity to describe God, for example, though Trinity is not a biblical word either.

12. We have no direct instructions in the New Testament to engage in strategic-level spiritual warfare. Does this not go beyond the established bounds of Scripture?

Evangelical Christianity has not established as a principle that we do nothing that is not explicitly directed by Scripture. There is, however, consensus that we do nothing that is *contrary* to Scripture. Many of us, therefore, worship on Sundays even though Scripture nowhere tells us to do so. The same could apply to celebrating Christmas and Easter. We build church buildings and organize Sunday Schools, and ordain clergy and hold city-wide evangelistic crusades, and advocate the freeing of slaves, and cast demons out of Christians even though we have no explicit directions for any of the above in Scripture.

What we do have for each of them, however, is enough knowledge about God's character and God's will, about the nature of the kingdom of God, and about principles of Christian behavior and ministry to do them all. All check out as not being *contrary* to Scripture. Therefore many of us, if not most of us, do them with no qualms. We should be aware, however, that every one of the things I mentioned above has received strong criticism from thoughtful brothers and sisters in Christ who feel that doing such-and-such is wrong and contrary to the will of God. They uniformly support their point of view by arguing that such behavior goes beyond the bounds of Scripture.

One of my friends told me that if Paul wanted us to do strategic-level spiritual warfare he would have said so in one of his epistles. He seemed surprised when I responded that if this were a principle we would have to apply it to evangelism as well. Nowhere in his epistles did Paul tell his readers that they should be soul-winners and attempt to lead their neighbors to Christ. My friend then saw that if he could not apply it consistently, it probably was not a good principle to begin with.

It may seem strange, but many look primarily in the epistles for biblical directions for ministry, particularly traditional evangelicals. They frequently interpret the Gospels and Acts from the framework of the epistles. Contrariwise, Anabaptists tend to start from the Gospels, while charismatics tend to start from Acts. I began as an epistle-oriented evangelical, but now attempt to give all three sources equal weight. If my friend had agreed, we would have discussed spiritual warfare and evangelism on the basis of what Jesus taught in the Gospels and what the apostles practiced in Acts and found that they are both there, even if they are not stressed in the epistles.

13. But we have examples of the apostles doing evangelism in the Book of Acts. Why don't we have examples of the apostles doing strategic-level spiritual warfare?

My response is that, in fact, we do have such examples in the Book of Acts. One reason we are not fully aware of this is that questions such as the ones we are discussing in this chapter were not in the minds of most biblical scholars who have given us the standard commentaries on Acts. Recognizing this, I am just now completing a twelve-year study of the Book of Acts and publishing my findings in a new three-volume commentary. I am finding substantial evidence for strategic-level spiritual warfare in my study.

One example is the first anecdote Luke records in the missionary career of the apostle Paul after he was sent out from Antioch. A dramatic power encounter occurs while Paul is evangelizing western Cyprus, recorded in Acts 13:6-12. He directly confronts a sorcerer named Elymas or Bar-Jesus. Confrontation with a sorcerer is clearly occult-level spiritual warfare. But was it also strategic-level? In this case it could well have been because of Elymas' relationship with Sergius Paulus, the highest official of the land. Paul demonstrates visibly that the power of God is greater than the occult spirits that empowered Elymas; he became blind, and the proconsul believed in Jesus.

Some may point out that in Cyprus, Paul dealt with a demonic force in an individual, not in a territory. It is not unusual, however, for a high-ranking spirit to attach to a person. The spirit named Legion whom Jesus cast out of a person may well have been one of these. For some reason Legion begged Jesus not to send him out of the *territory* (see Mk 5:10).

A similar example is the Python spirit in Philippi. This was a notorious spirit associated with the temple of Apollo in the city of Delphi. It proceeded from an identifiable seat of Satan in that part of the world. In Philippi Python chose to empower a slave girl, and there Paul directly addressed it by saying, "I command you in the name of Jesus Christ to come out of her" (Acts 16:18). Confronting this spirit had such an impact in the invisible world that the whole city of Philippi was shaken. As a result, Paul and Silas were thrown into jail. A flourishing church was subsequently planted.

I have already mentioned how the "great goddess" Diana of the Ephesians was overcome, not through the avenue of direct confrontation as was the Python spirit, but through ground-level and occult-level warfare. History records that the apostle John later engaged in direct confrontation with Diana in Ephesus, although this is beyond what is recorded in the Book of Acts.[13]

Do instances like these provide us an airtight case for saying that the Bible directs us to do strategic-level spiritual warfare? No. They do, however, indicate that biblical evidence is not *contrary* to a literal interpretation of Jesus' saying, "I give you authority... over all the power of the enemy" (Lk 10:19, NKJV).

14. How about history? Do we have examples in history where Christian leaders used strategic-level spiritual warfare as a part of their evangelistic advance?

We do not as yet have much evidence that our predecessors explicitly practiced what we call warfare prayer. Why? One reason may be that the research has not yet been done. New historical discoveries are constantly surfacing, and when historians begin looking for this they may well find it.

But even if they don't, it is not contrary to the nature of God to do a new thing. It is my opinion that we are now living in an unprecedented time, namely the final thrust of world evangelization. The enemy has been pushed back for almost two thousand years, the kingdom of God is advancing through the world, and Satan has his back to the wall. He is making his last stand, and in order for the kingdom of God to advance further, more supernatural power than ever before will be required. I believe that strategic-level spiritual warfare is one of the new "spiritual technologies" that God has seen fit to give to his people for these abnormal times.

15. If we examine standard Christian theologies through the centuries, we do not find sections on strategic-level spiritual warfare. Why is this?

If it is true that strategic-level spiritual warfare is a relatively new thing in the Christian movement, it follows that theologians would not previously have been asking themselves the questions we are now raising.

An interesting recent parallel is the theology of the ministry of all believers through spiritual gifts. Our standard theologies did not develop this point in any detail before 1970, even though it is almost universally accepted in the body of Christ today. Martin Luther, for example, rediscovered the biblical teaching on the *priesthood* of all believers, but he apparently never saw the biblical teaching on the *ministry* of all believers.

Our theologians do the best they can, but most of them, consciously or unconsciously, derive their theological agendas from ministry contexts. Only recently have we had ministry contexts in which questions regarding strategic-level spiritual warfare have been emerging.

16. Preaching the gospel has always been the divine method of evangelism. Only the gospel saves. Why should we add to it anything like spiritual warfare?

This is a very important question because it gives us a good opportunity to clarify that spiritual warfare is not evangelism. No one was ever saved simply by binding the strong man. The preaching of Christ and him crucified, repentance, and personal faith in Jesus as Savior and Lord is what brings the new birth and eternal life.

Few, however, are truly satisfied with the progress of evangelism in their cities and their neighborhoods today. What are the obstacles? The apostle Paul says that the major obstacle preventing the glory of Christ from shining on unbelievers is the god of this age who blinds minds (see 2 Cor 4:3-4). Strategic-level spiritual warfare is only a means to attempt to remove as many of these blinders as possible so that unbelievers can hear the gospel and respond to the wooing of the Holy Spirit. Spiritual warfare is not to be seen as an end in itself. The basic question is not how many satanic strongholds are torn down, but how many captives of the enemy are thereby released to the glory of God.

17. Directing so much attention to spiritual mapping and identifying territorial spirits can result in dissipating our energies and giving too much credit to Satan and the powers of darkness. Why should we be glorifying Satan?

Nothing we do should glorify Satan in the least. Our chief end, as the Westminster Catechism so eloquently says, is to glorify God and enjoy him forever. Some extremists may seem to have a tendency to become so fascinated with spiritual warfare that it becomes an end in itself. If it does, attention may be drawn to the enemy and not to God. We need to avoid such a thing, and for the most part we do.

First and foremost in any spiritual warfare initiative should be God's redemptive purposes for the city or other territory. God should have the highest profile. As I said in answer to the last question, dealing with the forces of darkness is only a means toward the end of God's purposes whether they be evangelism, social justice, or whatever.

I am grateful to John Dawson for his stress on the redemptive gift in *Taking Our Cities for God*. This is of utmost importance. In fact, I invite John to lecture in my Fuller Seminary courses on spiritual warfare on the first day to set a positive tone. I want God's purposes to reign supreme in my students' minds and I want them to learn to pray positively for God's kingdom to come to their communities.

18. Along those same lines, is it possible for publicity on spiritual warfare to empower the demonic spirits and to make them more dangerous?

I have never quite understood where this occasional question comes from. It almost sounds like the equivalent of raising the question as to whether we should research and publicize the way the HIV virus is transmitted for fear of causing more AIDS. The purpose of spending money on medical research is not to *glorify* a disease but to *eradicate* it. The more we know about it, the more we can fight it.

Exposing the "wiles of the devil," as Paul calls them in Ephesians 6:11, is a method of weakening, not empowering, the forces of darkness. "Wiles" is another word for strategies. Paul may not have been ignorant of the devil's strategies, but unfortunately, many of us today are. This only leaves us more vulnerable. Paul says that "lest Satan should take advantage of us... we are not ignorant of his devices" (2 Cor 2:11, NKJV). Since none of us wants to be taken advantage of, we do well to learn as much as we can about how the enemy operates.

The devil thrives on the "occult," which means "hidden." Secret societies know that if their rituals and activities become known to the public, they will be weakened and vulnerable to attack. Secrecy is a weapon of the devil because he is a deceiver by nature. We need to minister in the opposite spirit, which is full and open disclosure of reality.

19. Could strategic-level spiritual warfare simply be a fad? Are there dangers that it could turn out to be like the discredited "shepherding movement" which caused harm to the body of Christ?

Yes, the dangers are there and must be avoided. Since I was not involved in the discipling movement myself, I will turn to Paul Reid of Northern Ireland who was. Reid broke with the discipling or shepherding movement after he was deeply wounded by it, and he analyzes the experience in his book, *A New Easter Rising*.[14] In it he lists the three most prominent sinful aspects of the movement which he and others needed to repent of:

1) "Self-righteousness. We believed that we were better than other churches and fellowships." This is also a danger in strategic-level spiritual warfare. We must under-

stand and communicate to the general public that *only a few members of the body of Christ are called to and anointed for frontline warfare.* This calling is not based on some special attainment of spirituality or status with the Lord. It is as much due to the sovereign choice of God as was the selection of Gideon's three hundred, or just under 1 percent of the eligible warriors. When victory is won, the whole body of Christ shares the rewards equally.

It is a grave error to project the elitist idea that only the first-class Christians or churches engage in spiritual warfare, and that those who don't are somehow second-class Christians. God resists the proud but gives grace to the humble.

2) "Manipulation. Lives had been controlled through shepherding." I have not as yet seen indications of this in strategic-level spiritual warfare. In fact, the Spiritual Warfare Network is part of the A.D. 2000 and Beyond Movement and its United Prayer Track, which are intentionally structured as grassroots organizations to avoid any possibility of manipulation. I hope this continues.

3) "Idolatry. We had given to people the honor due to God alone." This is a temptation that I have found in almost every movement I have been associated with. In the Church Growth Movement pastors of large, growing churches are susceptible to receiving the glory. In the signs and wonders movement, those who receive most words of knowledge or see most people slain in the Holy Spirit are susceptible. In the strategic-level spiritual warfare movement those who see cities transformed socially and spiritually are susceptible.

If we are willing to learn from the mistakes of the discipling movement, mistakes that their top leaders now freely confess, we can avoid becoming harmful to the body of Christ and do damage only to the kingdom of darkness.

20. Isn't there a risk in confronting high-ranking princi-palities such as Paul and Silas did in Philippi? They ended up beaten and thrown in jail. Shouldn't Christians take a defensive posture and "stand" as it says in Ephesians 6:13? Most of the armor of God in that chapter is defensive.

The first thing to be said about this is that God does not call all Christians to risk the dangers of the front lines like he did Paul and Silas. Most believers are like the 31,700 who stayed home when Gideon battled the Midianites. They were where God wanted them to be, as were the three hundred who went to the front lines with Gideon. The remarkable thing about this case study is that there was no recrimination on either side. The three hundred did not complain that 31,700 stayed home, nor did those who stayed behind criti-cize those who went.

In today's context, I see myself as one called to the front lines. This is not some kind of spiritual merit badge, but sim-ply an honest belief that God has called me to do this and given me a personal desire to obey God's commands. I have no inclination to recriminate others whom God has called to stay home. They are warring with Satan on different battle-fields. Some have all they can do to keep a marriage together, to deal with dishonest business colleagues, to serve on an underfunded school board, to care for elderly parents, to pay next month's rent, to participate in a program to feed the homeless of their city, to plant this year's corn after a wet spring, or to resolve a conflict between the pastor and an elder. This is biblical. In the Bible itself, good reasons given for an Israelite not to go to war were building a new house, planting a vineyard, or marrying a fiancée (see Dt 20:5-7). Doing such things is God's best for many Christians, indeed the majority.

But God's best for my life, as it was for the apostle Paul, seems to be to move into the community and into the world on the offensive. Consequently, I attract others around me who feel a similar calling and we have formed the International Spiritual Warfare Network. I confess that my zeal for the battle may have come across to others as though I consider them less faithful to God if they do not join me. I am deeply sorry for this and I ask forgiveness. I need to improve the way I communicate, and I know that many of my friends would join me in this confession.

As we have attempted to follow God's marching orders, the thing that has hurt some of us most deeply is attacks on what we are doing by those who have been called to stay home and resist Satan in other ways. Some implicitly and some explicitly have suggested that we could be out of the will of the Lord. Some have argued that no Christian at all should move into confrontation with principalities and powers. Some have scolded us for exceeding limits of our authority. Some have caricatured strategic-level spiritual warfare as "the big demon theory" or "duking it out with the devil" or "railing at devils on street corners." Many of them raise the kind of question I am responding to here by advocating the defensive, rather than the confrontational, posture not only as God's will for them but for all other Christians as well.

Many of these critics speak from ignorance of what actually happens in responsible strategic-level spiritual warfare. They are largely unaware of the extensive preliminary research, the foundation of unity of local Christian pastors and leaders, the prolonged times of intimacy with the Father, the praise and worship that exalts God, the deep repentance that characterizes more than half of the prayer time, and the social and personal reconciliation that emerges as a fruit of the ministry.

To see the armor of God in Ephesians 6 as merely defensive is to misunderstand Paul's analogy. The Roman warrior to whom Paul alludes was never trained to see defense as an end in itself, but only as a means to an end of vanquishing the enemy. When Roman legions moved out to the frontiers, they did so with the explicit goal of extending the boundaries of the Roman Empire, not to huddle back and invite their enemies to attack them. Their armor was designed to enable them to do that very thing. Those whom God calls to strategic-level spiritual warfare today are to put on the whole armor of God as they seek the advance of the kingdom of God.

Is this risky? Yes. Paul says to Timothy, "You therefore must endure hardship as a good soldier of Jesus Christ" (2 Tm 2:3, NKJV). Every war has casualties, although we do our best to keep them to a minimum. But Paul, who is among the best of God's soldiers, speaks of his own tribulations, needs, distresses, stripes, imprisonments, and tumults (see 2 Cor 6:4-5). He also testifies to stonings, shipwrecks, perils of robbers, perils in the city, cold, nakedness, hunger, and many other hardships (see 2 Cor 11:23-27).

Many of my colleagues have suffered similar things. My own wife has been hammered hard by the enemy. But for the most part they "count it all joy when [they] fall into various trials" (Jas 1:2), and they get up and move into the battle once again. They know their calling from God, and they enjoy living in obedience to him, risky as it might be.

21. How do you respond to a public document that suggests that those engaged in spiritual warfare tend to substitute technique and methodology for holiness, evangelism, and Spirit-guided teaching?

Those who would frame such a document are obviously poorly informed. Among those I relate to in the field of strategic-level spiritual warfare, none would reduce their ministry to a methodology or technique. The closest I have seen to this is some authors in the field who print sample prayers for those involved in deliverance. Although I would not do this myself, I do understand that these prayers are not offered as some magical type of formula but simply as aids to those who are beginning and who have little experience. Most of the authors state this explicitly.

Rather than neglect evangelism, the contemporary Spiritual Warfare Network and the A.D. 2000 United Prayer Track are intensely focused on evangelism. As I have said, the kind of warfare prayer I am talking about is not regarded as an end in itself, but as a means to facilitate world evangelization, especially unreached people groups under the oppressive grip of the enemy.

Holiness is universally regarded by spiritual warriors as a personal prerequisite for moving into battle. Cindy Jacobs says that you can put on the armor of God, but without personal holiness you will have holes in your armor. A lack of purity and the fruit of the Spirit is an invitation to effective counterattacks by the devil.

Any teaching that is not guided by the Holy Spirit is obviously dangerous in spiritual warfare. This is why the most experienced of the front line warriors spend extraordinarily long hours in prayer, securing their intimacy with the Father. Having a realistic assessment of the power of the enemy forces them to do this. They would be foolish to go into battle without being filled with the Holy Spirit and seeking the Spirit's specific guidance as to the methodology and timing related to each case. They carefully study the written Word of God and also listen carefully for any specific word of guidance that the Holy Spirit gives them. The sword of the Spirit is the Word of God (see Eph 6:17).

Armed with mature knowledge of the Word of God and the fullness of the Holy Spirit, those who are called to the front lines can exercise the authority given to them by Jesus Christ, bind on earth what is bound in heaven, wrestle effectively against principalities and powers, and see God's kingdom advanced and Jesus' Great Commission fulfilled.

SIX

A Biblical Perspective

Tom White

From the early 1980s until now, there has been developing in churches and mission fields a strategy of ministry that focuses on active involvement in spiritual warfare. This term itself is very much in vogue, almost faddish. Followers of Jesus Christ do battle with "the world, the flesh, *and* the devil." Most of the battle is, in actual fact, with the flesh and false values. No one wants to give undue credit to the Evil One. Yet many people have moved from giving theological lip service to resisting evil to affirming that there must be a concerted strategy for it.

For the remainder of the church age, we live in the tension of Jesus' "already-but-not-yet" accomplished triumph over evil. "Already" because he destroyed the devil and his works (Heb 2:14; 1 Jn 3:8) and disarmed the principalities and powers (Col 2:15). "Not yet" because Satan and his forces will not be finally bound until the end of the age (Mt 13:37-43). The challenge for the believer is to "overcome the evil one" (1 Jn 2:12-14). The continued presence of evil provides a testing ground for both unsaved and saved.

The call is clear to personally overcome evil, to live the truth, and to be involved in setting others free from sin and Satan. However, the how-to of confrontation with ruling powers of evil is not so clear. I believe we must carefully guard against promoting extra-biblical methodologies that convey a "magic bullet" mentality. In the following pages I will suggest some biblical guidelines and models for discerning, penetrating, and overcoming the principalities and powers of evil.

ASKING THE TOUGH QUESTIONS

The sad truth is that often believers *react* to phenomena of evil too little, too late. A *pro*active mind set is urgently needed. We face today a widespread growth of the New Age agenda and of humanistic philosophies, a proliferation of cults and occult spiritism, the resurgence of militant Islam, and an alarming rise of blatant satanic ritual. At the same time, the Spirit is breathing a fresh courage into the church, equipping the rank and file for warfare. We have overindulged in theologizing and theorizing. It is time for more of us to take to the trenches.

In evangelism, we are accustomed to dealing with cultural barriers, intellectual resistance, and religious dogma. How skilled are we in discerning the invisible spiritual power that separates a soul from the knowledge of truth? How do we contend with it? How capable are we of identifying spiritual forces that contaminate the atmosphere over certain cities and regions? These are tough questions.

Consider the parable of the seed and sower. In some cases, when the word of truth goes forth, the "birds of the air" come along and devour the seed. These birds, according to Jesus, are the demonic powers that steal away the reception of saving truth (Mt 13:4, 19). Paul tells us that unbelievers are yet subject to the "spirit of disobedience" (Eph 2:2), and that the god of this age "has blinded the minds of unbelievers, so that they cannot see the light of the gospel" (2 Cor 4:4, NIV). We have not taken these verses seriously enough.

We read in Ephesians 6 about putting on the armor of God to face the struggle against the forces of evil. What, precisely, does "struggle" mean? We know from the context that Paul is depicting hand-to-hand combat. But there needs to be a fleshing out of the interpretation of this word.

What is Jesus describing when he illustrates the binding and plundering of the "strong man" (Lk 11:21-22)? He is speaking of the conquering of the kingdom of Satan. Does this merely refer to demonized persons in need of deliverance, or can it refer to a bold and aggressive penetration of territorial strongholds? What are the implications of Ephesians 3:10, where in some manner the mystery of redemption is being made known "*through* the church *to* the principalities and powers"? What about Jesus' commission to Saul to "turn them from darkness to light, from the power of Satan to God" (Acts 26:18-19)? Does this turning involve only sharing the truth with individuals, or is there a place for exposing and weakening the grip of powers of darkness that hinder response to the truth?

I believe that a more aggressive application of God's authority is necessary to enhance our effectiveness in the harvest. But let's be clear. This is more about intercessing before God's throne than outright confrontation of the powers. Decades ago, the role of leaders to apply this authority was described by theologian J.A. MacMillan:

To share a throne means without question to partake of the authority which it represents. Indeed, they have been thus elevated, in the plan of God, for this very purpose, that they may even now exercise, to the extent of their spiritual apprehension, authority over the powers of the air, and over the conditions which those powers have brought about on the earth and are still creating through their ceaseless manipulations of the minds and circumstances of mankind.[1]

We who are ambassadors of Christ have anointed authority over the powers themselves (see Lk 10:17-20), and over the various *effects* such powers have on people. This is a stirring concept! But the authority must be put into action.

In the early 1980s, the Hindu guru Baghwan Shree Rajneesh purchased land in central Oregon and began to build a city for his disciples. Over five thousand devotees came to sit under his teaching, which was expressly anti-Christian. Local residents, politicians, and law enforcement personnel tried different means over the years to get the group out of Oregon's backyard, all to no avail. In 1985 and 1986, I had the privilege of participating in two prayer meetings with committed intercessors who led out in strategic prayer, petitioning the Lord to weaken the grip of the spiritual force standing behind the Rajneesh commune. At the conclusion of these sessions, the participants felt that the ultimate removal of the Baghwan was a matter of time. I vividly recall praying David's powerful petition, "Contend, O Lord, with those who contend with me" (Ps 35:1, NIV).

In 1987, several of the commune's leaders were indicted on legal charges, and within weeks the guru was deported, leaving a few scattered followers. I believe it was the prevailing prayer of the saints that scattered the enemies of Yahweh.

Let me rephrase the issue in the form of two questions. First, *is it biblically sound and humanly safe to devise and carry out aggressive strategies for overcoming evil at the higher levels of the ruling powers?* There is a clear biblical mandate for exposing falsehood and false teachers, for delivering individuals from the binding powers of evil spirits (Lk 10:17-20), for taking a defensive and protective stance against satanic oppression (Eph 6:10), and for personally "overcoming" the Evil One (Rv 12:11). But is the church justified in escalating the conflict? Is it our place? In seeking to answer this question, I readily admit to a measure of personal hesitancy. One *must* have a scriptural place to stand here, and an unmistakable leading of the Spirit before storming hell's gates.

There is an eschatological consideration as well. To what extent can *we* realistically expect to weaken and eliminate territorial powers of darkness before the return of Jesus with his holy angels to judge evil men and bind Satan's power (2 Thes 1:5-10)? Will there not be an inevitable mixing of tares among the wheat until the reaping comes? Similarly, will there not be a permeation of the heavenlies with polluted principalities until the King of Kings ordains their removal?

The second question is practical. If in some qualified manner we can answer "yes" to the first question, we then inquire, *what does such an aggressive strategy look like?* It must be a supernatural strategy, initiated by God and infused with the potency of prayer and praise. Yet it cannot be elusively mystical. It must be tangible, pursuable. And it must be compatible with biblical limits, or it is not to be pursued at all. The risk here is high. The dangers should be obvious. Though Satan is a "pseudo-prince," he still wields a bona fide power that can take advantage of human, fleshly effort. What follows is an attempt to point in a safe and sound direction for those who feel called to do cosmic-level spiritual warfare.

STRIPPING AWAY THE VENEER: WHAT ARE WE UP AGAINST?

Having been personally involved in the study of the New Age teachings before conversion, I had an interest in understanding Paul's reference to "principalities and powers." I sought to answer this in my master's thesis at Asbury Seminary in 1975. Though the results of this study cannot be fully developed here, it is relevant to list some conclusions. What do we "struggle" against? Who, or what, are these "principalities and powers"?

We know from the contexts of Ephesians 1:21 and 6:12, and Colossians 1:16 and 2:15, that these are high-level, fallen angelic powers that operate in Satan's domain, opposing the redemptive purposes of God. The study of both Old and New Testaments, with corroborative evidence from certain Apocryphal texts, reveals two clear categories of fallen powers: 1) those angelic beings who fell originally with Lucifer at the time of his rebellion, and who are still active in the deception and affliction of all mankind, and 2) the "sons of God" (angelic beings) of Genesis 6:2 who committed such abominable acts of immorality with the "daughters of men" (women), that they were "bound with everlasting chains for judgment on the great Day" (Jude 6, NIV).

Paul brings light to the subject by describing the fallen angels at various operative levels: rulers/principalities ("archai"), authorities ("exousia"), powers ("dunamis"), and spiritual forces of evil ("kosmokratoras"). Though it seems reasonable that this list depicts the powers in descending order of authority, there is no textual evidence to confirm this. Through my research, I lean in the following interpretive directions. Daniel 10:13 and 20 unveils an Old Testament reference to the "archai" as high-level satanic princes set over nations/regions of the earth. The word "exousia" connotes both supernatural and natural parts of the government, in other words, there is a point of connection between the fallen powers and earthly authorities. Presumably, the "dunamis" operate within countries and cultures to control certain aspects of human activity. The "kosmokratoras," then, could be the many types of evil spirits that commonly afflict humanity, for example, spirits of deception, divination, lust, rebellion, fear, infirmity, and so on. These, generally, are the evil powers confronted and cast out in the majority of deliverance sessions. Even among them there is ranking, weaker spirits submitting to "strong men"

(Mt 12:29). Until the Day of Judgment, God allows these forces to remain in the heavenlies in spite of their disobedience. Mankind thus lives in the tension of a temporary, transitional situation where victory has been won, but where the redeemed also continue to struggle against evil. These insidious powers continue to work through human governments, religions, and select personalities to keep people in bondage to religious codes, social systems, and moral compromises that separate people from the knowledge of truth in Jesus Christ. Their role is to deceive the minds and pollute the wills of humankind, diverting them from redemption.

Several years ago we prayed with a new convert, a man who had grown up in West Berlin in the late 1930s. His grandfather and uncle had both been involved in the Nazi movement. He recalled secret meetings of German government officials in his home. With discernment and prayer, we exposed a stronghold of darkness in this new Christian. It seemed to be bound up with the very forces that fed the diabolical schemes of Hitler. Though the earthly movement finally failed, the spiritual powers of witchcraft and hatred of the Jew are still present. This man's life had particular strategic influence, so we battled for our brother's freedom over the course of a year. In the final session, a strong, dark spirit manifested itself, directly threatening my life. Holding firm in faith, with the sword of the Spirit, four other pastors and I prevailed to break Satan's claim on this man. It worked. Today, he and his wife are free to serve the Lord, witnessing to the grace of God as they set other captives free.

Exposing and dealing with higher powers of evil typically occurs when we press into kingdom ministry, for example, evangelistic penetration of a community, conducting individual deliverance, or engaging in authoritative intercession for a city or region. In the course of setting the individual souls free from the grip of darkness, we will regularly encounter lives that have been specifically targeted. In a sense, these are the valuable "chessmen"; winning them for God's kingdom draws the attention and stirs the anger of forces that have invested considerable effort in maintaining an evil stronghold. When such powers pressure a man of God to back off through fear and threat, it is time to stand our ground, claim ownership of the soul for Jesus, and speak judgment on the darkness. But as the Spirit guides, it is an imperative point of spiritual warfare that we *do not go looking for this level of battle, but that we let it find us.*

(When we speak of evil at this level, we are in a sense describing the "Boardroom of Hell," acknowledging that there are high-ranking CEOs [Chief Executive Officers] responsible for the major movements of deception and destruction of human life in our world. There are likely principalities that promote the proliferation of New Age metaphysics, the rise of ritualistic satanism, the production and provision of drugs, sexual perversion, and pornography. These are examples of the fallen forces of evil that seek to blind the minds [2 Cor 4:4] and bind the lives of the unbelieving world [1 Jn 5:19]. The question at hand is: *how are the ambassadors of Jesus Christ to wage war against the rising tide of darkness in the remainder of this century?*)

I believe we are first to be faithful to work at the overcoming of evil "from the bottom up." We "stand" as individuals, families, and local church bodies (Eph 6:10-18) against the devil's schemes. Some of us, however, will be called and equipped by God to stand more strategically against darkness. This activity, I suggest, is not common, or normative. It must be initiated by God himself, and sustained by his power.

COUNTERING EVIL POWER:
BIBLICAL PRECEDENTS IN THE OLD TESTAMENT

To find biblical precedents for cosmic-level warfare, it is wise to search Scripture for examples of confronting evil that go beyond person-to-person encounters. The Old Testament unveils Satan, the adversary, the one opposed to the purposes of God. Yet there is no development of the concept of resistance against him and the powers under his charge. Yet the seeds of later theological development are seen in Genesis 3:15, the judgment of Yahweh on the serpent: "And I will put enmity between you and the woman, and between your offspring and hers; he will crush your head, and you will strike his heel" (NIV).

As a result of Adam and Eve's yielding to the enticement of Satan, God imposes a condition of hostility between the human race and the demonic realm, to be resolved only by the appearing of the Messiah, the one who has authority and power to crush the serpent. The implications of Genesis 3:15 are not fleshed out in the Old Testament revelation. In Job 1 and 2, Daniel 10, and Zechariah 3:1, we see Satan in the background serving as accuser. But there is no direct confrontation with evil spirits.

We see idolatry, false deities that vie for the attention and adulation of mankind. The implication of the second commandment, "You shall have no other gods before me" (Dt 5:7), is that there *are* other gods that compete with the one true God. The challenge to Israel is to maintain commitment to their covenant relationship with Yahweh. But there is no clear mandate to war against supernatural forces, just Yahweh's role as "warrior" (Ex 15:3). There are exhortations, especially in the Psalms and Proverbs, to be separated from idolatry and evildoers. Evil is particularized with persons, places, and pagan nations.

Moses confronts Pharaoh. The first strategic, classic "power encounter" of the Old Testament occurs when Yahweh instructs Moses to go to Pharaoh with the command to let Israel leave the land. Moses has already struggled with the fear that Israel will not listen to him; now he is given the charge to go up against the seat of authority of Egypt: "Moses said to the Lord, 'Since I speak with faltering lips, why would Pharaoh listen to me?' Then the Lord said to Moses, 'See, I have made you like God to Pharaoh, and your brother Aaron will be your prophet'" (Ex 6:30-7:1, NIV).

Moses knew he was out of his league. He would need the direct impartation of divine authority and power in order to do the impossible: "I have made you like God to Pharaoh." Yahweh chose a vessel for a strategic purpose. The assignment was to strike at the heart of the source of power set over a nation. When Pharaoh took up the challenge and demanded a miracle, Aaron's staff turned into a snake. But the sorcerers and magicians of Egypt produced the same miracle! Yahweh countered by having his snake devour the lesser serpent, thereby demonstrating his superior power. We read about the remaining plagues and the deliverance through the Red Sea.

Moses was sent by sovereign choice. He did not go looking for, and did not want, an encounter with the powers of Egypt. In the face of fear, he wrestled with sacrificial submission to the will of God. In confronting Pharaoh, Moses and Aaron "did just as the Lord commanded them" (Ex 7:6, NIV). Moses clearly heard the voice of God. Then he was made to be "like God" to Pharaoh, granted an anointed authority guaranteed to succeed. Finally, he chose to obey and to submit to the divine will.

There is a profound point here: we dare not go looking for strategic power encounters—a man or woman must hear the voice of the Lord, and be sent. In the absence of this clarity, it is dangerously foolish to plunge into this level of spiritual combat.

Elijah and the prophets of Baal. The showdown with the prophets of Baal at Mount Carmel (1 Kgs 18:16-46) provides another Old Testament example of a man of God countering evil power. First, Elijah brought the issue into view: who really is God here? (v. 21). At stake was the submission of Israel to Yahweh as sovereign. He threw down a challenge to the prophets of Baal to demonstrate the power of their deities. The prophet, with taunts and mockery, then exposed the weakness of their god (v. 27). He pressed them into a corner, with a holy and confident boldness (personally, I think the taunting was more from Elijah himself than from the Spirit—I do not recommend this for our model). Elijah then prepared a *sacrifice*, the covenantal mode of pleasing God. But the key to success of the encounter came with a boldness in *prayer:* "O Lord, God of Abraham, Isaac and Israel, let it be known today that you are God in Israel and that I am your servant and have done all these things at your command. Answer me, O Lord, answer me, so that these people will know that you, O Lord, are God, and that you are turning their hearts back again" (1 Kgs 18:36-37, NIV).

Elijah's boldness was rooted in the clarity and confidence of *God's command.* He was prepared and prompted to make the challenge. The Almighty unveiled himself for the purpose of turning hearts back to him. Elijah was uniquely prepared and empowered. He had an unmistakable word from God to "go for it." The power of the Almighty was released by the faithful and fervent prayer of an obedient servant.

At this level of confrontation, there still was a personal price to pay. Under threat of his life by Ahab and Jezebel, "Elijah was afraid and ran" (1 Kgs 19:3, NIV). Humanly, he suffered from emotional exhaustion, the release of tension that follows a significant, stressful battle of this sort. Also, we can assume that the spiritual forces associated with the worship of Baal were enraged and sought revenge. In the unguarded moment of human letdown, the evil powers working through Ahab and Jezebel struck at his weakness. For such a profound victory, there was a price to pay.

Daniel and the satanic princes. In most conversations where the topic of cosmic-level warfare arises, the example of Daniel is cited. Again, as with Moses and Elijah, Daniel was a vessel uniquely prepared and chosen to participate in the unveiling of God's higher purposes for his people. Daniel was the recipient of visionary revelation that provided detail on the history of his people, the nations, and the coming of the Messiah. In the third year of Cyrus, king of Persia, another revelation was given to Daniel during a difficult, prolonged fast. A divine being, possibly the pre-incarnate Christ, came to Daniel in response to his prayer for understanding of a vision. There is also evidence that Gabriel, the messenger for earlier revelations to Daniel, is present with the Lord. I believe it is he who reveals the spiritual battle involved: "But the prince of the Persian kingdom resisted me twenty-one days. Then Michael, one of the chief princes, came to help me, because I was detained there with the king of Persia" (Dn 10:13, NIV).

It is unmistakable in the Hebrew that this "prince of Persia" is a powerful, territorial satanic angel on assignment to block the unveiling of the revelation. There is corroborative evidence that Jesus is present (cf. Ez 1:25-28; Rv 1:9-18). Daniel addresses this personage as "my Lord" (10:16-17). If so, there is a startling thing occurring here. The Christ, as Commander of the hosts of the Almighty, oversees the battle, yet delegates responsibility for the warfare to the archangels. There is an engagement of power, the outcome of which depends on the faithful service of the angels and the faith of a man of God in prayer. Verse 20 reveals that it is the assignment of Gabriel and Michael to fight against these princes. *Daniel had nothing directly to do with the battle at that level.* His role was that of prayer and humble submission to the will of God. The invisible battle raged on above him and about him, and was waged by the highest of the angels. And even at this level there was a significant struggle. Daniel's focus of attention was on the person of God, and his plan for Israel. He may have been keenly aware that spiritual forces were involved, but his energy was given to prevailing prayer.

After scanning these particular Old Testament power encounters, I conclude that these men were sent into strategic battle by God himself. They wrestled with the issue of submission. There was a connectedness to the divine will through prayer, for such encounters are strategic initiatives orchestrated by God. Success at this level of supernatural struggle comes solely by his strength and by the submission of his people to him as sovereign.

COUNTERING EVIL POWER: BIBLICAL PRECEDENTS IN THE NEW TESTAMENT

Jesus the Deliverer. The incarnation and resurrection of Jesus Christ brings to a focal point the whole of apocalyptic history. He is the promised one of Genesis 3:15 who has authority and power to crush the head of the serpent. He alone can deliver people from the binding oppression of demons. In the Judean wilderness, after his baptism by John, he enters into an encounter with Satan, and emerges victorious by standing on the strength of the Word of God: "It is written" (Mt 4:1-11). After this encounter, his ministry explodes with authority and power to proclaim the message of reconciliation, to heal the sick, and to cast out demons. He delegates his authority over evil first to the twelve (Lk 9:1-2), then later to the seventy-two (Lk 10:1), for the purpose of delivering individual persons from the devil's power, and for recording names in the Book of Life. He does say that this authority will overcome *"all* power of the enemy" (Lv 10:17). Jesus *did* confront and defeat Satan himself, but it was only when he was under attack. We never do see him looking for and initiating an assault on the adversary. Even when the sly one prompts Peter to divert Jesus from the cross, the Savior gives a straight rebuke, "Out of my sight, Satan!" (Mt 16:23, NIV). He did not seek out the devil for power encounters. It is my conviction that Jesus engaged in deliverance for the sake of those who were responding to his message of reconciliation. He shows us that the living truth further releases power sufficient to expose Satan as the "father of lies" (Jn 8:31-47).

Luke 11:21-22 records Jesus' description of attacking and overpowering the "strong man." He had just cast a mute spirit out of a man, and there was the blasphemous suggestion that he was doing this in the power of Beelzebub. After making the point that a kingdom divided against itself cannot stand, he uses the strong man story to illustrate that his authority is sufficient to break Satan's grip on a life and plunder his spoils. The section concludes with a description of an evil spirit leaving and then returning to a man who has not received the Holy Spirit to guard him from re-invasion. *The point is this: the focus of the illustration of the strong man is individual deliverance, the setting free of a soul as evidence of the coming of the kingdom of God.* There is weak justification here for using this passage as a launching pad for escalating the conflict onto a territorial level. The kingdom *is* manifested when hostages are freed. One thing is clear: the disciple of Jesus Christ is granted authority to cast demons out of individuals as a function of redemption, and for the secondary purpose of providing freedom from the devil's afflictive power.

Paul the apostle. Saul violently opposed the purposes of God as revealed in Christ. He was sovereignly led to salvation, and sent with a commission "to open the eyes and turn them from darkness to light, and from the power of Satan to God, so that they may receive forgiveness of sins and a place among those who are sanctified by faith in me" (Acts 26:17-18, NIV). Here again is one chosen to oppose evil for the freedom of souls and the glory of God. Again, the focus of the power encounter is on the salvation of individual people. In this commission, there is no indication of a holy crusade designed to cleanse the heavens of pollutive powers of hell. His calling is to be caught up with the miraculous mystery of the building of the church. Paul speaks of his role as "prisoner of Christ Jesus" in Ephesians 3:1-13. It is the building up of the body in love and unity that is to "be made known to the principalities and powers in the heavenly realms" (3:10, NIV); this is a tangible demonstration of divine community that exposes the emptiness and deception of evil.

I believe that Paul's words in Ephesians 6:10-18 primarily portray the Christian's struggle to "stand" against the relentless assault of evil, individually and corporately, that the armor is primarily defensive in nature. The presumption here seems to be that Satan is on the offensive, and that we are to stand our ground. Where, then, is the offensive exposure of evil and the expansion of goodness? Clearly, it is in the anointed presentation of truth (the "rema," the sword of the Spirit, the verbalized word) and the release of power in prayer. This is precisely what Paul was doing when he confronted Elymas the magician on Cyprus, "You are a child of the devil and an enemy of everything that is right!" (Acts 13:10, NIV). It is likely that Elymas consorted with evil spirits. But Paul, led by the Holy Spirit, spoke judgment upon the evil of the *man.*

The apostle makes a significant statement in his Letter to the Romans. After warning the church to watch out for those who cause division and strife, he injects a bold affirmation: "The God of peace will soon crush Satan under your feet" (16:20, NIV). He will be crushed under the feet of the body of Christ. But again it is *God himself* who has the role of doing the crushing.

What conclusions may we draw from the New Testament data? As representatives of Jesus, we are called to do what he himself did (Jn 14:12), proclaiming the news of reconciliation, making disciples, healing the sick, and casting out demons. Yes, we are to be more courageously involved in the work of deliverance. Yes, we are to expose evil when we discern it (Eph 5:11), yet speak blessing to the evildoer (Mt 5:44; Rom 12:17-21) in hopes of leading him into light. The church is to stand against and extinguish schemes of evil as they present themselves (Eph 6:10-18), being alert to such schemes (2 Cor 11:3, 14; 1 Pt 5:8). We are given practical instruction on how to "resist the devil" until he flees (Jas 4:6-10). The conditions for such resistance are centered on strengthening personal relationship to God. We are called to live the mystery of love, demonstrating the miraculous unity that is possible only in Christ (Eph 3:1-13). We are exhorted to earnestly pray for those in positions of governmental authority (1 Tm 2:1-2), that the gospel may be lived and promoted. The spontaneous, Spirit-led expansion of truth through the children of light is the normative means of advancing the kingdom. This will only occur in the context of bold, holy obedience.

If these are the normative strategies for God's people, what, we may now ask, are the extraordinary means of expanding light in the darkness? In the face of the flood of evil in our day, God seems to be leading his people at this time to recognize the higher sources of evil with more discernment, and to offensively restrain their influence. Based on the foregoing biblical precedents, I believe we may construct a model of kingdom expansion that will lead to a more fruitful co-laboring with our Lord in the building of his body in the spiritual climate of the time ahead.

God continues to call and equip pioneers and intercessors to press this battle. There are some who are bold in identifying and praying against principalities. It is not my role to be critical of others who pursue a more confrontational, aggressive approach. What I offer here and in chapter eight is a concerted effort to build a model consistent with our best understanding of God's revealed ways of overcoming evil.

SEVEN

How Satan Works at the Cosmic Level

John Robb

Jesus said, "I have given you authority to tread on serpents and scorpions and to overcome all the power of the enemy; *nothing* will harm you" (Lk 10:19, NIV, emphasis mine). His disciples returned from their first encounter with the demonic realm joyfully exclaiming, "Even the demons submit to us in your name!" (Lk 10:17, NIV). And the apostle John encourages us that, "The one who is in you is greater than the one who is in the world" (1 Jn 4:4, NIV). In spite of such statements, we can choose to live in blissful ignorance of our enemy and his tactics like children too afraid to venture into a darkened attic. Or with the light of God's Word and faith in his guidance and protection, we can seek to discover in a new way the power and prerogatives Jesus has given his followers to joyously and victoriously deal with the forces of darkness. In this chapter we will endeavor to better understand how our enemy works in order to more effectively combat him through learning what Scripture and the experience of God's servants around the world teach us.

SATAN'S OVERALL PROGRAM

Satan is a highly organized, intelligent spirit being dedicated to destroying human beings made in the image of the Creator he so deeply hates. He is the master deceiver and the author of idolatry, seeking to bring the whole world under his dominion by undermining faith in God, twisting values, and promoting false ideologies. He does this through infiltrating institutions, government administrations, communications media, educational systems, and religious bodies. He seeks to divert humankind's attention from worship of the Creator through substitution of money, fame, power, pleasure, science, art, politics, or religious idols. His three-point agenda is deception, dominion, and destruction. One of his primary objectives is to gain such control over nations and governments that he can turn them against one another to be destroyed through war or turn them against their own citizens to destroy themselves. We might think of the genocidal crimes of Hitler, Stalin, and Saddam Hussein, or the massive killing of the unborn through abortion, practiced increasingly in many societies.

Satan works through controlling spirits. Satan is not omnipresent or omniscient, but, as a master networker, he uses a vast organization of spirit beings who apparently communicate with each other and work in some sense cooperatively to undermine humanity's encounter with the kingdom of God. Toward this end these spirits attempt to gain influence over government leaders, legal and educational systems, and religious movements. Admittedly, Scripture is not entirely clear as to how these spirits are organized and how they operate, but there is enough scriptural warrant to draw some tentative conclusions.

Both Israel and the early church perceived that God had given his angelic hosts a special role in the administration of human affairs. The Septuagint rendering of Deuteronomy 32:8 says, "He set the bounds of the peoples according to the number of the angels of God." Biblical scholar F.F. Bruce writes:

The biblical evidence for the angelic government of the world is early: it goes back to the song of Moses in Deuteronomy 32....This reading implies that the administration of the various nations has been parcelled out among a corresponding number of angelic powers. In Daniel, these powers reveal themselves as both good and evil. Michael the Archangel is the great prince who has charge of the people of Israel, looking after their interests in the unfolding of history (Dn 12:1). The messenger of the Lord, presumably Gabriel, is detained by the prince of Persia against whom he must fight. The prince of Greece is also mentioned. Apparently these last two high-level angelic powers were standing in resistance against the revelation made to Daniel about the future of God's people Israel.[1]

Theologian Walter Wink wonders at the power of these evil beings who are able to hold God's messenger back for twenty-one days: "The angels of the nations have a will of their own and are capable of resisting the will of God. God is perhaps omnipotent but certainly not able to impose the divine will on recalcitrant powers due to God's own self-limitation: God will not violate the freedom of creatures."[2]

How and why did some of the angels turn against the Lord their Creator? We don't know exactly, but may surmise that they joined Satan in his rebellion, and since that time have become foes of God and the nations of humankind, whom they seek to hinder rather than to help. In much of the Old Testament we see their baleful influence as the false gods of the nations—the gods of Egypt, the Amorites, Canaanites, Edomites, and others—whose worship, Israel was warned, would bring oppression, slavery, foreign invasion, and poverty (Jgs 6:6; 10:6-16). The Lord is portrayed as bringing judgment upon the gods of Egypt under Moses (Ex 12:12) and "driving out nations and their gods" from before Israel during the conquest (2 Sm 7:23). Of course, in relation to Yahweh, the incomparable Creator, they are not really gods, but only demons impersonating deities worshiped through the medium of idols. "For all the gods of the nations are idols, but the Lord made the heavens" (Ps 96:5, NIV), and in 95:3, he is referred to as "... the great God, the great King above all gods." Later the apostle Paul acknowledges the reality of these spirit beings and their deception of the Gentiles (the nations), whose sacrifices to idols are made to demons (1 Cor 10:20), and who are slaves to those who by nature are not gods (Gal 4:8). Scripture, therefore, seems to indicate that these corrupted angels have joined Lucifer in seeking to deceive the nations so they will not recognize the true God.

Their agenda is achieving dominance. Domination and control appear to be the main objectives of these demon gods that the apostle Paul appropriately calls "principalities, powers, thrones, dominions" (Eph 6:12). The acquisition of power and influence over human beings and their societies is their obsession. This dominating nature may be revealed in their very names. For example, the meaning of Molech, god of the Ammonites, is "ruler." He managed to get such control over the people of Ammon that they offered their firstborn children to him as sacrifices by fire. Chemosh, the national god of Moab, may mean "subduer," perhaps a reflection of the degree of dominion he had obtained over this people, as well as of the successes he gave Moab in wars against its enemies.

Missionaries of today can also give testimony to the kind of control that these spiritual beings have over pagan peoples. The late Ernest Heimbach, formerly a pioneer missionary to the Hmong people in Thailand, described for me how the chief spirit of the tribe dominated it for centuries, using the fear of sickness, death, attack by evil spirits, and opium addiction to keep the people in his grip.

Lest we think these demon gods, these controlling spirits, these principalities and powers, are only still operative in far-off pagan tribes, we need to take a harder look at our own society. Aside from Charles Manson, Jim Jones, and the Branch Davidians, who seem more obvious examples of demonic deception, what about our own national policy and culture? Theologian Walter Wink urges us to discern the demonic installed at the heart of our own national policy, infiltrating the CIA, government administration, and armed forces to ensure continued American political and economic dominance over weaker nations. Commenting on the blind allegiance so many citizens give to their national self-interest, he writes,

> What makes nationalism so pernicious, so death-dealing, so blasphemous is its seemingly irresistible tendency towards idolatry. In the name of this idol, whole generations are maimed, slaughtered, exiled, and made idolaters. One hundred million lives have been offered on the altar of this Moloch, thus far in the 20th century.[3]

Wink, Berkhof, and others help us to see that the powers are still very much with us, injecting their influence over culture, public opinion, ideology; coloring our assumptions, worldviews, values, and behavior. As Christians who want to rightly discern the activity of the powers of darkness in our society, Berkhof helpfully suggests, "The church's great question is always which Powers are now attempting to get life under their control."[4]

Are they "territorial spirits"? Should we call these spiritual powers "territorial spirits" as they have been almost faddishly described lately? Certainly geographical territoriality is part of how Scripture describes their influence. The Canaanite god Baal, who was a continual scourge to Israel because of Israelite involvement in Baal worship, had several localities named after him: Baal-Peor, Baal-Gad, Baal-Hermon, and others. "The etymology suggests that Baal was regarded as the *owner of a particular locality....* These local Baals were believed to control fertility in agriculture, beasts, and mankind. It was highly important to secure their favor" (emphasis mine).[5]

This was accomplished through ritual prostitution, child sacrifice, and other detestable activities (Jgs 2:17; Jer 7:9; 19:5).

The Lord continually warned Israel through his prophets to forsake worshiping foreign gods like these if they wanted to remain in their land; otherwise God would bring the peoples against them in judgment *"against this land* and its inhabitants.... This whole country will become a desolate wasteland" (Jer 25:9-11, NIV, italics mine). When judgment finally came upon them, a primary reason God gave for this judgment was that *"they have defiled my land* with the lifeless forms of their vile images and have filled my inheritance with their detestable idols" (Jer 16:18, NIV, italics mine). Other nations who were guilty of enshrining false gods on their territory also incurred his wrath. The prophet Zephaniah mentions how God will be awesome to the Moabites and Ammonites when he "destroys all the *gods of the land"* (Zep 2:11, NIV, italics mine). Philistine lords were told that if they returned the Ark of the Covenant to Israel, the Lord might "lift his hand from you and *your gods and your land"* (1 Sm 6:5, NIV, italics mine). Yahweh's prophets saw a link between the "gods" and the land, a link that was activated by or reinforced by the worship of people.

In the New Testament, geographical territoriality is only hinted at. The mob of demons speaking out of the Gadarene demoniac begged Jesus that they "not be sent out of the country," perhaps because that was the territory to which they had been assigned (Lk 8:26-39). In Acts 19:35 the Ephesian city clerk attempted to quiet the screaming mob by affirming: "The city of Ephesus is the guardian of the temple of the great Artemis and of her image which fell from heaven." The fact that the mob had been shouting in irrational unison for about two hours, "Great is Artemis of the Ephesians," may indicate some kind of collective possession by a "territorial spirit" though Scripture itself does not make this analysis.

Other cities mentioned in the Bible are described as having connections with Satan or demonic gods. Pergamum, location of one of the seven churches of Revelation, was "where Satan has his throne" and "where Satan lives" (Rv 2:13). It was a known center in the ancient world for the worship of the spirit of Rome. In declaring allegiance to the emperor, citizens burned incense at the foot of his statue. Also, Dionysius, god of vegetation, and Asklepios, god of healing, were worshiped locally. Snakes and the handling of reptiles were associated with the cults of both these gods. An ancient coin from Pergamum shows the emperor, Caracalla, standing before a great serpent twined around a tree and saluting it in the manner for which the Nazis later became known.

Spiritual territoriality probably does take an urban form, but a more subtle form than is often recognized in the spiritual warfare movement. Whether we can identify the spirits over cities as "greed" for New York City, "power" for Washington, or "pornography" for Los Angeles, as one American evangelist recently did, is highly questionable. After all, aren't these just the sins of some of the people who live in those places? Couldn't greed be equally applied to Los Angeles as well as New York? Or pornography to Washington as well as Los Angeles? Much of the discerning of "territorial spirits" seems both oversimplified and naïve.

Are they organized hierarchically? I believe we must be careful of making unwarranted assumptions about the way in which the principalities and powers are organized. One of the most frequent of such assumptions is that they compose a hierarchy in a pyramidical sense, with Satan at the top and various gradations of spirit beings ranked in descending order down to "ground-level spirits," the kind that indwell individuals. The idea of a possible hierarchy stems from attempts to decipher the apostle Paul's understanding of the principalities and powers. Berkhof points out that the apostle was influenced by Jewish apocalyptic writings that conceived of classes of angels on higher and lower levels who influenced events on earth. He also points out that Near Eastern nature religions of Paul's day also believed in a hierarchy of demonic beings arrayed at various levels between God and the world. But he stops short of identifying a definite hierarchical structure in Paul's depiction of the powers, since the functions and names of the various terms Paul uses ("principalities," "powers," "thrones," "dominions") are never clarified: "We rather have the impression that Paul means to suggest broadly by the variety of expressions the number and diversity of the powers."[6] F.F. Bruce agrees. Commenting on Colossians 1:16, he says, "They probably represent the highest orders of the angelic realm, but the variety of ways in which the titles are combined in the New Testament warns us against the attempt to reconstruct a fixed hierarchy from them."[7]

Walter Wink has demonstrated that the terms Paul used in describing the powers were the same ones used to describe human authority in the New Testament.[8] Because human authority is generally organized in a hierarchical manner, perhaps Paul also conceived of the spirit world in a hierarchical manner. But we must not categorically assume this to be the case. Are there other models that may give us a better handle on understanding their organizations? Given their anarchic self-centeredness and total depravity as fallen spirit beings, could they instead operate like a band of unruly guerrillas or an urban street gang, terrorizing, vandalizing, and running on to the next place where an opportunity presents itself to do destructive things? In this case they would constantly be deploying and redeploying to take advantage of unfolding situations. Just as terrorists' or vandalists' activities are affected by the arrival of soldiers or the police, so these roving bands of evil spiritual forces are put to flight by the intervention of God in answer to the prayers of his people. Wouldn't this characterization fit more with the apostle Peter's description of Satan as "prowling around like a roaring lion, seeking someone to devour" (1 Pt 5:8-9)?

Though we must be careful of constructing a theology of the spirit world based on pagan belief systems, the possibility of a hierarchy of spirits may be borne out by the perceptions of animistic peoples. Animists typically believe in a hierarchy headed by a supreme god, who is remote and unknown, and in a pantheon of lesser deities, superior spirits who exercise great power over a wide range of affairs. Beneath these are the lesser and the more immediate spirits of their ancestors, and finally, the evil spirits. The Burmese believe in *nats*, supernatural beings arranged hierarchically with control over natural phenomena, villages, regions, and nations. The cult of guardian spirits in northeast Thailand involves both village and regional spirits, the village ones being subordinate to the regional. In India, Hindu goddesses serve as "guardians" of villages and regions. They are often associated with disease, sudden death, and catastrophe. Kali, goddess of destruction, is a regional deity widely recognized to exert influence over West Bengal and the Bengali people.

A missionary in Thailand believes he has identified the national principality that reigns over the whole country. It is a being known as Phra Sayam Devadhiraj, which means "greatest of the guardian angels of Siam." It is believed this deity has kept Thailand from being overrun by invaders. King and queen preside over a royal homage-paying ceremony, with the whole nation joining in the worship of this spirit, whose image resides on a throne in the royal palace.

Heinrich Schlier contends that the apostle Paul had no

interest in speculating about the spiritual powers' organization and operation. (Perhaps that should serve as a caution to us as well.) He finds that the names Paul gives to the powers are "to a large extent interchangeable"; that is, principalities, spirits, demons, gods, and princes are all used of one another. Schlier finds only one distinction emphasized among them. Whether demons, spirits, or principalities, they are all subordinate to Satan and manifest his power: "The numerous powers all derive from one fundamental power which is called Satan; they may be regarded as emanations and effects of that power."[9]

He may be right. Perhaps we should think of Satan and the demons as being more closely joined together and interdependent. Most likely, given their freedom from the restrictions of the dimensions of space and time, they can be both many and one at the same time. How else could up to six thousand demons (the size of a Roman legion) inhabit the Gadarene demoniac and speak with one voice, "My name is Legion... for we are many" (Mk 5:9, NIV)?

We can conclude that Satan works to exercise dominion through a vast organization of other spirit beings. But whether he and his spirit henchmen operate as a network, a hierarchy, or a more free-flowing configuration, we cannot definitively surmise from Scripture. Certainly they are "territorial," but I prefer to use the term "controlling" since the achievement of control is the essence of their purpose and since they seek control not primarily over geographical areas, but first and foremost over *people* and all that concerns them politically, institutionally, culturally, and religiously. In other words, they do not care about real estate, but about those who own and live on it. Both as many and as one, they participate in the destructive agenda of the one Jesus described as the original liar and murderer (Jn 8:44). For this reason alone we need to gain a better understanding of how they gain control over individuals and societies.

SATAN GAINS CONTROL THROUGH
THE ACTIVE COMPLIANCE OF HUMAN BEINGS

From the original episode in the Garden (Gn 3) where the original humans allowed Satan to gain control over them through deception, sadly, the whole history of our race attests to willing cooperation with the efforts of Satan and his evil spirits to gain control over individuals and societies. Indeed, one theologian places the blame for the fall of angels on humanity rather than the other way around: "The fall of angels must not be seen independently from the sin of man...the two are interwoven. The angels fell because they were tempted by man who was prepared to sell his soul to authorities other than Yahweh."[10] In other words, instead of saying "the devil made me do it," we may need to change the saying to "we made the devil do it!"

The Israelites not only forgot their God and served the Baals and Ashteroth, the gods of other nations, they refused to listen to God's prophets, despised his statutes and covenant, and stubbornly opened the door for satanic occupation of their society. The Bible lays the blame squarely upon the Israelites themselves rather than on Satan:

All this took place because the Israelites had sinned against the Lord their God.... They worshiped other gods and followed the practices of the nations....They did wicked things that provoked the Lord to anger. They worshiped idols though the Lord had said, You shall not do this. They would not listen and were stiff-necked....They rejected his decrees and the covenant he had made....They followed worthless idols and themselves became worthless....They forsook all the commands of the Lord their God....They bowed down to all the starry hosts....They sacrificed their sons and daughters in the fire. They practiced divination and sorcery and *sold themselves to do evil* in the eyes of the Lord. 2 Kings 17:7-17, NIV (emphasis mine)

John Dawson sees the same principle operating today. He states: "Satan is an invader and usurper operating in our territory. God did not give demons authority over your city. Demons have infested the earth's atmosphere since before the creation of mankind, but they can only extend their authority into a town or institution when people sin."[11]

One Christian worker who served in Mauritania thinks the people there have opened the door to a "spirit of divorce" through serial polygamy and adultery. The tragic result is child abandonment, leading to the severe malnutrition and death of many children. The main obstacle to spiritual growth for the tiny number of Christians is temptation through divorce and adultery. Three national believers of the estimated twenty in the country have already fallen away from the faith for this reason, and the marriages of expatriate Christians have also been troubled.

After World War II, German pastors mentioned the role of the demonic in the events which befell their fatherland by saying, "You cannot understand what has happened in Germany unless you understand that we were possessed by demonic powers.... *We let ourselves be possessed* (emphasis mine)."[12]

From his more socio-political perspective, theologian Walter Wink believes that demons became "the actual spirituality of Nazism manifested in the political forms of the Hitler Youth, the SS [Hitler's bodyguard], Gestapo, the unwitting cooperation of churches, the ideology of Aryan racial purity, and the revival of Norse mythology." He also mentions the "collective possession" prevalent in modern times in which "the demonic has taken the form of mass psychosis," when humankind en masse gives itself up to evil.[13]

The reverse of the above is also true. McCandlish Phillips writes: "Fidelity to God and his Word breaks the power of evil spirits and erects barriers to Satan. This can be true in a life, in a home, in a nation." He relays the story of the failed attempt by the Theosophical Society in 1926 to bring the Hindu guru, Krishnamurti, to prominence in America as a "world teacher" who would combine all religions into one and make radical changes in American civilization. After he arrived in New York harbor, he complained of "electrical atmospheric intensity" and said he doubted he would be able to meditate successfully. Plans to speak throughout the country were cancelled when he became incoherent, stripped of the powers that had worked for him in India and complaining of "bad atmospheric conditions prevailing in this country." He ultimately went into seclusion and renounced his pretensions as a new messiah. Apparently, God had put a hedge about America through his people's faithfulness and general commitment of the wider society to keeping his ways.[14]

Would that this were still the case in our society! Unfortunately, the general unfaithfulness and disobedience to God's ways have opened the way for a literal invasion of evil spirits in various forms of Eastern mysticism, the New Age movement, and especially through declining moral standards relating to honesty, integrity, and sexual purity.

SATAN GAINS CONTROL
THROUGH DECEPTIVE PATTERNS OF THINKING

In keeping with his character as the arch-liar and the father of lies, Satan's major strategy for the world involves massive deception. He has "blinded the minds of unbelievers so that they cannot see the light of the gospel of the glory of Christ" (2 Cor 4:4, NIV). His most pernicious attacks are directed at the minds of people, and in this effort he "masquerades as an angel of light" (2 Cor 11:14, NIV). *Time* magazine, in reviewing the film *The Exorcist*, observed that the devil presented therein was an "easy devil." Far more dangerous and destructive are the shared wrong notions about reality with which hundreds of millions of human beings live. The apostle Paul warns both the Galatians and Colossians about being "taken prey" by deceptive philosophies and becoming slaves again to the "elemental spirits" (Gal 4:3; Col 2:8-9). The Book of Revelation depicts worldwide satanic deception that results in gathering all the nations for that last great battle of Armageddon (Rv 16:12-14).

Richmond Chiundiza, a church leader from Zimbabwe, describes how in that country the demonic powers came to subvert the Shona people's legends concerning Nehanda and Chaminuka, two of their heroes from the past. The spirits of these heroes are now being consulted by Zimbabwean government officials. Other demonic spirits influence the teachings of the various Shona clans requiring animal sacrifices and festivals and through the use of individuals to speak their will. Clan members fear leaving the clan territory without asking the permission of these spirits and must wear charms for protection, and continue appeasing them daily wherever they happen to be living.[15]

Referring to 2 Corinthians 10:3-5, Francis Frangipane says, "There are satanic strongholds over countries and communities. There are strongholds which influence churches and individuals. Wherever a stronghold exists it is a *demonically induced pattern of thinking...* a house made of thoughts which has become a dwelling place of satanic activity" (emphasis mine).[16]

Culture is made up of many commonly held patterns of thinking, developed through generations and passed down to children as the normative way in which a society operates. For example, many Japanese, though outwardly highly technological and materialistic, are still bound up with occultism. Two-thirds of the population attend Shinto shrines, every school child carries an amulet, and Shinto priests dedicate each new building. The recent coronation of the new emperor called for ritualized intercourse with the sun goddess, the national deity of the country.

The Bozo people of Mali believe it is necessary to sacrifice animals and deformed people, such as albinos, to ensure the blessings of the spirits for abundant harvests. When twins are born, they kill one or both of them since, in their belief system, two people cannot share one spirit. An animistic Bantu population in Somalia believe the land will not yield an abundant harvest without the shedding of human blood. To guarantee the fertility of a field, all the men rush to meet at its center to beat each other with clubs. Thus, numerous injuries and deaths provide enough blood to bring a good harvest.

Cindy Jacobs, a noted intercessory prayer leader, characterizes the "Western mind set" as being:

> A stronghold that Satan has built within the culture of the United States and other countries that denies the supernatural and relegates reality to what can be proven scientifically or what can be known by the physical senses. The result upon the Western church is one of disbelief of the work of territorial spirits, thus Satan's kingdom is protected from attack by disbelieving Christians.[17]

Indeed, this may be one of the devil's most effective subterfuges, blinding the Western church to the way he operates by getting us to buy into the same unbiblical, materialistic worldview held by the rest of our society.

HOW SATAN MAINTAINS AND STRENGTHENS HIS CONTROL

Through animistic practices. Animism, which Philip Steyne calls the "basic underpinning of all non-biblical religions,"[18] is the search for power sources by which human beings can manipulate the spirit world. People do this to gain control over their environment and destiny so that they become, as it were, their own gods (cf. Gn 3). In nearly all religions and cultures animists manipulate spirit beings to make rain, get abundant crops, get a new job, get healed, become fertile, or pass school exams. Employing shamans, charms, and rituals, they seek protection from disease, evil spells, catastrophes, and witchcraft. Baal worshipers of old and modern-day New Agers alike seek success, happiness, and security through the involvement and manipulation of spirits, usually not realizing they are the ones being manipulated.

Through human intermediaries. Satan uses *political leaders* to carry out his agenda for a whole society. Leaders of Israel such as Jeroboam "enticed Israel away from following the Lord and caused them to commit a great sin" (2 Kgs 17:21-22, NIV). On the part of his people he created an idolatrous cult involving the worship of two golden calves which launched the northern state of Israel into a downward spiral, culminating in its destruction by Assyrian invaders. It was widely known that Ferdinand and Imelda Marcos of the Philippines were deeply involved in the occult through daily consultations with a soothsayer, and that Cory Aquino did not want to live in the same palace because she felt there were evil spirits there. Is it any wonder, then, that the Marcoses exploited their own people to the tune of billions of dollars, intensifying the poverty and suffering of millions? Pol Pot exterminated two million of his own Cambodian people. Hitler, Stalin, Saddam Hussein, Jonas Savimbi, Slobodan Milosevic, and many others could also be mentioned.

Spirit mediums are Satan's "hatchetmen," human instruments by which he extends his dominion and tightens his control in a society. Simon the sorcerer was an instrument of Satan to get control over the people of Samaria. "All the people, both high and low, gave him their attention and exclaimed, 'This man is the divine power known as the Great Power.' They followed him because he had amazed them for a long time with his magic" (Acts 8:10, NIV). Elymas, a sorcerer and false prophet, used his influence to oppose Paul's proclamation of the Good News to the proconsul of Paphos and tried to turn the proconsul from faith in Christ (Acts 13:6-11).

Peter Wagner mentions the case of a former high-ranking occult leader in Nigeria known as "St. Thomas the Divine" to whom Satan assigned control of twelve spirits, each of which controlled six hundred demons, a total of over seven thousand.[19] Occult practitioners played a part in the early rise of Hitler and Nazism. Erik Hanussen was a dealer in astrology who ran "The Palace of the Occult" and was known as the "Prophet of the Third Reich" because of his influence over its development.[20] Filipino shamans or *babylan* are experts in things relating to spirits. They claim the power to heal or kill, to prepare amulets for warding off evil spirits and getting blessings.

According to Cindy Jacobs, Satanists and witches, Western forms of spirit mediums, send people to purposefully seduce pastors and leaders of Christian churches. In so doing they use spells, love potions, and charms. They use magic to "ensnare people" (Ez 13:17-23, NIV) through divination. They also use the tools of unholy intercession and the unholy fast to unleash demonic powers to distress Christians. Very dedicated to their lord, they serve him either through fear or a desire for power. The higher their rank in the satanic church, the more demonic powers they control. In cooperation with the spirits they can bring curses upon the unsuspecting, even causing disintegration of the physical body. Ed Silvoso speaks of a spiritist group in Argentina who made a pact to break up a church by praying for strife among its leaders. In my own community of Upland, California, efforts have been made by spiritists connected with a New Age cult to curse local churches and their pastors in order to bring division or other harm to local congregations.

Fortunately, there is growing evidence that the presence of praying Christians interrupts, or breaks altogether, the link of mediums with their controlling occult powers. Mediums in the Malaysian town where I served as a missionary were unsuccessful in calling the spirits to possess them during the period a Chinese Christian worker was waiting for the bus outside their festival grounds. The mediums eventually came out and appealed to her to leave the area so that the spirits could come into them! A Ghanaian pastor told me that the witch doctor in the area they were evangelizing lost his occult abilities once the local Christians began to pray in unity for the area. More will be said about the power of this kind of praying later.

Through places or objects set apart for infestation by spirits. A missionary friend from Thailand, Joy Boese, described the increasing spiritual oppression she felt, accompanied by an inexplicable apathy on the part of the people with regard to the gospel. "Spirit pillars" had just been erected in her town. She writes in a letter, "From our local people I've learned that many cities have a protective and ruling/controlling spirit residing in a recognized pillar. The provincial governor decides to erect a pillar and invites a spirit to come and inhabit that pillar to protect his city or province."

Pam Seaward, another missionary friend from Nepal working among Tibetan Buddhists, described her confrontation with a "god" of Tibetan Buddhism who appeared to her as she was praying for the people. She rebuked its ugly image, but it remained because as it explained, "My things are here." Seaward discovered Tibetan Buddhist religious paraphernalia which her landlord had left in a nearby closet. Until she got rid of the demon's "things," it would not leave.

Peter Wagner concludes, "Real demons do attach themselves to animals, idols,... trees, mountains, and buildings as well as to any number, or variety of manufactured and natural objects."[21] Also, because spirit beings are extradimensional, not confined by the same space-time limitations we experience, they should have no problem attaching themselves to any number of objects at the same time, provided these objects have been set apart for this purpose.

No wonder God through Moses commanded Israel not to bring any "detestable things" into their homes because of the destructive effects they would bring upon them. The ruthless actions of reformer kings like King Josiah to rid the land of the high places, shrines, and other occult objects used in the worship of foreign gods are now fully understandable (Dt 7:25-26; 2 Kgs 23).

Through rituals of worship sometimes involving human sacrifice. Rituals of worship to the spirits are one way their control is strengthened. In parts of West Africa, human sacrifice is sometimes used to gain stronger power with the spirits. The Lebu of Senegal are believed to make such sacrifices on an island off the coast. They are perceived by other tribal groups as having, as a result, an inordinate degree of political, economic, and spiritual power. The Dionka tribe of Mali worship *Komo*, the god of killing. Local Christian workers told me that in some areas strangers have been killed in sacrifice to this god.

Lest we think that our society is more advanced or immune from such practices, Dianne Core, founder of Child Watch, writes of Devilfish, a coven of satanists connected with the Ordo Templi Orientis, a national organization in the United States with over forty branches. Their book, *The Secret Rites of OTO*, gives instructions on how to do human sacrifice in order to increase satanic power.[22]

Ted Gunderson, former FBI director for Los Angeles, shocked the participants of a seminar on occult crime with his claim that the FBI has over 100,000 "missing persons" in its files, half of which he estimates have ended up as victims of occult sacrifice.[23] Even if he is only 10 percent correct, it is cause for grave concern.

Through blocking God's people from interfering with his dominion. As we have already noted in passing, the prophet Daniel faced a "great conflict" as powerful spirit beings sought to prevent his receiving a revelation that would cast a spotlight on the purposes and plans of the principalities and powers in their future interaction with political realms. It was a word that also revealed God's sovereignty over all these future events, as well as a warning to his people Israel regarding the dangers of deception and the need to prepare for persecution (Dn 10-12).

I have also mentioned that Artemis, the controlling principality of Ephesus, may have stirred Demetrius the silversmith and his trade union members to provoke a riot in order to hinder the spread of the truth. Also, Satan himself is spoken of as hindering Paul's mission plans (1 Thes 2:18) and throwing Christians into prison and tribulation (Rv 2:10). And in 1 Peter 5, he is portrayed as the roaring lion, who brings suffering to all God's people.

A Youth With a Mission missionary from Principe/Sao Tome reported an encounter with a "demonic prince." This being threatened him and the fledgling church to stop their missionary activities in his area. Subsequently, an outbreak of cholera tragically claimed the lives of several of his first converts.

Hector Torres, an Arizona pastor, rightly observes that Satan seeks to neutralize the power of God's people by attempting to wear out the saints through discouragement and infirmity, by discrediting ministers and ministries, and especially by bringing division in the church and family relationships. He writes, "I believe Satan's tactics are to destroy the three institutions established by God: the family, the church, and the nation." Torres especially emphasizes Satan's attack on families since they are "the foundation for all relationships."[24]

WAYS TO OVERCOME SATAN AND HIS TACTICS

More than one biblical expositor has interpreted the Book of Joshua as portraying in the physical realm what the church is to do in the spiritual. Just as Joshua and the people of Israel took the territory that God had given them in the land of

Canaan, so God's people today are to take back "territory" from Satan and the forces of darkness. Jesus has told us, "Occupy till I come" (Lk 19:13, KJV). The implication is that we are to be an influence for him in our jobs, in our communities, wherever we find ourselves. Joshua's question could well be asked of us also: "How long will you wait before you begin to take possession of the land that the Lord has given you?"

There are several ways in which we as Christians can overcome Satan and his tactics in order to take back territory from his domain:

Reoccupy lost territory through intercessory prayer. There is considerable evidence, both biblically and in the history of the church, that prayer through the power of the Holy Spirit is used by God to overthrow demonic forces seeking to gain or maintain control over individuals and societies. One key to Joshua's victory over Israel's Canaanite enemies, all of whom relied upon demonic gods, was his prayerful dependence on the Lord's intervention on Israel's behalf at Jericho, Ai, and in other crucial battles. It was the intercession of Samuel that brought God's thunderous response against the Philistines, throwing them into such a panic that they were routed before the Israelites. Thus, the territory the Philistines had captured from Israel as well as neighboring territory was restored to God's people (1 Sm 7:7-14). Judges such as Gideon and kings such as David, Jehoshaphat, and Hezekiah experienced God's deliverance and the reclamation of territory due to their dependence on God through prayer.

Prayer in the power of the Holy Spirit always undergirded and extended the missionary outreach of the early church. In the Book of Acts alone, prayer is mentioned over thirty times, usually before major breakthroughs in the expansion of the Christian movement. Looking back over the history of Christianity, Robert Glover observed, "All the mighty spiritual revivals which constitute the mountain peaks of missionary annals had their roots in prayer."[25] Jonathan Goforth, missionary to China, described the powerful spiritual awakenings that brought many tens of thousands to Christ in Korea and China during the early part of this century. It was "intense believing prayer that had so much to do with the revival which in 1907 brought 50,000 Koreans to Christ. We are convinced too that all movements of the Spirit in China which have come within our own experience may be traced to prayer." He added that one missionary remarked to him, "Since the Lord did so much with our small amount of praying, what might he not have done if we had prayed as we ought?"[26]

Wesley Duewel described to me the agonizingly slow work of his mission's church-planting effort in India during its first twenty-five years. Only one church per year came into being as a result of all the missionaries' efforts. As a result of heart-searching evaluation, the mission recruited one thousand people in their home countries to pray fifteen minutes per day for the work. He reports that this prayer effort turned the tide, and in the next few years, the number of churches went from 25 to 550 and the number of believers from 2000 to 73,000. One national leader told him afterward, "All of us are seeing results beyond anything we could have imagined!"

The great revival and ingathering among the Telugu outcasts of India in the mid-1800s is linked with what happened on "Prayer Meeting Hill," an elevated area overlooking the city of Ongole. In 1853, when their mission board was on the point of abandoning the work for lack of response, a missionary couple and three national coworkers spent the night in prayer for the Telugus. They battled through to a sense of shared assurance that their prayers had prevailed. Gradually the opposition to the gospel broke and when the outpouring of the Spirit took place, eight thousand came to Christ in a six-week period. In one day over two thousand were baptized and the church there became the largest in the world at that time.[27]

David Yonggi Cho, pastor of what is today the world's

largest church, recounts the demonic oppression over the Korean village where he pioneered during his early ministry. The key to the breaking of spiritual bondage was months of prayer, culminating in the casting out of a demon from a woman who had been paralyzed for seven years. With her healing and deliverance, the church exploded with growth. As he puts it, "The sky above the village was broken open and the blessings of God began pouring down."[28]

Why does God require our prayers? We learn from Scripture that the prayer of intercession is key to the fulfillment of God's gracious purpose for the peoples of the earth. He invites us, "Ask of me and I will make the nations your inheritance and the ends of the earth your possession" (Ps 2:8, NIV). Ezekiel reveals that God looks for someone to "stand in the gap" for the land (Ez 22:30). And through Isaiah the Lord says he has posted watchmen on Jerusalem's walls who will "never be silent day or night," giving themselves and the Lord no rest "till he establishes Jerusalem and makes her the praise of the earth" (Is 62:6-7, NIV).

Why does God, the Almighty, limit himself by reliance on his people's prayers? Admittedly, it is a mysterious matter, but I believe it goes back to his giving humankind dominion over the earth. This dominion, as we have seen, both at the Fall of man and subsequently, has been surrendered to Satan and his demonic cohorts. But through Christ's redemption, this dominion is being restored. And through prayer, we as his redeemed people reassert our God-given dominion over the world, ruling and reigning with Christ "far above all authority and dominion" (Eph 1:21; 2:6). Through believing prayer, we open the door for God's intervention in our troubled world. The Holy Spirit shows us how to pray, indeed, prays through us in accordance with God's will (Rom 8:26-27). Jesus has given us a virtual blank check to exercise through united prayer with other believers: "Again I tell you, that if two of you on earth agree about *anything* you ask for, it will be done for you by my Father in heaven" (Mt 18:19)...."And I will do *whatever* you ask in my name.... You may ask me for *anything* in my name and I will do it" (Jn 14:13-14, NIV, emphasis mine).

In Mark 9, when confronted by the need to cast out an evil spirit, Jesus told the disciples, "This kind cannot be driven out by anything but by prayer" (v. 29). If this holds true for the demonization of at least certain individuals, does it not also hold true for the spiritual oppression of societies? That is why united, believing prayer by God's people is so important for the breaking of demonic bondage over cities and nations. In this connection, Hendrik Berkhof speaks of the gift of the discerning of spirits that God gives to his people as they pray. He says that "this involves especially the discerning of the Powers which hold the hearts and actions of men under their sway in specific times and places."[29]

Dick Eastman described the part focused prayer played in a literature distribution effort carried out by Every Home for Christ. In one community where they distributed literature, they experienced a 10 percent response without prayer. In another place, where the staff prayed for the community as a whole, there was a 55 percent response rate. In a third community, where the staff prayed for each home as they distributed the literature, eight out of ten families responded (an 80 percent response).[30]

A word of caution and critique. Though we mention the importance of the discerning of spirits in connection with intercessory prayer, we need to exercise caution when it comes to focusing offensively against or "binding" principalities and powers. Scripture never explicitly teaches that we do this nor do we see examples of this in the ministries of Jesus, Paul, or other biblical figures. B.J. Willhite of the National Prayer Embassy has written:

It does not seem that the apostles spent much time teaching people about these unseen forces. Not once that I am aware of did Peter, Paul, James, or John... instruct that Christians were to identify these spiritual forces and command them to be bound.... How can we account for this lack of understanding on the part of the early disciples? Had Jesus left them in the dark about such things? Were they too immature for the Holy Spirit to reveal things of this nature to them? Or did they perhaps believe that Satan's power had been broken by the cross of Jesus?... that when a person turned to Jesus the power of Satan was bound in that person's life. That when a city experienced revival Satan could no longer rule in that city.[31]

It seems reasonable that such an exceedingly important matter would have been taught more openly and demonstrated clearly for us somewhere in the New Testament. Instead we see Jesus and the early disciples focusing their energies on ministry to *people* and only when necessary dealing with demons as they manifested themselves, normally in individuals. Their focus was never intentionally on the demonic. It always seemed incidental to their main mission, the proclamation of the Good News of the kingdom to human beings. Paul urged that the subject of prayer be people, especially for kings and others in authority, because God wants all people to be saved and to come to the knowledge of the truth (1 Tm 2:2, 4, NIV). As we have seen above, this kind of praying has brought astonishing results in terms of spiritual revival and the reclamation of individuals and whole societies from the dominion of darkness.

The pain-free, easy approach to putting "territorial spirits" to flight advocated by some Western, especially American, prayer leaders who see themselves as operating on the cosmic or "strategic" level can be presumptuous and dangerous. Presumptuous because we can make unwarranted claims for a one-to-one correlation of our prayers and a specific political or historical change, taking credit for that change, when in reality the dynamic interplay between divine, human, and demonic factors involved in every such change is much more inscrutable. And the danger of spiritual pride, the very sin Lucifer was guilty of, is always present. For example, some American intercessors have declared that they bound territorial spirits over Russia during special prayer meetings at Red Square and, by implication, made possible *glasnost, peristroika,* and the great Russian revival! Glamorous stories of this kind often appear in glossy newsletters. But the activities described are at best likely to be only a part of the reason for such happenings since thousands of others have also been praying, often over long periods of time, for the same thing.

(The downfall of Communism in the former Soviet Union and the amazing spiritual openness involving millions is, I am convinced, God's sovereign answer to the prayers of tens of thousands of Russian Christians who suffered and prayed for decades while imprisoned in Stalin's gulags. One of these Christians, Pastor Nikolai, told me of his many long years in a cell without sunlight and without a Bible or book to read. When I asked what he spent his time doing, he said, "I prayed for this city." Is it any wonder that the city for which he poured out intercession is now an epicenter of spiritual revival?)

Of course, the Lord can and will use the prayers of American jet-setters as he will those of any of his people who pray. But let us not be guilty of oversimplifying the breaking of spiritual bondage. In keeping with our American culture of convenience, we like to provide instant, easy solutions when local believers have not only travailed in prayer but also suffered great hardships over many years.

We should also heed the tiny Book of Jude's big warning about those who "slander celestial beings" (v. 8). Even the archangel Michael spoke respectfully to Satan, "The Lord rebuke you," and he "did not dare to bring a slanderous accusation against him" (v. 9, NIV). If God leads us to bind principalities of evil in prayer, we must do so carefully and respectfully. The safest posture in the absence of clear scriptural warrant is to take a cue from the archangel. Like him, ask the Lord to do the binding and the rebuking. After all, he is "Lord of hosts," the only one whom Satan and the demons really fear and must obey.

Proclaiming Christ's Good News. It is clear from the Gospels that the primary purpose of Jesus' ministry was the itinerant proclamation and demonstration of the Good News of the kingdom. He was always hastening to move on to other towns which had not yet heard his message for, as he explained to the disciples, "That is why I have come" (Mk 1:38-39). It was only in the course of evangelization and out of compassion for its victims that he took on the demonic realm. His work of deliverance usually happened in a reactive, responsive way when demons actually manifested themselves, and in order to free those who were held in bondage. His focus appeared to be on liberating people, not on getting embroiled in a high-level confrontation with the powers of darkness.

An Indian leader of the Friends Missionary Prayer Band told me their missionaries never go looking for the demonic; it always finds them as they busy themselves with proclaiming the Good News. When it confronts them, as it invariably does, they deal with it as part of their evangelism efforts. B.J. Willhite agrees:

What is this war about? Is it not taking souls which have been held captive by Satan? We do not release them by speaking to Satan. We release them when we tell them the truth about Jesus.... It seems to me that there is a danger in making the binding of such spirits the prerequisite for harvest. Jesus did not tell his disciples to go into all the world and bind demonic powers in the heavenlies. He said preach the Good News to every person.[32]

The apostle Paul had a similar approach to ministry. He spent two years in preaching and teaching at Ephesus until "all the Jews and Greeks living in the province had heard the word of the Lord" (Acts 19:10). This preaching led to deliverance of people from the power of darkness when many burned their sorcery books and articles publicly. Only later, when Demetrius and the other craftsmen felt threatened and were provoked into rioting against the Christians, was there anything that could be construed as confrontation with a "high-level spirit" (vv. 23-41). The apostle's concern was to proclaim the gospel of Christ and spread the knowledge of him everywhere. For him spiritual warfare meant a battle for the souls and minds of human beings that they might be saved, brought from darkness to light and made into all that God meant them to be (Acts 26:17-18; 2 Cor 2:12-15). In this pursuit, the aim of Paul's preaching was to demolish "strongholds," those wrong patterns of thought in his hearers that were due to satanic deception (2 Cor 10:3-4). This task involved persuading people through reasoning with them from God's truth.

Charles Finney, the American revivalist, often insisted that prayer together with the sharing of Christ's truth is the combination that God uses to bring spiritual revival. God uses our prayers to restrict forces of evil and our proclamation of Christ's Good News to fill the vacuum left by their departure. It is through preaching the Good News of Jesus Christ that the principalities and powers are exposed for what they are. The power of illusion by which they seek to control humanity is broken. As Berkhof puts it: "Unmasked, revealed in their true nature, they have lost their mighty grip on men. The cross has disarmed them; wherever it is preached, the unmasking and the disarming of the Powers takes place. Though they are still present, where Christ is proclaimed and believed in, they are limited in what they can do."[33]

Richmond Chiundiza agrees that our focus must be on reaching people. "The mistake churches sometimes make is to attack the system and structure of the territorial spirits," he says. "The church must preach a liberating gospel and be involved in the subsequent power encounter."[34]

Living God's way. Obedience to God and his standards is a potent part of spiritual warfare. Often we define spiritual warfare in too narrow a sense. Actually, Scripture seems to take a much broader, more holistic view. The apostle Paul looked back on his entire life as a servant of Christ as being a "good fight" (2 Tm 4:7). He describes his struggle to serve God as requiring

> great endurance; in troubles, hardships and distresses; in beatings, imprisonments and riots; in hard work, sleepless nights, in hunger; in purity, understanding, patience, and kindness; in the Holy Spirit and in sincere love; in truthful speech and in the power of God; *with weapons of righteousness in the right hand and in the left* through glory and dishonor; bad report and good report; genuine, yet regarded as impostors... beaten and yet not killed; having nothing and yet possessing everything.
>
> 2 Corinthians 6:4-10, NIV, emphasis mine

Spiritual warfare for Paul encompassed all these things because all were necessary in his war against the Prince of Darkness to win the peoples to Christ.

The apostle enumerates here in 2 Corinthians and elsewhere in his epistles his manifold struggles. These demonstrate the costliness of true spiritual warfare as opposed to the very narrow idea that has recently been promulgated by some American prayer leaders, who have it down to essentially a "no fuss, no muss" approach. In their thinking, spiritual warfare consists only of cosmic-level praying against spirits. But in taking this line, could we be guilty of oversimplifying and over-spiritualizing the matter of spiritual warfare in a way it was never meant to be?

Israel was continually told their primary responsibility was to obey the Lord, to be careful about following his ways, and he would take care of their enemies. "If my people would listen to me, if Israel would follow my ways, how quickly would I subdue their enemies and turn my hand against their foes" (Ps 81:13-14, NIV; cf. Ex 14:14; Dt 1:30). McCandlish Phillips believes that obedience to God and his Word is the main bulwark of defense Christians have against the devil. He notes that satanic takeover of a nation begins with its people being drawn away from faith in God and his Word. It moves on, secondly, to increased indulgence in sin; thirdly, to false worship and supernaturalism; and fourthly, to tyranny and dictatorship. He suggests that America is in the third stage now. How important it is for us as Christians to live as God would have us live. It may be the most potent form of spiritual warfare we can practice! As Schlier puts it:

> The struggle against the principalities fundamentally begins with and in myself. If I am to resist and drive out the devil and not merely to strengthen his power, the struggle can only be waged by denying myself to him, and choosing and abiding in truth, justice, peace and hope…. The evil one is powerless against the sacrifice of ourselves in godly living and, if necessary, in death for Christ's cause.[35]

Working for social reform: doing justice and loving mercy. As mentioned above, Scripture seems to take a much broader view of what constitutes spiritual warfare. It is a battle against evil in all its forms. And since the wrath of the powers is against human beings, we must look for their activity where there is injustice, including exploitation of the poor and those who are weak. Psalm 82 tells us, "Defend the cause of the weak and fatherless; maintain the rights of the poor and oppressed. Rescue the weak and needy; deliver them from the hand of the wicked" (vv. 3-4, NIV).

Israel had the same problem that many American evangelicals have: they spiritualized commitment to God as the fulfillment of certain prescribed, purely religious duties. They were guilty of turning a blind eye toward human suffering in their own society. God, through Isaiah the prophet, denounces this narrowing of their spirituality, and says that the kind of fasting he endorses is "to loose the chains of injustice and untie the cords of the yoke, to set the oppressed free and break every yoke,...to share your food with the hungry and to provide the poor wanderer with shelter—when you see the naked, to clothe him" (Is 58:6-7, NIV).

Through the prophet Amos, God sounds a similar note: "I hate, I despise your religious feasts; I cannot stand your assemblies.... Away with the noise of your songs.... But let justice roll on like a river, righteousness like a never-failing stream" (Am 5:21-24, NIV).

Is struggling against injustice a form of spiritual warfare? Is working for the reform of unjust, exploitative social structures part of spiritual warfare? If understood in a more holistic sense, it certainly is, since those who engage in this kind of warfare are fighting against spiritual darkness as it is embodied in social structures.

Wink understands social protest against evil to be a "form of exorcism" when there has been a collective possession of a society. He regards the Civil Rights movement and the efforts of Martin Luther King during the 1960s (especially the march across Selma Bridge) as exposing the "demon of racism, stripping away the screen of legality and custom for the entire world to see." He raises the question of what might have happened if German pastors and churches had staged "ritual acts of protests" outside Nazi death camps. Could history have been different? He takes, as a biblical model, Jesus' act of cleansing the temple, an example of the collective exorcising of an institution which had been perverted from its original purpose (Mk 11:11-19). Wink affirms that exorcism understood in this light "answers to the problem of ideological blindness." Our involvement in evil, he says, "goes far beyond our conscious volitional participation in evil. To a much greater extent than we are aware, we are possessed by the values and powers of an unjust order."[36] That is why each of us as an individual is responsible for the way our nation responds to the needs of the powerless for food, clothing, shelter, medical care, or fair treatment.

Do we Americans suffer from this kind of "ideological blindness"? Have we reflected on the fact that, though we are just 6 percent of the world's population, we consume 40 percent of its resources? Our greedy multinational companies have exploited the natural resources and cheap labor of other countries in order to raise cash crops and inexpensive goods for our consumption. For example, American hamburger chains buy up and use the best land in some poverty-stricken areas of Latin America to fatten beef for the U.S. market while local people live on the brink of starvation. Think about that when you eat your next Big Mac!

Around the world an estimated twenty-five to thirty million homeless children wander urban areas. Roughly two hundred million work as virtual labor force slaves, often for eighteen hours per day, in unhealthy sweat shops. Countless others are exploited for prostitution and pornography. An estimated one billion of the world's population live in absolute poverty without adequate food, clothing, and shelter. Forty thousand children per day die from malnutrition and easily preventable diseases. Is it not spiritual warfare to fight against the horrific conditions that oppress much of the human race? Can we not discern the activity of the powers of darkness in these things? It is a truism that advancing telecommunications have made us a "global village" and, with enhanced awareness of world need, conferred on us a heightened responsibility to love and care for those who suffer, and to fight against the forces that oppress them. This may include nonviolent social protest, lobbying political leaders, participating in relief and development, as well as intercessory prayer, proclamation of Christ's Good News, and living out the values of the kingdom of God.

In 1979, during the Cambodian famine crisis, when the

Vietnamese authorities refused to let relief convoys pass into the hinterland, a massive effort was mounted by Christians of many different denominations. We prayed, gave, lobbied our political representatives; some of us took part in a demonstration at the United Nations, dropping off thousands of signed petitions at the Vietnamese and Russian consulates to bring pressure on the authorities in Cambodia. God used all of these efforts along with those of many others in a marvelous synergy to change the situation. The Vietnamese occupiers of Cambodia relented, and the relief convoys were allowed through. Starvation was averted for up to two million people. This certainly was spiritual warfare holistically understood in the broader sense in which Scripture portrays it. How we need to see the practice of spiritual warfare in this wider light as integrated with Christians' efforts to advance Christ's kingdom in the total scheme of things, rather than focused on a narrow slice of a purely "spiritual" reality.

In C.S. Lewis' *The Chronicles of Narnia*, four children crawl timorously through a wardrobe into a whole new dimension of reality. It is a world dominated by the evil White Witch, who holds all its creatures in bondage through the cold winter of fear. The four children themselves initially feel intimidated by her dominion. But later they realize that Aslan, the great lion, has all ultimate power and is their friend, ready to deliver them and to gift them so that they can join him in the battle against the witch and her cohorts.[37] Like the children of Lewis' imaginative series, we also have nothing to fear because our Lord comes with "all power in heaven and on earth" to gift and enable those who join the fray against the dark powers of our world. There is no doubt who has ultimate power and control and where true victory lies, in spite of the tactics employed by the Evil One. May God give us true discernment and childlike boldness in taking up these weapons he has put at our disposal.

Hallelujah! Christ is Victor!

EIGHT

Advancing God's Kingdom

Tom White

To use the current terminology, there are examples of spiritual "SWAT Teams" springing up in various areas. Individual Christians who recognize the preponderance of evil and feel led to do warfare against it are developing strategies for both defensive protection from and aggressive penetration of enemy strongholds.

In my own community, for the past twelve years I have been leading prayer walks, implementing deliverance ministries, and praying over the cities of our county from a nearby mountaintop which is a place popular for witchcraft ritual. When I'm asked to minister in foreign cities and countries, I call for a "muster of the cluster" of saints already stirred by the Spirit to enter the battle for souls at a deeper level. We petition the Lord for an outpouring of his Spirit to stem the tide of evil in our cities and nations. These are large, long-term petitions.

In obedience to Jesus Christ, as representatives of his kingdom and endowed with his delegated authority, I believe we are called to take a visible and verbal stand to actively *expose* schemes of evil operative within our spheres of ministry, confrontationally *engage* demonic powers with authoritative prayer, and *expel* darkness from individuals, churches, and Christian organizations. Further, we must be committed to stand against and restrain the influence of evil forces set over cities, regions, people groups, and nations. In proposing an operative model for this warfare, there are vital principles that need to be understood. There are numerous new methodologies and modes of spiritual warfare afoot. Let's be sure we have a firm footing on the biblical fundamentals before leaping into a campaign against the gates of hell.

PRINCIPLES AND PERSPECTIVES

The spiritual soldier must gain and maintain a high view of *God's overarching sovereignty over evil*. With Job, we must affirm that "no plan of yours can be thwarted" (Job 42:2, NIV). Broadly speaking, we understand God's sovereignty over the outworking of human history. At the individual level, however, I believe there are battles for souls to be won or lost, depending on our obedient availability to the Holy Spirit and our effectiveness in evangelism. In line with Jesus' word to his disciples (Lk 10:17-20), *we must hold to the preeminent focus that the central part of kingdom work is the writing of names in the book of life*. Cosmic-level warfare, like any other aspect of ministry, should not become a preoccupation. There is the danger here of a holy crusade to rid the world of evil strongholds. If the vision of the heart of God aching for the lost is buried by a commando operation to storm the gates of hell, we miss the point of the Great Commission.

We must *allow Jesus Christ, as Commander of the hosts of the Lord, to stage and wage our spiritual battles*. Pride and fascination with power creep close by the tent of the warrior. We must let genuine dependency on the Almighty expose and check any fanaticism that can flow from fleshly zeal. As Jesse

Penn-Lewis pointed out, there are demonic "eagles" that hover about the peaks of Christian leadership, stirring up pride, power, and self-importance.[1] Grandiosity has no place in spiritual warfare.

This ministry is not for the untested. The ones called to it should have experienced the sanctifying grace of the Spirit in areas of sin such as lust, anger, pride, deceit, and ambition. Further, they should have undergone emotional healing that seals cracks of vulnerability (fear, false guilt, depression), and must experience the empowerment of the Spirit for this specific work. Such men and women should be among the ones who are considered spiritual "fathers" (1 Jn 2:12-14): mature, stable, submitted, and selflessly committed at any cost. Potential casualties will be minimized by a straightforward culling out of eager novices as well as those whose motivation is tainted.

This type of resistance requires *two distinct orientations.* The first is Godward—a sensitive abiding in and listening to the Source, a receiving of clear impressions and directions from Jesus Christ himself. A lifestyle of prayer is enhanced by the regular practice of praise (Eph 5:19-20), and the out-breathing of petition and the inbreathing of the Spirit's ministry of peace and empowerment (Phil 4:6-7). The second dimension is Satanward—a resistance rooted in authority and activated by prayer, empowered by objective truth. This resistance is not itself "prayer." It is encounter, engagement, "struggling." We do not "pray at" the devil. We fight him with heavenly weapons. For this reason, many of us use the term "power encounter" for this aspect of our work.

Successful strategic praying has several necessary elements. Genuine unity of heart among the participants is presumed, a relational commitment to one another as well as to the "cause" (Acts 1:14; 4:32). In seeking God's mind, there must be agreement in Jesus' name to ask according to his will and purpose (Mt 18:18-20; Acts 4:30). The faith level of the group is to be visionary and unwavering (Mk 11:22-25). And there must be the sober realization that an advance against Satan's kingdom will be tested—we persevere through persecution, trial, even death (Lk 18:1-8).

I discourage an approach to power encounter that "takes on" the principalities of evil with a view to staging a knock-out punch that will drive them out of a territory. Rather, it is my view that a proper interpretation of "struggling" means entrance into a deeper, prolonged form of prayer, a laying hold of God that prompts him to act. It means a commitment to oneness with fellow believers and a commitment to bold incarnational truth, which weaken the effectiveness of evil. For example, substantive reconciliation of racial prejudice, ministries of mercy to the poor, or offering pre-abortion counseling to a community can objectify the superior power of the gospel. This takes perseverance, spiritual courage, and a radical commitment to live according to kingdom values. In light of Ephesians 3:10, God is making known the "mystery of Christ" (in the building of the church body) to the ruling powers. This occurs when the church is living *in* the dynamic koinonia of the Spirit and living *out* the lordship of Jesus in daily life.

This is not big splash stuff. Most flashy agendas are of human origin. God reserves the paradoxical right to choose the weak to boggle the minds of the wise. Something dynamic and eternal occurs in the heavenly realm when truth is lived. It is not usually immediately apparent or measurable. Christian character, distilled through trial, demonstrates the superiority of the way of Jesus and puts evil in its place.

TOWARD A WORKING MODEL FOR KINGDOM ADVANCEMENT THROUGH POWER ENCOUNTER

Power encounter ministry should be but one dimension of the church's overall commission for evangelization and discipleship. This outline is preliminary, and is intended to point a direction for spiritual warfare strategies in the context of the Great Commission. It is presented as a phased approach, covering an experimental span of three years. The length of time, however, is contingent upon such variables as intensity of spiritual resistance, health of the local body of Christ, and level of faith.

The elements of the model are flexible, and must be adapted to each context. The outline is neatly linear, in keeping with our Western mind set. In reality, entrance into battle will be predictably unpredictable, and may need to be approached in quite a different form than that recommended here. This is simply a framework, a place to begin. *Above all, follow the flow of the Spirit.*

PHASE I: PREPARATION (six months)

Form a core community. It is assumed that a particular individual or a small group will be moved by the Spirit to adopt a more aggressive ministry posture. This may come through the reading of Scripture, prompting in prayer, desperation and discouragement in the face of resistance, or the reading of a book or article treating the topic of strategic warfare. A small core group (minimum three to four persons) should commit itself to mutual accountability and initiate the regular practice of body life, ministering in God's grace to one another through the Word and prayer. Ideally, this should be a group of local leaders, "city elders." This core group may well cross denominational and theological boundaries.

Pursue normative ministries. The work of ministry along the lines of gifts, callings, and roles must be maintained (e.g., pastoring, teaching, evangelizing, discipling, counseling, and so forth.). Chasing after principalities must not be the focus.

Maintain scriptural kingdom ministries, such as sharing the Good News, teaching its content, setting souls free from direct demonic bondage, healing the souls and bodies of those in need, and making disciples (Is 61:1-3; Mt 9:35-10:8). Keep in mind that *power encounter is a specific application of spiritual authority that goes alongside existing ministries.*

Appropriate the Lord's protection. Apply the full provision of the armor of God (Eph 6:10-18), and receive protection through the blood of Christ, the shielding of the Spirit, and the ministry of the angels. *This is not automatic*—in taking a strong stand against evil, the soldier must repeatedly request protection and power for himself and for family members. Recognize that those endowed with dark power might intentionally send evil your way; curses are real. Naïveté and ignorance may allow for such spiritual assaults to harm us.

Develop resources. The core groups must commence and sustain a commitment to study the best books, articles, and cassette and video tapes available on subjects of authority, gifts of the Spirit, prayer, evangelism, discernment, deliverance procedures, and intercessory prayer. This challenging area demands the best of our mental and spiritual abilities.

1. Appoint a study committee and designate a director responsible for searching out and securing the best of available materials.

2. Set apart a two- or three-hour block of time monthly to review "in-house" critiques of materials. Ask the Spirit to bring consensus on what rings true—keep the wheat, toss out the chaff. Develop biblical/theological and stylistic guidelines that fit your group. There must be agreement on this level if the core group's vision and practice are to hold together for the long haul.

Begin research. Generally, in any given culture or people group, there are ideologies, religious practices, particular besetting sins, and other factors that allow for continued demonic bondage. Further, there are cities and territories that may have a distinctive type of spiritual atmosphere. Good research will identify original conditions upon which a nation, territory, or city was established. Are these people or is this place generally characterized by greed, violence, immorality, incest, occultism, crime? For example, at the Presbyterian Bible College in Hsinchu, Taiwan, students were experiencing disturbing visitations of spirits at night in the dormitories. It was later discovered the college was built on a Buddhist burial ground. After this discovery, prayer removed the influence.

Seek the Lord for the revelation of strongholds. Note the intentional use of the word "revelation." Insight and information must be received from the Spirit, with confirmation. The question: what specific strongholds, human institutions, ideologies, and cultural sins are the channels through which hidden principalities could operate to promote deception and bondage of souls? What seem to be the specific types (or demonic archetypes) that govern the anti-Christological agenda in this place? The Spirit may choose to impart this data by several means:

1. Gifts of the Holy Spirit. It is expected that there will be at least one (ideally several) on the team who are cultivating the gift of discerning of spirits, or "spiritual sight." Corollary gifts of prophecy (promptings from the Spirit), word of knowledge (instructions for ministry), word of wisdom (applied scriptural truth), and faith may serve also as primary sources of guided insight, or may confirm or disconfirm discernments.

John writes in his epistle that the believers have an "anointing from the Holy One" allowing them to know the difference between false teaching and truth (1 Jn 2:20). Anyone indwelt by the Spirit has this anointing, and thus may generally sense when a particular content, circumstance, or person is *not* of the truth. This is "standard equipment" for a Christian; I call it *general discernment.*

There is also a specific charisma which could be called discernings of spirits (1 Cor 12:10, note: *diakrisis*, plural). The same word is used in Hebrews 5:14: "Solid food is for the mature, who by constant use have trained themselves to distinguish good from evil" (*pros diakrisin*, "toward a discerning"). It is a process of cultivating a sharpened judgment. *A gift of spiritual discrimination enables a believer to judge specifically whether a source of power is human or satanic or divine. The ability is cultivated over time by practical experience and by a deepening sensitivity to the Holy Spirit.*

It is important to note that one so gifted will "read" not only the active agency of evil spirits, but also the corruptive agency of a human spirit tainted by pride, deceit, control, criticism, and bitterness. The gift functions to see past surface things, identifying not only *that* something is wrong but *what* is wrong. This is a vital gift for protecting the body from counterfeit and corruption, and also for detecting sources of evil power in a community or country that serve to divert people from truth in Christ (see Paul's dealing with Elymas, Acts 13:4-12).

Within such specific discernment, we may point to two kinds of methodology. Either one or both may lead to precise spiritual diagnosis. The first may be labeled *inspirational induction*, a method that relies heavily on the direct revelatory work of the Spirit. This method moves from specific revelation (either via Scripture or Spirit-guided impression) outward to the situation. It involves giftings of "discerning of spirits," "word of knowledge," and perhaps "prophecy." There is great advantage and also danger in this approach. The advantage is that if what is perceived is genuinely from God, it is unquestionably reliable information, the right application of which results in redemptive fruit. If, however, the perception is not from God, there is great danger of going ahead of God or without God altogether. The key to success here is the active practice of humbly and prayerfully waiting upon God.

The second method may be labeled *observational deduction.* This method is used by the reasoning saint who feels more at ease with a sort of "sanctified scientific approach." Undergirded with scriptural truth, this method moves from observation of the general revelation (circumstances, phenomena, demonic manifestations) back to a presumed cause (a certain territorial spirit). This approach gleans such data as information from deliverance sessions; observation of the type of spiritual bondage suffered by both Christians and non-Christians in a certain city, region, or country; and interviews with key leaders in a particular environment. The advantage of this method is that it is much safer than pure inspirational induction, but can also be enormously slow. The drawback is getting bogged down in observational detail.

2. Observations. Take note of the obvious. What is happening in this community or country that points to a predominant negative spiritual influence? Examples (these come out of the author's own experience and personal discernment):

    a. Homosexuality (San Francisco Bay area)
    b. Metaphysics (Seattle: a major center for New Age teachers and teachings)
    c. Appeasement of Idols (the temple and ancestor worship climate of Taiwan)
    d. Sensuality/Witchcraft (Bogota, Colombia)
    e. Religious Strife (Israel: Islamic "Intifada" that targets Israel for destruction)
    f. Violence/Fear (Los Angeles)
    g. Despair (India: the hopelessness of the caste system and Hindu philosophy)

Ask the question: Based on what I see in the lives of the people and what I sense intuitively, what are the spiritual powers that presumably shape and dominate their attitudes and actions?

3. Knowledge of Scripture. When engaging in strategic-level warfare, it is imperative that one develop a reservoir of biblical knowledge of revealed supernatural forces. Instead of being quick to grab or guess at the identity of a fallen power, let's look first to the Word. For example, a cursory look gives us the following major "spirits" of darkness: Dagon (Jgs 16:23), Molech (Lv 20:2), the Queen of Heaven (Jer 44:17), Ashteroth (1 Kgs 11:33), Artemis (Acts 19:24-35), Zeus (Acts 14:11), Hermes (Acts 14:11), the "Princes" of Daniel 10, and Apollyon (Rv 9:11). Such demonic deities require such human responses as the seeking of knowledge and power, human blood sacrifice, sexual indulgence.

Since we are dealing here with immortal angelic creations, there is nothing new under the sun. The supernatural beings against which Israel wrestled are the same forces encountered in our time. They may merely change their names and create a new "front of operation" suitable to modern sophistication. The point is this—we shouldn't have to guess at this with human reason. For example, we see that in the end times, "the great prostitute...Babylon the Great" of Revelation 17 is in fact the final manifestation of occult religion existent from early history. We need not grope to detect the principal players of hell's boardroom already unveiled through revelation.

4. Interview key leaders. Question leaders who have been engaged in ministry in this place. These should be pastors who have lived in a location at least five years, native pastors or evangelists in a foreign context, leaders of parachurch groups, and so on. To get more specific, ask the following:

- What kinds of moral and spiritual problems come up with the greatest frequency?
- Could you identify a spiritual "wall" or source of resistance that seems to have been impenetrable during your ministry?
- Identify persons or organizations that have been sources of resistance.

(Note: In the majority of Third World cultural contexts, nationals will know and readily identify the sources of spiritual power commonly known to the people, e.g., certain guardian spirits, tribal or temple deities, shamans, elemental spirits.)

5. Note forms of oppression. What are the kinds of spiritual pressures and hassles that the saints encounter in this ministry context? Do hard times of illness, depression, extreme discouragement, ministry team dysfunction coincide with religious festivals or encounters with persons endowed with negative spiritual power? It may be possible to trace specific effects back to causes.

Encourage corporate repentance. Unconfessed sin is a chief hindrance to revival and a source of satanic oppression. There can be no effective movement forward until there is accountability for sin in the camp. It is appropriate for the core team and pastors in a city or missionary leaders on a field to go before God to name and confess the sins of the people, asking the Spirit to bring conviction and cleansing of individual sin. Often, this type of prayer must precede direct advancement against strongholds. (See Nehemiah 9 and Daniel 9 for models of this type of identificational intercession.)

Where sin has occurred in the leadership of a church, parachurch, or missionary organization, and has not been resolved through repentance or church discipline, such compromise may open a door of advantage (2 Cor 2:11) for satanic influence. God's blessing may leave and oppression may settle in. Often, mere ignorance of Satan's schemes or theological skepticism allow for the penetration of demonic power into the life of a church. People may perceive the heaviness: hindrance of worship and prayer, strife in relationships, confusion in discerning the mind of God, a high occurrence of sickness among the staff, or an overall spirit of discouragement. If there is cause to suspect such an institutional "foothold" (Eph 4:27), the following procedures are advised:

1. Deal with the sin. If it is recent or recurrent, confront and resolve it according to Matthew 18:15-17. If it is in the past, the core leadership should speak corporate confession of the "sins of the fathers," and seek restoration of the Lord's blessing (see Lv 26:40-42).

2. Call for special seasons of fasting and prayer. The leadership should encourage people to seek the Lord's face afresh, asking him to remove spiritual hindrances.

3. Cleanse the property. Leaders and others gifted with discernment and faith should walk through the facilities, claiming each room for God's use and glory, naming the name of Jesus, cleansing the premises with the potency of his blood, pronouncing all enemy oppression broken, and commanding evil spirits to depart. Invite the Holy Spirit to sanctify and fill those places consecrated to the kingdom work.

4. Remove curses and occult oppression. In authoritative agreement in prayer, apply the blood of Christ to directly break the lingering effects of any curses placed upon the former leadership specifically, or the church generally. (This is not "hocus pocus paranoia": there has been sufficient documentation of this problem from pastors and missionaries.)

Move ahead with intercession. In united, prevailing prayer, moving in the principles of Matthew 18:18-20 and Mark 11:22-25, ask God to loose the Spirit in the following directions:

1. To strengthen, protect, heal, bless, and empower his servants and leaders in this locality. The focus here is on lifting up key servants, petitioning the Lord to provide a shield of protection, pour out grace, and give power for the work (Eph 6:18).

2. To bring conviction of sin and prompting to repent. Only the Spirit himself can convict souls of guilt in regard to sin, righteousness, and judgment (Jn 16:8-11).

3. *To remove the influence of evil spirits* away from unbelievers so they are able to respond to the gospel: to subdue their power, silence their voices, and separate their power from people, allowing for response to truth (Acts 26:17-18).

4. *To work according to Acts 4:29-30,* asking God to enable his servants to proclaim the Word with boldness, and to stretch out his hand to perform miracles through them in the name of Jesus, thus validating the truth and potency of his Word.

Active power encounter may occur at any point in this process, either by the leading of God, or by the sabotage of Satan. If the encounter is initiated by the devil, remember that failure may occur unless the believers are well-prepared and well-trained, not operating in the flesh. The Lord allows us latitude here to be human, to make mistakes, and to learn from experience.

PHASE II: THE SHAPING OF STRATEGY (one year)

Continue body ministry. Whether in a local church setting or as an interdenominational team, meet regularly to minister to one another in love and mercy. Keep current with personal needs and vulnerabilities. Troubleshoot. Deal with any oppressive assaults. Gather around together and pray for those who request prayer.

Gather ministry data. Document significant power encounters, insight gained through deliverance sessions, and patterns of spiritual bondage observed in counseling cases.

Build discernment through dialogue. Set times to analyze observed data, discuss materials read, and compare notes on spiritual impressions. Ask the two questions: What are we perceiving, and is it correct?

Begin to identify power sources. Identify first any individuals, organizations, cultural practices that seem to be the locus of negative spiritual power. Then attempt to gain a general descriptive label for the force that presumably works behind and through them. Match these observations with impressions gained from the Holy Spirit and from interviews with local church and ministry leaders. Sit on this data awhile—ask the Spirit directly to confirm or discount the information. After personal prayer, come together again to sharpen the accuracy of what you come up with.

Begin active training. Identify those clearly called and gifted for power encounter ministry, and provide opportunities for apprenticeship training. (Avoid recruitment campaigns. This ministry tends to draw those fascinated with power, or those needing to be a part of something "big and important" for their own ego needs.) We must trust the Lord himself to raise up those called and gifted by him for the work. Those beginning to operate in the necessary authority and gifts will be led alongside those already adept at prayer, discernment, and deliverance techniques. Training in spiritual warfare occurs more through doing battle than through didactic instruction.

Begin to identify and employ strategies. What do we do with all this data? Some suggested strategies follow:

1. Regular intercession. There will always be those who are clearly called to closet prayer, the behind-the-scenes wrestling with the devil and prevailing with God that releases real power on visible planes of activity and ministry. The historical models at the end of this chapter illustrate the nature and function of true intercession.

2. Develop a back-up prayer team. Cultivate a group in another locality to be a spiritual "watchdog" to provide blanketing prayer, and to be a source of "discernment at a distance" for the encounters you are involved in. The prime example here is a prayer group in a sending church that is in touch with the spiritual warfare dimensions of a missionary's work. God may often give guidance, warning, or encouragement in this way.

3. Faith walks. In view of Abraham's charge to "walk about the land" and claim it for his possession (Gn 13:14-17), and Joshua's instruction to walk about Jericho, the Lord may direct small groups of prepared saints to walk through a city and actively claim it for God's glory. On such walks, expect the Spirit to sharpen your discernment, stir your faith, and prompt you to loose his power to penetrate darkness. Keep in mind that such a walk is part of a long-term, visionary endeavor.

4. Doing justice. It is clear from Scripture that God honors and blesses deeds of caring for the poor, tending to the needs of the helpless and fatherless, and ministering to the oppressed. Thus, evil may be exposed and weakened through faithful involvement in prison ministries, inner-city mission work, orphanages, anti-abortion efforts, and drug or alcohol rehabilitation. There is no substitute for the hard, sacrificial obedience of doing God's work.

5. Evangelism. Allow the Spirit to teach you how to cooperate with him in the binding of spiritual forces that prevent people from receiving the truth that leads to salvation. We should become more accustomed to exercising authority to *subdue, silence, and separate* satanic influence from the one being drawn to Jesus by the Holy Spirit. In leading a person into salvation, we should be more thorough in breaking and forsaking specific areas of satanic advantage, allowing for more immediate practical freedom in addition to positional freedom from the enemy.

6. Praise marches or rallies. These are positive and visible proclamations of the lordship of Jesus Christ. Not designed to confront evil directly, marches and rallies demonstrate the joy and unity of believers who acknowledge Jesus as King. Examples are park concerts, parades, or special days of prayer. Recently, while visiting Cambridge University on a Saturday, I was delighted to observe a praise parade pass through the Quad, with instruments, celebrative singing, and a banner declaring "JESUS IS LORD." I felt it was a tasteful, appropriate expression of faith.

7. Implement deliverance ministries. Ideally, this is done in at least one local church. Deliverance ministries do not necessarily need to be conducted within the local church, but those involved must be under the authority of a local body. Deliverance prayer must be offered within the context of skilled psychological insight, medical expertise, and the availability of persons gifted in emotional healing.

8. Be prepared for isolated power encounters. You may be thrown into battle at any time. In Colombia, a Bible translator visiting an unreached village awoke in the night choking, with a sensation of hands gripped around her neck. She audibly spoke out the name of Jesus. Two days later, when she met the tribal shaman, he looked at her in amazement and said, "I could not harm you. Why?" Within a week, she led him to accept Christ. The power of the spirits sent to destroy her was broken by her response of faith.

9. Special seminars. These are informational seminars for believers related to aspects of spiritual warfare, which help to raise people's awareness of the reality of the battle. Professional and leadership training seminars may deal with issues of discernment, intercessory prayer, counseling the oppressed, satanism, ancestor worship, sexual abuse, and other matters.

10. Radical obedience. Some may be called to actively resist the legal system. Examples of this would be acting in conscience to resist the practice of abortion, or exposing the identities of producers of pornography. This may involve a choice to smuggle Bibles into closed countries, or an individual decision by a Chinese believer to defy martial law and participate in the democracy movement.

11. Written communications. One effective way to expose evil is to produce high-quality written work. The pen is a potent weapon for the clear communication of Christian truth. Editorials in local newspapers, periodical articles, and books may serve to instruct believers and challenge unbelievers. In the United States, the work of Dr. James Dobson to expose the pornography industry is exemplary. Written testimonies relevant to each culture can also be powerfully used.

PHASE III: MOBILIZATION (one year)

Maintain and fine-tune the practice of body life. The core team should continue to meet regularly for dialogue, sharing in the Word, and ministry to one another. The ideal core team should be a local grouping of pastors and leaders committed to regular prayer and worship. In light of Paul's exhortation in Ephesians 6:18 to "be alert and always keep on praying for all the saints" (NIV), it is imperative that we help each other in our personal struggles and any spiritual assaults that may arise. Discouragement, disillusionment, and confusion need to be replaced with faith, joy, and clear thinking with the help of the Holy Spirit, especially for a core team involved in such strategic spiritual warfare.

Guard against that dreaded development of "sin in the camp," especially in the form of attitudinal sins of pride, envy, jealousy, criticism, and resentment. During the early part of this phase, I recommend a two-day fasting retreat to "clear the deck" through repentance and confession. Too often vital ministries have been sabotaged through sin that is exploited, if not caused, by the Evil One.

Also, inject laughter and lightness into the heavy job of doing battle. There will always be "driver," goal-oriented personality types drawn to spiritual warfare. To have times when we take ourselves and the burden of the battle less seriously is spiritually therapeutic and necessary for sustaining the troops. In the prayer movement in my own city, we have blessed moments of "holy hilarity," a healing release of joy.

Continue training. By this point there should be up and running four major groupings of saints committed to the penetration of strongholds: the leadership core group that provides vision and administrative decision-making, the intercessory prayer team, deliverance teams, and various functional ministry teams (street witnessing, media outreach, written communications, youth ministry, and crisis counseling). Those confident in power encounter will be bringing others into an apprentice relationship to demonstrate the necessary reliance on the Spirit, authority, and gifting.

Envision the kingdom. In Mark 11:22-25, we read Jesus' teaching about moving mountains with the prayer of faith. In faith, we can visualize the establishment of the kingdom in our particular ministry locale. Ask the Spirit to come as light that exposes and dissipates darkness, as a purifying presence that cleanses corruption, and as the Spirit of truth that challenges falsehood. God will initiate the outpouring of his power to advance his kingdom to the degree of our prevailing faith. Continue to petition the Lord to honor the prayer of Acts 4:29-30.

Target specific strongholds. Sharpen your strategic focus on two or three strongholds, reconfirming your discernment. This may be a particular person (political figure, New Age

proponent, witch doctor), a human institution (local government, religious body, social service organization), or revelation
of a demonic stronghold over an area (sexual perversion,
witchcraft, gambling, violence).

A serious question must be asked here: How can we know
if the spiritual influence that pollutes any given environment
originates primarily from the heavenlies downward, or from
the corrupt hearts of men outward? Before we plunge into
active resistance and weakening of "territorial spirits," we
must consider that the greater point of bondage may rest
with the wickedness of the human heart itself. Supernatural
deception would not succeed were it not for human vulnerability to its power. How can we be so sure that a cultural preoccupation with greed, lust, or violence points unquestionably toward a supernatural entity? Several years ago I saw a
map pinpointing the ruling spirits over counties and cities in
the San Francisco Bay area. Over San Jose and the Silicon
Valley was listed "Self." Though there is no doubt that the
problem labeled "Self" exists there, is it because there is really
such a personal spirit being hovering over that area? Or is
what is being identified simply a prominent manifestation of
human fallenness?

Whether strongholds are of human or satanic origin, *my
conviction is that we are to become so broken, yielded, and sensitive to the Spirit's movement that we do not move into aggressive
prayer against strongholds unless we are "picked up" by the Lord
and placed into a place of compelling action.* Historically, only a
few believers have been so sovereignly moved. This suggests
to me that strategic warfare is not meant to be a populist phenomenon.

One thing we know: prayer is always the right thing. As we
pray, then, our primary focus needs to be on the exposure of
strongholds *within* the church (unbelief, bitterness, disunity)
that inhibit repentance and revival. A parallel burden compels
us to petition God for a release of the Holy Spirit's power to
convict the unsaved of their sin and the inevitability of judg-

ment (Jn 16:8). If it is truly inspired and guided by the Lord himself, intercession moves the hand of God to expose and diminish the influence of satanic strongholds "in the heavenly places," and will surely enhance both revival of the church and redemption of the lost.

Use effective methods of intercession. We are applying Christ's authority to expand his kingdom, believing and asking God to work through his Spirit and the angelic hosts to penetrate and push back the influence of evil powers, enhancing the harvest and growth of the church.

Prayer at this level is visionary, bold, and prevailing:

Pattern Prayer: Lord, you alone are the Almighty—we affirm your sovereign dominion over _____. By faith, we write the triumphant name of Jesus above this (church, town, nation), and claim it for your glory. The scepter of the wicked will not remain over the land you have given to your people (Ps 125:1-2). The battle is not ours but yours (2 Chr 20:15). We ask you to penetrate and weaken strongholds of evil (name them if known). Thank you for scattering the enemy. We praise you for your faithfulness.

We should follow the prompting of the Spirit to do any "on sight" prayer, such as praying at the site of an abortion clinic, pornography shop, or New Age bookstore. We might also be led by the Spirit to arrange a face-to-face encounter with a person identified as a source of power in the community.

Watch carefully for counter-opposition. One thing you can count on in some form is the "counterpunch" of the demonic realm. This may range from the obvious resistance of an individual or a local institution, to obvious harassment of a person or family on the team, to the more subtle assaults on areas of emotional weakness and besetting sin. The quicker these strategies are detected, the easier they are dealt with. The goal is to "trace it, face it, and erase it" with anointed, authoritative prayer. Repel suspected curses with application of the blood of Jesus and speaking a blessing toward the one presumed to have sent the curse (Rom 12:21). Watch particularly for the following symptomatic indicators of oppression: uncontrolled fear, extreme discouragement, a wedge of anger or mistrust between team members, undiagnosed ailments or illnesses, inability to get clear leading from God, interruption of sleep patterns, and excessive temptation in the area of a besetting sin. A caution: guard against overreaction here. Do not attribute the problems of normal life to demonic harassment. Expect the Spirit to instruct you when spiritual resistance is required. He will be faithful.

PHASE IV: EVALUATION AND REPLICATION
(six months)

Evaluation. Because the nature of this activity is focused on the supernatural, measurement of advancement and success is difficult. It is a dangerous thing to rely on mere subjective impressions to answer the question, "How are we doing?" There have to be some objective criteria by which we can determine movement in the right direction. Ask the hard questions, rejoice in the successes, and honestly assess the failures.

Evaluation Questions:
- Where has our discernment been incorrect?
- Are we slipping into any doctrinal error? Can we better strengthen the ministry with Scripture?
- Has anyone carried an assignment he or she should not have?
- Have there been casualties? What can we learn from them?

Measurement of the Ministry:
- Has there been a significant, noticeable increase of unity

of heart and commonality of purpose among the believers in our community, or on our team?

- Is there a deliverance team ministry up and functioning? Are captives being set free, followed up, and discipled?
- Are there visible signs of the breaking up of strongholds (closing of pornography shops, decrease in the occurrence of types of ungodliness, collapse of organizations opposed to the gospel, legal and political victories)?
- Are we seeing a measurable growth of the churches throughout our community or area? Can we honestly say that the kingdom is advancing, and God is receiving glory?
- Are believers more in love with Jesus, or overly preoccupied with fighting Satan?

Replication. At this phase, there will most likely be others who have been aware of your efforts in this area. No doubt team members will have already spoken or ministered in other areas, sharing elements of the model and teaching the principles and practice of strategic resistance. I would make some recommendations:

1. Document in writing that which has been developed, and put it in a format that may be transferred to similar ministry teams in other communities.
2. Trust in the Lord to appoint and anoint those on the team gifted in teaching and preaching to move into other communities or areas (including overseas fields) to replicate the principles and practice of strategic prayer.

HISTORICAL MODELS

I am convinced that down through the age of the church there are both single souls and small groups of faithful saints who have waged spiritual warfare on behalf of the kingdom in the secrecy of their own prayer closets. Most of these prayer warriors will not be known until the Great Day. We are prone to limit our evaluation of success to human standards. The Lord knows those pioneers who have laid hold of him in prevailing faith, wrestled with the Evil One, and opened the doors for the penetration of the gospel.

Recently, in rural India, I sat at lunch with a man in his late fifties. Augustine was his name. He didn't eat. He conversed very little. He sat in the corner of a pastor's porch poring over the Word of God. Later I was told that he walks through India, petitioning God to breathe out his power to save his people. He spreads out maps of regions of India, and prays over territories. He walks the streets of the Punjab, the militant Muslim province, speaking peace in the name of Jesus. I praise God for such "secret agents"!

Here are three examples of singular souls who have gone before us and who have dared to place unshakable trust in the promises of God, and stand against the devil.

Pastor Johann Christoph Blumhardt. Though his name is not commonly known in Christian lore, Pastor Blumhardt stands out as a soldier of the highest caliber. In a ministerial report given to the Lutheran Synod of Germany (*Blumhardt's Battle: A Conflict With Satan*, translated by Frank Boshold), Blumhardt recounts his experience with a young German woman named Gottliebin, who first came to him in desperation in 1841. She was born into a family heavily involved in black magic, and had been targeted to be the recipient of powers of witchcraft. Complications arose when Gottliebin was exposed to the gospel, and responded with a desire to follow Jesus. Pastor Blumhardt then entered into a bizarre supernatural struggle that lasted two years. He enlisted the help of a medical doctor to document the strange effects of the witchcraft. Alongside the doing of normal ministerial duties, he clung to God in faith, praying and hoping for victory for this tormented soul. Because the intrusion of the supernatural was so unexpected and unknown to him, his theology of evil was often inaccurate, but his focus and response were admirable:

> If Pastor Blumhardt was not right in every single conclusion he drew from his experience, or in every single interpretation of the events and their implications, yet his main thrust was unwaveringly in the right direction, to despoil the enemy with the weapons God has given the believer: faith and more faith, prayer and fasting, and a steadfast holding to the Word of God. Blumhardt was a pioneer in the true sense. He opened up once more the frontier for the true believer, a frontier which has been enlarged steadily since his days at the expense of the devil and his supernatural schemes against mankind.[2]

After two agonizing years of battling with hell, Christmas of 1843 brought victory. Surprisingly, a powerful spirit manifested itself and spoke to Blumhardt through Gottliebin's sister, Katharina. The being identified itself as a "prominent angel of Satan, the chiefest of all magic" (p. 55). It was arrogantly angry that because of Blumhardt's tenacious faith, a deadly blow to magic had been wrought throughout Europe. At two o'clock in the morning, the spirit departed with a roar heard throughout the community, "Jesus is Victor, Jesus is Victor!" The battle for a human soul, and a greater battle for the gospel in Europe, was won.

Blumhardt himself identified three phases of his experience: 1) the battle itself, passing through the test of faith, 2) repentance and awakening in his region that followed the breakthrough, and 3) an established authority in prayer that led him into a healing ministry for the balance of his days. Often throughout the report, Blumhardt described the "special grace" God imparted to him for this battle. As we have already seen with biblical characters, he was chosen and sent into the battle. Sovereign grace was imparted to strengthen him and ensure success. He was subject to his own weakness and occasional error. But the Lord, for his preordained purposes, carried his servant the distance, enabling him to prevail against the strongest of powers in the devil's arsenal.

Reverend Charles Finney. There are few books on revival as stirring and awe-inspiring as *The Autobiography of Charles Finney.* Some believe he did more to purge our continent from evil than any other single man. His theology was right, his heart pure, his preaching ability superlative. But the preeminent secret of the revivals lay in the practice of prevailing prayer:

> I have said, more than once, that the spirit of prayer that prevailed in those revivals was a very marked feature of them.... Not only were prayer-meetings greatly multiplied and fully attended, not only was there great solemnity in those meetings; but *there was a mighty spirit of secret prayer.*[3]

Finney had an occasional partner in his revival work, the Rev. Daniel Nash, who "gave himself up almost continually to prayer" (p. 122). It was customary for Finney and Nash to retreat to the woods and cry out to God for hours on behalf of a town, or on behalf of a soul particularly resistant to the gospel. Surely, we would presume, the devil was in strong opposition to these revivals. No doubt this was true. But Finney rarely mentions directly dealing with the devil. Rather, the emphasis is on faith in the divine promises, and a relevant, straightforward proclamation of those promises. What comes across in the reading is a thorough dependence on the agency of the Holy Spirit to bring conviction and reap the harvest. The successes are ensured by the sovereign hand of God. Instead of concentrating on dealing directly with the devil, it is striking to see how Finney (and others like him) majored on obedience to truth, labor in prayer, and dependence on the Spirit.

Finney gives this description of his preparation for revival meetings in Antwerp, Ohio:

> In passing around the village, I heard a vast amount of profanity.... I felt as if I had arrived upon the borders of hell. I had a kind of awful feeling, I recollect, as I passed around the village on Saturday. The very atmosphere seemed to me to be poison; and a kind of terror took possession of me.[4]

In comparison with some of the ministry assignments I've faced in the past years, this sounds all too familiar. Finney's response was better and quicker than my own. No doubt he *was* standing against a significant stronghold. But he immediately gave himself to prayer until the fear lifted, the peace of the Spirit came upon him, and he had received a relevant word for that town. The next day, with confrontational preaching, the resistance broke, and many souls yielded to Christ. For Finney, the preeminent keys to the breakthrough were a faith-filled reception of God's promises through prayer and a faithful proclamation of the Word.

Rees Howells. When speaking of individuals who exemplified a distinctive walk with the Spirit, Rees Howells of England comes quickly to mind. After living a life devoted to intercession, Howells found himself in the late 1930s receiving a peculiar burden for the Jews. He sensed, early on, the enormity of the evil of Hitler, and purposed to stand against the forces of Nazism in prayer. In his journals and verbal statements, he often proclaimed that God must destroy Hitler if the Great Commission was to be fulfilled. The last chapters of Norman Grubb's book, *Rees Howells, Intercessor,* are nothing short of an account of the waging of the battle for Western Europe in the prayer closets of Howell's training college in

England. In his own words, "The world became our parish and we were led to be responsible to intercede for countries and nations."[5] In the face of threatened invasion of England in 1940, Howells recorded the following:

> I think what a glory it is that we don't need to change our prayers one bit, in spite of the present developments. I am so glad that it has been the Kingdom we have had before us all the time in the last nine months, and I haven't a single regret. The Lord has said, "I am going to deal with the Nazis." It has been a battle between the Holy Spirit and the devil, which we have been fighting for four years.[6]

In light of our study of the lives of Moses, Elijah, Daniel, and Paul, it is important to note here the Lord spoke a clear word to Howells that *he* was waging, and would win, the battle. Howells had been uniquely prepared, and prompted into participation with the will of God at this strategic level. We see in the account also that at times his predictions and statements were either wrong or ill-timed. He remained human. He recognized, however, that the battle was between the Holy Spirit and the devil, but that he and his colleagues were drawn into collaborating with the Spirit in a struggle for the survival of the free world. At the point of apparent defeat by the Nazis on May 18, 1940, this man recorded a rather profound observation: "It is not you struggling, but God doing, and you coming to know what God is doing."[7]

In all of our current human zeal to scale the strongholds of the enemy, to stand against the New Age movement, or to penetrate the wall of Islam, this point must not be lost: it is God's business, and his divine action that alone will lead us to victory.

These great souls show us the necessity of clearly hearing God's call into the fray, and a dependence upon the presence of God to sustain one through each battle. Jesus' words ring loud and clear. "*I* will build my church, and the gates of

Hades will not overcome it" (Mt 16:18, NIV, italics mine). If the Lord of the church is doing the building, we cannot fail. If the church moves out ahead of the Head, we are destined to fall. May there be more and more men and women among us who exemplify this level of maturity and genuine spiritual authority.

A PARTING PERSPECTIVE

You may have come upon road signs warning: "Bumpy Road: Proceed with Caution." This is my message as well. It may have appeared to be mixed: on the one hand, "Don't do this, there are dubious biblical precedents and it is dangerous," and on the other, "Here is a model for doing it."

Strategic warfare intercession is appropriate and powerful if God is in it. The kingdom is to be wheat that grows up among tares. Let us understand that we will not be rid of evil until God deals with Satan. Remember that even cities and countries that have seen profound revival have, several generations later, slipped back into ungodliness. There can be no permanent, geographical expression of the kingdom short of the King himself coming.

If God prepares and prompts a particular person or group to get involved in strategic intercession that targets strongholds, do read the warning stamped on the assignment: "Danger: Handle with Prayer." If there are "commandos" currently ready for this mission, then I say *proceed with courage*. Keep accountable and open to correction. Keep your perspective. This is not a witch-hunt, but a divinely ordained means to increase the harvest of souls.

A few years ago I was in Taiwan, where I was involved in training pastors in deliverance and intercession. One evening, with forty or fifty who indicated a readiness to move into aggressive prayer, we identified a major deity of materialism recognized throughout Taiwan. After a period of praise and worship, the group listened for the Lord, in silence. Then, one by one we petitioned him to penetrate and weaken the grip of greed in the land. A very strange thing then occurred. This track of prayer continued only for about fifteen minutes. Then I noticed that several were getting involved in an intense personal dialogue, diverting the direction and diminishing the momentum. I recall thinking to myself, "Oh no, we were finally getting some strategic stuff here!" I asked my translator what was going on. He listened for a while, and was drawn into the intensity himself. He then related that there were both mainlander and Taiwanese Chinese present, and that strong feelings of hurt and hatred were surfacing that traced back to the struggle for Taiwan's independence. Suddenly, resentment, hatred, and mistrust were confessed. The honest, painful exchange went on for several hours. There were tears of forgiveness and reconciliation. The Spirit was tending to priorities, mending the broken body. At first I left the room feeling rather defeated. "The body is just too self-occupied and divided to do this kind of praying." But as I reflected on the evening, the real meaning of Ephesians 3:1-13 came to light. Here was the true victory, the miracle of reconciliation. This is what is to be "made known to the principalities and powers," and to the watching world—the supremacy of love that demonstrates the goodness and glory of God. If we could but love one another with the same intensity and fervor with which we tackle problems and projects, there would be more damage done to evil than by all of our zealous agendas combined.

May the strategic discernment and penetration of strongholds *not* become another fanatical agenda, a misplaced priority. Instead, may it be an endeavor entrusted to healthy bodies whose priorities are right, and who are ready to pay the price of prevailing in the presence and power of the Most High God to participate in major advances of the kingdom.

PART IV
Putting Strategy to Work

NINE

From Death Camp to Freedom

Mark H. White

Often, God uses ground-level spiritual warfare to bring deliverance and conversion to a person. Many times, as believers, we are called to use the weapons that the Lord has given us as we battle for the lives of unsaved persons living in enemy territory.

Ground-level warfare as it has been discussed in this volume is generally done person-to-person. It is a highly relational undertaking. We must never forget that the central object of God's affections are individual human beings, male and female, who have been created in his image. As we do ground-level warfare in and around persons who have not yet come into a relationship with Christ, it is essential that we remember God's view of people and so treat them with the utmost love, care, and respect.

INTRODUCING ANN

A few years ago, I was working with students at a major university in the United States. During that time, I became acquainted with a woman I'll call Ann who, through the course of the next six months, would become a good friend and, as well, would help me to understand more of the "ins and outs" of ground-level warfare.

Ann was one of my coworkers, in charge of a women's dormitory on campus. A Bible study I was teaching on campus met in her building. She had had several years of experience and ran a tight ship with the girls in her dorm. In order to get to know her better, I had lunch with her one day.

In the course of our conversation, the subject of my previous summer's missions experiences in Europe came up. Religion thus became the topic and Ann briefly, but matter-of-factly, explained that she was a Jew descended from the tribe of Levi. I expressed an interest in her faith as a Jew and then shared briefly my own experience of religion as a Christian. I discovered that her Jewish heritage through her father goes back some twenty generations. Her mother, however, had been raised Roman Catholic but had converted to Judaism.

When she was a young girl, Ann's family had been taken prisoner by the Nazis during the Holocaust period of World War II. She had been a prisoner in three of Hitler's "hell-camps"—Auschwitz, Gross Rosen, and Dachau. Tragically, she and her twin sister had become a part of Joseph Mengele's "twins experiments." The Nazis had experimented on the girls by removing one of Ann's kidneys and attempting to transplant it into her sister's body. All of this was done while they were both fully conscious, without anesthesia. Ann's sister died during the operation. They wheeled Ann, still alive but in great pain, into a cold, dark room. There, she began calling out to God, asking him to allow her to die as well.

At that moment, Ann reported, a bright light suddenly invaded the room where she lay. As Ann described the light, she said it was formed in the shape of a man and a voice said to her, "You will heal as I have healed you," and then disappeared. It was this vision that enabled Ann to endure the recovery from the operation and the remainder of her captivity in the camp. This vision had since become a landmark experience in her memory, but she had never fully understood that it could have larger implications for her relationship with God.

After World War II, Ann related the "man of light" experience in the concentration camp to several psychiatrists. Each of them told her that it had been a schizophrenic delusion brought on by her difficult circumstances. Believing it was real, however, she decided not to tell anyone further until years later she found herself relating the story to me.

Ann's openness in sharing had opened up the door for me to share more deeply my faith in Jesus. She seemed to be open to hearing me explain my faith. I told her how Jesus Christ actually lives inside of me and how he had been changing my life ever since I received him as a young boy.

Ann countered my thoughts with her own opinions of Jesus. They were markedly conciliatory, but also demonstrated the fact that she had chosen to distance herself from this man. But Ann had one final thing to say during that conversation. Curiously, she blurted out, "I don't know what it is about you, but I can tell there is something real in your life. Something deeply personal, something concrete. I can't put my finger on it, but I can sense that Christianity is not just a religion to you. What you have is real."

I invited Ann to our Bible study and, to my surprise, she agreed to come. Ann brought a fresh perspective to the passages we were studying. Her questions were insightful and interesting. And her comments from a Jewish perspective helped us to understand the Scriptures more fully. Sensing her openness to the gospel, we began giving her assignments in reading and studying specific Scripture passages. The Book of Hebrews became Ann's favorite and she soon developed a powerful affinity for it. Jesus as the "priest forever in the order of Melchizedek" (Heb 5:6) became one of her favorite verses. Other passages intrigued her. She was a learned woman who identified readily with the elevated language and complex ideas presented in Hebrews. We committed ourselves to more intense intercession for Ann. Prayer supporters in other states were soon praying regularly for her salvation as well.

Ann continued coming to our meetings as a full participant. At the close of one of our worship times one evening, Ann reported that two different sentences had "popped" into her mind as she worshiped. She thought they were from the New Testament but she wasn't sure. She could picture them in her mind and, in a sense, "read" them to us. The sentences were, "For God so loved the world, that he gave his only begotten Son, that whosoever believes in him should not perish but have everlasting life," and, "Come to me all who are weary and heavy-laden and I will give you rest."

As we sat there in astonishment, she asked, "Do you know what these mean?" We tried to explain that both of these verses were invitations from Jesus for her to be in a relationship with him. The Holy Spirit was speaking directly to her and Ann was getting closer and closer to coming to Jesus.

As far as we know, these two verses of Scripture came to Ann directly without prior knowledge of them on her part and without the help of the actual written Word in front of her. God personalized the gospel for her.

Several months passed. Ann's attendance at the Bible study fell off. She seemed distracted and evasive at times. We stepped up our prayer efforts for her, but nothing seemed to bring the walls down. Then one day a student named Karen and I sat with Ann at a luncheon and asked her how things were going. She was not doing well. Both physically and emotionally, she seemed drained and hopeless. She had been having heart problems and had received some unpleasant news about her physical condition. Furthermore, she had had heated words with her boss and was fearful of losing her job. On top of all this, her two-year old grandson had fallen out of a second-story window that morning and had been hurt.

With all of this on her mind, Ann gladly consented to Karen's and my offer to return to her apartment to pray with her. We again witnessed to her, explaining that Jesus wanted to help her to be released from her pain and frustration as well as from the intense anger that kept bubbling up and getting her in trouble. We talked specifically about what she would have to do to make that happen.

As it neared the time for Karen to go to class, we decided to pray. Our prayer time was short, but powerful. After the prayer, Karen got up to go to class, and I felt I should be going as well. Something kept me in my seat, however, and we continued to talk after Karen had left.

DEMONIZED?

Suddenly, and without any prompting from me, Ann looked me squarely in the face and said, "You know, Mark, sometimes I feel like I have a demon." I asked her what she thought the names of the demons could be. Without hesitation, she replied, "Suicide and Murder," and began relating to me the history of her interaction with these two demons. Sometimes they manifested themselves in her life as angry and violent thoughts about others. Often, when she was angry with someone, she would rip them to shreds in her mind in some sort of violent scenario. At no time did she ever give in to these images by physically hurting someone, but she felt the spirits might be behind some of the uncontrollable anger in her thoughts as well as in the difficulty she had in managing her tongue.

Other stories poured forth. Like the time they found her husband wounded in bed one morning after having been beaten in the head during the night with some sort of blunt object. They later found the object underneath one of the beds in their house. To this day, no one knows who actually did the beating but they assumed it was someone in the family. Other stories were equally bizarre.

DELIVERANCE

I had had no previous experience with deliverance, so the only thing I knew to do next was to pray and ask Jesus to take the spirits out of her life. I knew nothing of the importance of doing inner healing to deal with the areas of brokenness in her life before or in conjunction with deliverance. I also did not know of the importance of leading her to Christ before I attempted deliverance. It is usually very important to have the Holy Spirit as an ally within the person when attempting to deliver them.

I briefly explained that I was about to pray and that I was going to cast these spirits out of her life. She agreed that it was the right thing to do. So, with all the courage I could muster, I prayed, "Lord Jesus, in your Name, I command the spirits of suicide and murder to leave this body right now." Immediately, Ann's body was sent into a mild convulsion. Her eyes rolled back in their sockets. She began moving back and forth in her seat, gently shaking. I panicked a little and headed for the phone to call a friend to come help me. But the friend didn't answer. Apparently, God wanted me to seek counsel from himself alone.

So I gathered my wits and sat back down on the couch with Ann, who was now beginning to come out of the shaking. I watched as the last few moments of the deliverance were taking place. Ann's eyes rolled back to normal. The body movements subsided. She looked at me with a bewildered expression on her face, paused, and said, "What was that?" Now feeling more girded up by the Lord, I explained to her that what was going on inside of her was a battle between the forces of darkness and the forces of light. And at that moment, and the forces of light had won the battle. The demons had been cast out. But in order for Jesus to keep on winning and for the demons to stay away, Jesus had to be given the place of honor on the throne of her life as her personal Lord and Savior. She had not yet given herself to Jesus.

Our time that day was coming to a close. Ann had an appointment and had to go. I decided to leave, telling her that I would come back and check on her. That was on a Friday. On Saturday, I decided to visit her. She still looked haggard and worn out. I gave her some more salvation-oriented Scriptures and assured her that we were praying for her.

In the meantime, I was continuing to raise prayer support for her salvation. Friends, relatives, and supporters from all over stepped up their intercession for Ann. Students in the Bible study were rallying for prayer. It was evident that we were in a spiritual battle for Ann's life. She was very close but not yet over the threshold.

Since I was new to this kind of warfare, I consulted the pastors of my church. They counseled me to remain in supportive dialogue with Ann in whatever she decided to do next, but to make it very clear to her that she was on borrowed time as an unbeliever who had been delivered. Without the filling presence of the Holy Spirit to take the place of the demons, she was a sitting duck for further and potentially even more devastating attacks (Mt 12:43-45).

By Monday, I felt I needed to take charge of the situation. So I asked Ann if she would come and spend some time with me and one of my pastors. She agreed quickly, so we made an appointment for early Tuesday morning.

On Tuesday she looked more rested and seemed to be in a little better condition both physically and emotionally. On the half hour drive to the church, however, Ann began to share with me what was really going on inside of her. She said, "Mark, I think I am going absolutely crazy. For the past several days, I haven't been able to find my anger anywhere."

She continued, "It used to be such a big part of my life. I had a real relationship with it. And now I feel like there is a big hole inside me and I don't know what to do to fill it up." It surprised me to see that she was visibly upset over not being able to find her anger.

She went on. "I called a friend of mine that I really don't even like this weekend and I apologized to her for some things I had said. That's not like me! What has happened? I feel like I'm going absolutely crazy!"

I paused, prayed, then asked, "Ann, don't you remember on Friday when Karen and I were praying for you in your apartment ..."

She stopped me short. "You and Karen were in my apartment?" she asked in disbelief.

"Yes, we were in your apartment on Friday. We prayed with you and commanded some demons to leave. They were the source of your anger. You feel like you have lost your anger now because the demons were commanded to leave you!"

Ann was incredulous. This talk of demons, deliverance, and prayer in her apartment set her mind swimming. She leaned back in her seat with her mouth wide open, staring at me over her glasses as if I were the most clever liar she had ever met. Apparently she remembered none of what happened on the previous Friday. In reaction, she turned in on herself again, accusing herself of going absolutely mad.

Her next statement, however, suggested to me that she was becoming more open to my story being true. She said she had awakened that morning, for some reason, with a "strong sense," accompanied by a picture in her mind, that Karen had been in her apartment sometime that weekend. But she had no conscious recollection of the actual event.

Mostly, though, Ann was still in a state of disbelief. So beginning with the luncheon on Friday, I related to her the details of our time together. With each sentence, Ann gasped, let out a squeak, and accused me of lying to her, interrupting so often that I had to ask her to be quiet so I could finish the story. She told me later that she didn't actually believe me until I mentioned what she had told me about her husband being mysteriously beaten during the night. She had never told anyone that story before, so that in itself was proof enough to keep her in the car till we arrived at the church.

BREAKTHROUGH

We met my pastor, Alan, and entered his office for what would be a three-hour session leading to Ann's salvation and deliverance. My pastors ministered regularly in deliverance and so I felt more comfortable in this setting than I did ministering alone.

We began by having Ann relate to Alan the events of her life, beginning with the vision in the concentration camp and ending with our conversation on the way out to the church. When she had finished, Alan shared some thoughts on his perception of how God had been working in her life. He likened Ann's experience in the concentration camp to Paul's vision of Jesus on the road to Damascus. And he carefully explained that Jesus was both seeking out Ann for a relationship with himself and wanting to affirm the fact that she is Jewish. "He is not calling you to give up one set of religious rituals for another set of religious rituals," Alan explained. "But he is calling you to be completed and fulfilled in your Jewish faith. He wants you to experience the fullness of both covenants as God has intended for you in a relationship with himself."

Ann's response was, "I just believe that either Jesus was who he said he was or that he was the biggest charlatan that ever walked on the face of the earth." Alan agreed and lovingly based his sharing of the salvation message on the implications for our lives of how we view the person and claims of Jesus. After about two hours, Ann paused and said, "You know, I just really have this deep love for Jesus. He has to be more than a good teacher. I think I really admire him. I think I really do love him."

Alan responded, "Then why don't you just tell Jesus that you love him right now?" She agreed and began to try to talk to Jesus. Talking *about* him was one thing, but now she was talking *to* him in prayer. The spiritual dynamics were suddenly altered. She had considerable trouble getting the words out. Something was blocking her. She struggled, "JJJJJeee [breath], JJJJJeee [breath]." We were praying for her with fervency now. "JJJJee, JJJJee." Still, she could not say his name. She gasped in frustration and Alan encouraged her to relax and try again. Finally, with all of her physical strength, will, and emotions focused on uttering that one crucial name, she was able to relax, overcome her fear, and quietly say through tears, "Jesus, Jesus, I love you, I love you, I love you!"

Whew! The tension broke in the room and a wonderful stillness came over Ann's spirit. We could see the glory of the Lord shining on her smiling face. Alan then led Ann to pray and receive Christ as her personal Savior and Lord. It was a glorious time. We spent several moments just basking in the beauty of this salvation experience. Ann had passed from death to life right before our eyes.

We took a few minutes for a break and then Alan wanted to make sure we prayed for Ann to be even more filled with the Holy Spirit (Eph 5:18), and as well, to pray once more for deliverance. He began by relating to Ann a brief history of evil in the world from the Fall on up to the present time. Alan quoted Billy Graham to the effect that in the early seventies he believed Satan had been allowed to release an even larger barrage of evil into the world and that we were now in the midst of an even fiercer battle for the lives of women and men.

Alan then explained to Ann some of the "ins and outs" of demonization. He told her that the place in her that had been taken up by suicide and murder was now filled with the Spirit of Christ, but that other demons might be present and she would need to continue in deliverance for a period of time.

Ann agreed and submitted to Alan's suggestion that we lay hands on her and pray for her at that time.

We began to pray and asked the Holy Spirit to fill Ann even more fully with his presence. We then prayed for further deliverance. Alan commanded any demonic presence to leave Ann's body. The same physical manifestations Ann had had in her apartment praying with me occurred at that time. There was more shaking, then all was quiet. Great rejoicing began again. Ann was now a completed Jew in Jesus. All that the old covenant pointed toward in the new covenant of Jesus Christ now resided within her newly regenerated person.

Our drive home and the weeks that followed were filled with rejoicing over Ann's salvation and deliverance. All of those who had been praying were notified of the victory and Ann shared her testimony at the next Bible study. I asked her several weeks later, after her baptism and one additional deliverance session, "Where is Satan in relation to you now?" She replied, "He's gone. He is no more in my life the way he was. I have no conscious sense of his presence here with me anymore. I can now concentrate for the rest of my life on being the bride of Christ in my new marriage to Jesus!" Praise God! Ann was free from the grip of Satan!

Someone in the group had a verse from the Lord for Ann that summed up her long-term experiences with Jesus: "Bear in mind that our Lord's patience means salvation" (2 Pt 3:15a, NIV). Jesus had been pursuing Ann for many years and now she had finally heard his voice and answered his call. Ann was free. She had finally come home.

TEN

From New Age to New Life

Lora Elizabeth

The foundation of all New Age doctrine is the belief that humanity can attain godhood. This belief is central to all the teachings on the road to "self-enlightenment." The idea that each person contains the whole universe, all of the answers and all of the creative power of the Creator himself is very appealing. These ideas are nothing new. They are the same lies the Serpent spoke to Eve in the garden. But they are dressed in new clothing to appeal to today's people. "For God knows that the day you eat from it, your eyes will be opened and you will be like God ..." (Gn 3:5, NIV).

The following pages may be shocking to some. These things are happening not just in someone else's town but right where we live. The following account is not a fictional story; it is a nonfictional testimony written from experience. "The Spirit clearly says that in later times some will abandon the faith and follow deceiving spirits and things taught by demons" (1 Tm 4:1, NIV). Though it may seem hard to believe that people would follow doctrines taught by demons, this story is a clear example of exactly how the Bible forewarns us.

MY STORY

I sat in the center of a room slowly drifting into a deep trance. Rose incense clouded the air. It smelled so thickly sweet it was almost nauseating. My breathing became so slow that it was almost imperceptible. My eyelids fluttered slightly like one who is dreaming. Other followers watched anxiously, waiting for more changes to take place.

I began to tremble. My head jerked rapidly from side to side. I slowly fell forward from the waist, as if being crushed by the weight of gravity; my forehead touched the floor. Suddenly I sat straight up, filled by new power. "Ashtanka," my inner guide, had arrived. You could see him in the unblinking stare I fixed upon each follower in turn. "Greetings, my beloved ones," Ashtanka began. The voice coming from my lips was so deep and powerful, it couldn't possibly be my own.

This small group had been gathering weekly for three months to hear Ashtanka's teachings. The teachings became more intense and more demanding over time. Ashtanka told them that others were being raised up all over the nation to do the "work of the light" and that they were his "special chosen ones" who were to begin the "thrust of clearing energy into this area." Their goal: "liberate mankind from the bondage of old thinking and outdated religion."

They were reminded that the only way to experience true freedom, love, and joy was to "find their god within." They were to "reclaim their birthright," to "become gods themselves." Ashtanka threatened them, "All who refuse to grow and evolve will die. Any who stand in the way will be removed."

Fearful that they might perish because they couldn't really understand him, the group carried out Ashtanka's demands to the letter. They gave their allegiance to him and to the returning "ascended masters" he said would help them.

Through my hands, Ashtanka touched each group member to establish a "permanent mind link" between himself and each follower. Each felt a tingling sensation at the top of his or her head where he touched them. They discovered that they could hear his voice in their minds even when he was not using Mishabae to speak.

THE BATTLE IS REAL

When I was Mishabae, the spirits spoke to our group of their plan to usher in the "Golden Age of Humanity." The spirits promised that through our hard work and our commitment to "enlightenment," mankind and our planet would be saved from destruction.

These spirits were actually Satan's demons at work. The kingdom of darkness—his kingdom—is organized to work at a frenzied pace. The battle is real. And willing or not, we are all a part of it.

Satan is the "father of lies," an expert at deception. He knows where humanity is the weakest and just what to offer us to keep his unwitting victims blind to his true purposes—to deceive, entrap, and destroy.

"But woe to the earth and the sea, because the devil has gone down to you. He is filled with fury, because he knows his time is short" (Rv 12:12, NIV). The demons themselves know that with Christ's return they will no longer have free reign and dominion here on the earth and that all their work will come to nothing.

I continued to follow Ashtanka's teachings and found myself in the middle of a spiritual odyssey that had promised me everything but left me with nothing. The year was 1985. With my health failing, my heart full of depression and despair, and a deep, soul-felt torment, I prayed daily for death to release me.

DRAWN INTO THE NEW AGE

My introduction to the occult began in a Unitarian church in the small Massachusetts town where I grew up. The church was a social club more than anything else. It drew liberals and "free thinkers" who wanted the parishioners to create their own belief systems. The name of God was never heard. Jesus was never mentioned.

Our children's group took hikes, had picnics, and did art projects. Later, during that time, the leaders announced that we would begin a study on Extra Sensory Perception (ESP) and paranormal experiences. They began to administer a series of tests that would tell who among us had a gift in this area. I rated higher than anyone else in my class. I was particularly adept in telekinesis, the ability to move objects with your mind. Having come out of a home where I was usually ignored, I was delighted to be the center of attention. No one had ever called me special or gifted before. Satan, knowing my rejection and my longing to be noticed, was beginning to draw me in.

When I was in fourth grade, our class was invited to visit a spiritist church in Boston. The teacher thought it was a wonderful opportunity for us, so off we went.

As we got there, I felt a strange stirring within. I just knew that the medium had a message for me. He did! I was the first one to be called on that night. A spirit spoke to me of a special purpose in my life, saying that I was called to a spiritual path. It then instructed me to begin studying meditation and philosophies. I was again told that I was special, gifted. Through my desperate need to be needed, and a longing to be loved, I was hooked. I had finally found my little place in the sun. I began to develop my whole sense of self-esteem around my newly found gifts.

Fascinated by what I had seen, I decided to try contacting spirits on my own. I would get my friends together to hold make-believe séances, and I was always cast in the role of the medium. When demonic manifestations actually began to occur, we became very frightened and vowed never to play any séances again. However, the doors to satanic influence had been opened in my life. From that point forward, Satan was in subtle, and later very blatant, control.

As the years went by, I read everything I could find on yoga, meditation, and various philosophies. I had a deep hunger for truth, but with no religious training or foundation in my life, I was forced to draw my own conclusions and create my own truth at a very tender age. My parents boasted that I had come from a long line of atheists. They encouraged me to educate myself, but to follow no one. "To follow is weak," they told me. Between the ages of eleven and fourteen, I became deeply involved in the practice of yoga. I fancied myself a loner and preferred to spend hours in meditation rather than engage in normal social activities.

At twelve, my one close friend introduced me to drugs in the form of marijuana and LSD. From that time on I constantly struggled between Eastern asceticism and falling into drug use. It was after I began using drugs that I found I could leave my body for short periods of time. Through meditation and drugs, I had become completely opened up to demonic influence in my life, and Satan had more and more reign over me.

For a while, everything faded into the background as I got caught up in the whirlwind of teenage activities. But the darkness was always at the edge of my consciousness, guiding the events of my life, waiting for the right time to step in.

The next turning point wasn't reached until I was twenty years old. Desperately searching for the peace that had eluded me for most of my life, I plunged back into Eastern philosophy. It seemed odd to me that at this time I started experiencing nightmares that would leave me shaken for many days.

I began having disturbing visions of the future that frightened me terribly. I wasn't sure if I wanted to live. It was then that a demonic spirit began to appear in my room at night. It threatened to consume me. Realizing I had no knowledge to protect myself, I left my ordinary studies behind and began to study sorcery. I learned to use the power of my will to influence others. I found that I could control people and manipulate events to my own liking. (I now know that I was deceived and the power was not mine, but was demonic.) As I became adept at these practices, the visitations stopped. They had served their purpose well, leading me deeper into Satan's plan through fear.

This went on for some time. I sought fulfillment, but each path I followed only led me onto another path of emptiness. Bit by bit, Satan was seeing to it that I would develop all the qualities he needed me to have.

I could now see and read "auras," colorful energy fields that surround the human body. They have an appearance similar to heat waves rising off hot pavement in the summer. My intuition was honed to a razor's sharpness, and my abilities in the psychic realm reached a zenith—I discovered channeling. This meant that I could gain information from spirits living in what they told me was "the light" and contact the "dead."

My guides came to speak to me with amazing clarity and accuracy concerning many topics of which I had no personal knowledge. I now felt that I had arrived! But I had only arrived at the beginning of what would have led to a miserable end had it not been for the divine intervention of God himself.

Satan "blessed" me with a measure of the acceptance and fame I had craved for so long. I became well-known for my gifts of healing as well as for my kindness. Most of the time I refused payment because of a sincere desire to help people. I was so thoroughly deceived that I truly thought I was serving God. The things I was doing only seemed to bring good to those who sought my help. I understand now that Satan was using me to deceive as many people as possible. Because I was gentle, kind, and soft-spoken, it made the deception easier. Through helping those who had found no help anywhere else, Satan was luring more people into his bondage.

At this time, I became involved with an organization whose main goal was to teach channeling to the masses. They sent me all over the state to lead workshops and perform healings. My mother even bragged about my activities to her office mates. But a few of her coworkers happened to be Christians. They tried over and over again to convince my mom that what I was doing would lead to disaster. They told her that my activities were demonic, and that I was possessed. But they couldn't reach either of us. We were deaf to their warnings and message of salvation. As a result, they decided to commit themselves to pray for me, not only individually but with their churches. Before long, I was on permanent prayer lists in churches all over the state.

God also put me on the hearts of believers all over the town where I was living. People who saw me felt the urge to pray, and many prayed faithfully for this woman whose name they didn't even know. I wasn't yet aware of it, but God had begun to draw me out of the darkness and into his light.

A HIGHER AUTHORITY: GOD INTERVENES

At first gradually, and then with increasing speed, everything I had worked so hard for began to deteriorate. The spirits became cold and distant. Channeling sessions became painful, leaving me sick and exhausted. I began to develop allergies to almost everything, especially food. I felt as if all of creation was rejecting me, and wondered why. I was becoming so weak that I couldn't hold down a job, and could no longer do readings or channeling for people.

My friends were shocked to find that I couldn't even heal

myself. As I was the one to whom people usually came for help, I had no one to turn to. When I asked the spirits for help, they answered me only with silence.

During a meditation, one of my "guides" spoke to me for the last time. He informed me that none of "them" could stay with me any longer. I was devastated! "Why?" I cried to them. "Why?"

Their answer surprised me: "You belong to a higher authority," they said angrily and agitatedly. "One much more powerful than we."

"Who is he? How will I find him?" I begged them to tell me.

"He is so powerful that we cannot even utter his name," they answered. Weeks of silence followed. I was lost, confused, and frightened.

Looking back, I now understand that in answer to the prayers of his people, *God had begun to intervene* in my life. As a result of prayer, the demonic beings who for so long had ruled my existence were being bound up and cast away. God's people had laid claim to me for God's kingdom. The work had been started and God would answer. The demons, realizing that defeat was at hand, were doing their utmost to kill me before I could come to God. This would have secured me for Satan's realm for eternity.

I was plagued with depression, sickness, and thoughts of suicide. I began to drink heavily to escape the horrible nightmares that were visited upon me any time I tried to rest. At this point, Satan made a final attempt to claim me.

I had barely lain down one afternoon when a commanding voice spoke to me. It asked if I was ready to know the truth. I thought that my new teacher had finally come to rescue me. I readily answered "Yes!"

In less than a second, my room was filled with a foul smell and a noise that sounded like a thousand angry hornets buzzing. Satan himself appeared in my room. My ears began to ring, and I went numb from the top of my head to the tip of my toes. He had a crushing grip on one of my feet. I struggled desperately but to no avail.

"You fool!" he shouted. "The truth is that you have been deceived!" he laughed. "You actually thought that you had power? You actually thought you had knowledge?" he bellowed at me. "You are worthless, nothing. Not even as valued as a blade of grass. You shall be plunged into darkness for ten thousand, tens of thousands of years before you will regain even a glimmer of what you once were!"

With that, he pulled out a large double-edged sword. "To sever you from this life," he said, raising his arm high for the blow.

I screamed and wept. I called on every power known to me that was supposed to protect me from evil. I called on the name of every spiritual "master" who had ever lived. Nothing worked. Finally, in desperation, I called the name of the one I had never known, never loved.

"Jesus!" I cried out, "Jesus, God, help me!"

In an instant I was alone in my room. Satan had fled.

Thus began a long battle to bring me to the Lord. I was completely confused, and still full of rebellion. I told God that if he was really who he said he was, if Jesus was the answer, and if he really wanted me to become like one of those Christians who I had for so long despised and slandered, that he would have to bring it about. I was too tired and hurt to ever believe in anything again.

So, God sent believers into my life. I began to bump into them everywhere. I finally consented to study the Bible with a few of them.

Finally, after many long talks, and trying their patience beyond the limit and back again many times, I began to see the light. I broke down and wept when I realized that they were telling me the truth. I knew that they were right, and that I had been horribly wrong.

I received Jesus into my life. As this book goes to press, it will have been about five years since that great day. God has had to do a great deal of work to clean out my mind, continuously breaking me of rebellion, and healing the damage done by years of fear and bondage.

A dear brother in the church came to me shortly after I had been saved. I was struggling hard to know God's love and to understand his Word. This man had a word from God for me. He told me that there was a fierce battle raging over my soul, but to fear not for God had already won.

How I clung to those words! They helped me through many a battle as I would claim victory through Christ in my life. "Satan," I would say, "God has already won this battle! I have been sealed into his kingdom by the blood of Christ! Now leave me alone!"

God gradually taught me to stand in him. When I came under attack, he gave me the gift of praise and prayer. As I would stand and praise the Lord with all my heart, the demonic oppression would lift. Demons would actually flee. I saw then that the battle belongs to the Lord. I saw that by knowing my rights as a Christian, rights that I have through my union with Christ, God could reign victorious in my life.

I began to trust him in all things, and love him with my whole heart. "What then shall we say in response to this? If God is for us, who can be against us?" (Rom 8:31, NIV). The answer is "NO ONE!" Not even Satan can destroy a believer standing firm in the faith. I thank God daily for his forgiveness and salvation, for the miracle of him in my life. Mishabae is forever dead, but Lora will live in eternity with God forever! "Therefore if anyone is in Christ, [she] is a new creation, the old has gone, and the new has come" (2 Cor 5:17, NIV). But our enemy is still very much alive and working hard to entice us often.

THE SUBTLE DECEPTION OF THE NEW AGE

Our Adversary wants us to believe that God is holding out on us. Because the seeds of rebellion have been planted, we turn to a multitude of false prophets and doctrines in an attempt to claim what we have been led to believe is ours.

Many "New Age" teachings have their roots in Hinduism. The Hindu belief that God is within each individual who is constantly evolving toward godhood is rapidly being adopted by the Western world. Also, the promise that all beliefs contain basic truth and will eventually lead to God creates a unity that allows New Age thinking to cross many religious and cultural barriers.

Twisted and inverted truths tempt and tease us. Deceiving doctrines lie waiting to devour the unwary. Without the foundation of God's Word to test these doctrines, it is very easy to fall prey to deception. As we are warned in Scripture, "Be self-controlled and alert. Your enemy, the devil, prowls around like a roaring lion, looking for someone to devour. Resist him, standing firm in the faith" (1 Pt 5:8-9a, NIV).

Infiltration of the New Age movement. In 1985, the spirits told us that within five years channeling and other occult practices would be widely accepted. This, and more, has already come to pass. Satan, through his overt attack on society, is effectively desensitizing us to demonic manifestations and power. He plans for this whole generation to grow up accepting occult practices as normal, a generation devoid of conscience.

Satan is doing this by introducing his methods of wickedness into every realm of our lives. Many practices are no longer "occult," or hidden. He has succeeded in coming out of hiding directly into the mainstream of professions of all kinds. For example, Satan, through the New Age movement, has infiltrated the health profession, the media, schools, and even some churches. Following are some instances of this infiltration.

In almost every New Age technique advertised to the general public there is one common denominator—they all require individuals to open up to an unnamed "universal energy." It is often referred to as the "source," the "light," or a "higher self." Whether involved in healing or positive affirmations for successful living, the power comes from the same source: not the "Light," but from the forces of darkness. Individuals are led to believe that the power comes from within themselves. They are advised not to question the process, not to analyze how it works. According to these teachers, over-intellectualization would stop the "energy from effectively moving."

Health sciences. Like a cancer, the New Age movement has spread into many of our traditional institutions. One woman is a medium (channel) and a massage therapist. She makes no attempt to hide her beliefs or practices as she teaches workshops in healing massage to obstetrical nurses at the local hospital.

Her workshops incorporate a mixture of creative visualization and meditations. The nurses, in turn, will teach their patients. These techniques are meant to awaken the "innate healing power" believed to be latent in each individual.

Nurses and patients are also taught to tap into their own "higher power" or "spirit guide" to enhance their own healing ability. They are taught to use their bodies as conductors. The power moves through the body and into the recipient of the healing. This is done by inducing a trancelike state through the use of yogic breathing techniques. Once the trance state is achieved, one simply wills the energy to move through the body by repeatedly visualizing it. These techniques have their roots in yoga, a practice that comes from Hinduism. Many, out of a sincere desire to help others, are falling into the trap of believing that the gift of healing can be cultivated by their own power.

Many professionals are beginning to blend traditional with new, or alternative, therapies. Anyone using a chiropractor or a massage therapist should thoroughly check his or her credentials. These professions lend themselves easily to the subtle use of some highly questionable practices.

A friend of mine I will call "Peggy" had been ill for quite some time. Her doctor seemed unable to pinpoint the cause of her troubles. As a result, she sought the help of a certain nutritionist, on the advice of an acquaintance.

During her visit to the nutritionist, Peggy was offered spiritual counsel along with dietary suggestions. The nutritionist told Peggy that it was useless to try to heal the body without healing the spirit as well. She went on to tell Peggy that she was a channel (medium) for two "Angelic Beings" who could see into her body on a cellular level and give a more accurate diagnosis than even the most sophisticated medical equipment now in use.

Out of desperation and ignorance of the psychic realms, Peggy agreed to allow the "angels" to examine her. The nutritionist led her into a hypnotic state, enabling the angels to move throughout her body. Their findings were shocking! Peggy was told that she had an undiagnosed cancer in her stomach and the first stage of AIDS. They warned her that if she didn't do exactly as she was told that she would most certainly die and so would her three-year-old daughter "Jessie."

One of Satan's most powerful tools is fear. Through fear, my friend fell immediately into bondage. She began a strict dietary regimen and continued to consult the "angels" for progress reports on her health. Occasionally the nutritionist would phone Peggy telling her that the "angels" were pleased with her, or to deliver another warning.

During this time, Peggy became aware of an ever-watchful, hostile presence in her home. She found herself constantly looking over her shoulder, expecting to find someone or something there. She was becoming tense and irritable. Her daughter Jessie began to act strangely. She frequently talked to invisible friends. One she referred to as her "other mother" and the other one she simply called "him." These conversations would be followed by bursts of hyperactivity and aggressive behavior.

Not knowing any of this, I had volunteered to babysit little

Jessie. One evening after a prayer meeting, I went over to their home to take care of Jessie. Soon after Peggy left, Jessie became extremely agitated. She began talking to her "other mother" and running around the room laughing hysterically. She stopped suddenly, looked me right in the eye and said, "He's here. He's here." I gently held her by both hands and asked, "Who's here, Jessie? Who's bothering you?" I could feel the growing hostility in the room. The air was suddenly very cold. Out of the mouth of this sweet three-year-old came the answer: "Satan. Satan is here."

My heart was pounding, and I felt as if my blood had turned to ice water. It was only by God's grace that, although I was terrified, I could still think clearly. I grabbed Jessie in a tight hug and began to pray aloud, pleading the blood of Christ over her mind, body, spirit, and soul. I went on to pray that God's protection and grace would be on her and that one day she would come to truly know and love Jesus. I stood and asked God to send his angels to guard this home and claimed Jessie and her mother for the kingdom of God. Jessie calmed down and seemed to be exhausted. She looked up at me pleading, "Pray again. Heal me." I explained that I couldn't heal her, but that Jesus could if she would only ask him. Together we prayed and asked Jesus to touch her and watch over her.

Later, in relating the incident to Peggy, it became clear that this was a case of demonization. Theirs was not a religious home where prayer, healing, or Jesus were talked about. Neither had Jessie been exposed to TV programs or horror movies in which Satan had been mentioned. The three-year-old's knowledge of Satan and healing could only have been gained from the spirit realm.

Children have very sensitive spirits. If a parent is not strong in the Lord, or is engaged in some kind of psychic activity or heavy drug use, the doors to the demonic open not only for the parent, but the child as well.

I asked Peggy if she knew where she might have opened

herself up to influence from the demonic realm. She immediately told me about the nutritionist. Because of the practices of a seemingly trustworthy professional, Peggy became an innocent victim. People are accustomed to trusting their doctors and other health professionals.

Peggy has now given her life to Jesus and the demonic visitations have stopped. She also went to a doctor to be checked for cancer and AIDS. Both reports came back negative.

The media. Satan's growing contact in our nation is most easily seen in the media. Theatrical movies and television sensationalize his power, often making his works look desirable. He has raised up likable celebrities to claim that their personal success is due to becoming "enlightened through channeling, astrology, past life regression, etc.... "

Celebrities like Shirley MacLaine have become powerful advocates for Satan because of their influence over so many people who idolize them. Unfortunately, the more highly esteemed a person or publication is, the more readily the public will accept what they have to say, blind to the hidden agenda.

In the past few years, *Time-Life* launched a crusade to educate their readers about the wonders of the supernatural realm. They have a number of TV spots promoting their new series of books. These books explore psychic places, mystic powers, dreams, out-of-body experiences, and phantom encounters. They encourage us to explore these topics and find parallels in our own lives. The commercials are clever. They try to goad us into acceptance, or convince us that every normal person has psychic experiences and abilities. They try to make us believe that there is something abnormal in being disinterested or inexperienced in these matters.

Even Saturday morning cartoons are not exempt. Vulnerable children are being exposed to Eastern religious philosophies and also direct demonic contact through the many Saturday morning cartoons. Have you taken a good look at cartoons like

Thundercats, Beetlejuice, or *Ghostbusters* lately? The majority of the kids' cartoons out today depict societies in which magical powers, psychic experiences, and consorting with demons is normal. The object is to normalize these activities in the minds of the viewers, and in the case of children, repetitive imitative play can often open the doors to satanic influence.

The schools. Schools are also being used as an entry point for initiating children into evil practices. Elementary school teachers in a small town were asked to participate in a workshop introducing Creative Visualization and Meditation into the classroom. Yoga and meditation for kindergarten students is said to be extremely beneficial in lengthening attention spans, and in controlling hyperactivity. These techniques have already become popular in a number of "open" or "free" schools elsewhere in the same state.

Some of the books used were *Guided Imagery and Education,* published by Humanistic Psychology, and *200 Ways to Use Imagery in the Classroom*, published by Trillion Press. Teachers may be introducing these techniques under the guise of "new educational programs." To the children, they appear to be a time of quiet play.

The objective is to encourage the use of the whole brain, and stimulate the "creator-like power" which is said to be latent in every individual. The process begins with a series of exercises that might go something like this:

All right class, now that you are relaxed, I want you to take a few deep breaths to clear your minds. Now, imagine that you have opened your eyes. What you see in front of you is an empty field waiting for you to fill it. Let's all take a good look at the field. Does your field have flowers? What color are they? Now, notice the brook just over to your left. Walk over to it. Listen to the water splashing over the stones. If you are thirsty, take a drink from the brook. Is everyone with me? Good. Now look into the distance. There is someone approaching you. Who is it? He's right next to you now. Take his hand and walk further into the field with him. He is your guide. He will help you. Whenever you need his help, all you need to do is ask him to come.

After this kind of experience, the teacher tells the class that what they just saw was real. "In order to see it," she might say, "it has to exist somewhere in a place not too different from here. Now that you know how, you can take yourself there whenever you like... "

This clever ploy brings children right into the heart of New Age influence in one quick jump. Through meditation and visualization the children are put in direct contact with evil spirit beings, without being aware of the consequences.

Universities. In a day and age when people so strongly object to simple prayer in the classroom, it is amazing how easily Eastern mysticism has found acceptance. Often labeled "science" rather than anything to do with spiritual matters, it has found a place in college psychology curricula. It provides students with what appears to be an interesting diversion from what is often a dry topic.

During my involvement with the occult community, I became acquainted with a group of people studying Eckankar, the science of soul travel. Among them was a prominent psychology professor from the state university. Knowing I was adept at astral travel and used dreaming to counsel my clients, she asked me to be a guest speaker in her course for the honors program. Under the banner of self-discovery and dream analysis, I would lead her class through studies fundamental to the practice of Eckankar.

I was delighted at the opportunity to offer these future counselors what I perceived to be highly effective tools for a healing practice. Class times were used for a series of meditations and visualization exercises. Our purpose was to develop the students' intuitive abilities as well as open them up to psychic activity. The students learned about different levels of existence and the numerous spiritual forces with which we co-exist. Explaining that these forces affect us on a conscious or subconscious level, I would then show them how awareness of the supernatural was key to healing the whole person. These opening exercises would culminate with meditation techniques that provoke out-of-body experiences.

Some students had trouble crossing the threshold to the astral plane. They complained that a strong barrier was standing in their way. At this point, I would endeavor to set them free. I used a series of clearing techniques (a form of hypnosis) to erase the old thought patterns and belief systems (that is, traditional religion and values) that were hindering their progress. Many were struggling against their Christian upbringings. They had been taught to follow Christ rather than to seek self-fulfillment and find their own "god-given" power within.

This classroom gave me the perfect platform to express my own twisted views on Christianity as well as to dispense channeled information about Jesus. I counseled these young seekers to renounce all ties with the Christian faith. This was the barrier that stood in their way. It was time to cast off the bondage of guilt and fear and to embrace a fuller, more radiant new life! A few of the most stubborn and "growth-resistant" students left. I felt sorry for them. They were missing the opportunity to evolve. I considered *them* to be truly blind and doomed to repeat their lives again and again here on earth in other incarnations until they attained enlightenment. The rest of the class broke through and began to experience astral projection. As they did this, I would channel their personal spirit guides. These astral guides would continue to be a source of protection and information to the students as they traveled down this new road of self-discovery.

These teachings were pointedly anti-Christian. Any other faith was not so viciously attacked. No other faith has the power to close the doors into the psychic realm that have been opened through the use of visualizations, meditations, and attempts at soul travel.

We were using the psychology department to recruit some of the university's brightest students into Eckankar as well as build up our own healing practices. Looking back on this episode of my life, I shudder to think how many people I affected by these teachings. Young people enter college with eager open minds. I can now acknowledge what we did as a grievous breach of trust. I was under such a strong deception that I felt it was my responsibility to free as many people as I could from what I perceived to be spiritual slavery to a selfish god. In the name of freedom and enlightenment, I helped set many feet on the road to hell. Reader beware! There are more people just like I used to be, still at work to gain the trust and allegiance of this nation's youth. The structure of the state university obviously offers little or no protection from teachers of false doctrines.

The churches. Churches are one of the last frontiers in main-streaming the occult. Alternative churches are springing up everywhere. Even sects such as Eckankar, which used to be secretive, are building temples with the traditional Sunday service in order to more easily attract new members.

The Unity Church is gaining popularity across the nation. It preaches a watered-down gospel, mixed with metaphysics and the Hindu theory of a god within ourselves. Self-enlightenment and self-love are the basis for all its teachings.

The Unity Church insists that all its doctrine is based on God's Word, yet it refuses to acknowledge Jesus Christ as God, and that the only way to the Father is through him. Christ's teachings are considered merely a good stepping stone on the way to "higher truths."

A member of the Unity Church paraphrased the Bible to me: "Ye shall know the truth and it shall set you free" (Jn 8:32, NIV). He explained that one must realize that the truth is not found in following another, but in finding the God, or

Christ, within. He also referred to learning the "science of astral travel" as being the "truth which sets you free." He shared his excitement about being able to travel into the heavenlies and absorb all of God's knowledge, directly from him.

New Age thinking has made deep inroads into the heart of our nation and the souls of her people. Professionals of all kinds have become infected by deceptive doctrines in their quest for power. The darkness is at work in our schools and the truth is being twisted in our churches. How can anything but chaos reign when humanity is submitted to no other god but each person's self-god, each of which becomes increasingly tied to the enemy of all human souls?

Christians need to remember that it isn't what we know about the occult that will set people free. It isn't our strength or wisdom that will save. It is the power of God's spirit activated through prayer and his living, active Word that will penetrate hearts of stone and impart new life. That's what won me. And that's what will win others from the enemy's delusions.

While I was still a captive, God appointed believers to come into my life. These people knew next to nothing about witchcraft. What they did know was Jesus Christ. Their intimate relationship with him spoke to me. Their obvious joy shone out like a beacon in the night, shedding light on the darkness that bound my soul. Their unshakable faith made me hunger after what they had. The fact that no matter what the world had to offer, they would choose Jesus over and over again impressed me. They were able to help me to see God's unfathomable love and mercy and to believe that his grace is sufficient for any who would seek his forgiveness—even me. I finally saw how beautifully simple it would be to act on it and to receive Jesus as my Savior.

Rejoice with me in our relationship with Christ. Share his goodness, grace, and mercy. Shed his love abroad wherever you go. Step out in faith in the Lord's wondrous ability to save and free. It really is a matter of life or death.

ELEVEN

Argentina– Evangelizing in a Context of Spiritual Warfare

Edgardo Silvoso

For our struggle is not against flesh and blood, but against rulers, against the powers, against the world forces of this darkness, against the spiritual forces of wickedness in the heavenly places. **Ephesians 6:12, NIV**

Learning to put the principles of spiritual warfare into practice is not an easy thing. The Christians of Argentina were no more prepared to do so than are most North American Christians. What follows is an account of some of the things the Argentine church is learning about what needs to be done at both human and spirit levels, involving both ground- and cosmic-level warfare.

We started by *observing* what was going on. We observed, of course, many problems. But in observing the problems, we discovered that there were some things going on that were proving effective, and decided to learn from the effective approaches and to apply what we learned. This led to a second step, the *analysis* step. We analyzed two things: 1) the Scriptures, to see if there were any precedents there, and 2) the experience of those ministries that were effective. We asked questions such as, "What are these successful ministries doing that seem to be contributing to their success?" and, "Is what they are doing within the parameters allowed by Scripture?" Next, we asked if any of the biblically allowable strategies being employed by the successful ministries could be taught and used by others. Once we decided that they probably could be, we began the *action* step, "Plan Resistencia."

Observation, analysis, and action are what this case study is about. As I point out toward the end of the chapter, we now feel we did not do everything right in the city of Resistencia, but we learned enough that it has become a major part of the present ministry of our mission, Harvest Evangelism, to share what we have been learning with Christian leaders throughout the world.

WHAT DO WE DO NOW?

A perplexed group of elders and the pastor of a Baptist church struggle through the night battling against the powerful spiritual forces that have taken control of a woman. The leadership of this Argentine Baptist church has never seen anything like this before. It is a bizarre and gruesome manifestation of hellish power displayed by the masters of this unfortunate woman. They challenge the authority of the elders and proclaim that they will never leave her. She was, the demons said, "delivered" to them by a leading surgeon in town who also doubles as a priest in the occult Macumba religion.

Questioned by the church leaders, the demons boast of

how they acquired the right to control the woman's body. They tell the incredible tale of the doctor's pilgrimage to a Brazilian Macumba temple where he was recruited. He was instructed to sew microscopic fetishes, such as enchanted hairs and nail shavings, inside his patients' flesh. These fetishes provided the demonic equivalent of "spiritual remote control." Like bugs planted inside embassy walls, they can be activated or deactivated according to the will of whoever planted them.

Nothing these Baptist leaders had ever learned from experience or Scripture prepared them to deal with this kind of problem. This experience, however, began to alert them to the fact that there is a war going on, a war that they are part of whether they like it or not, and that they need to learn how to conduct themselves in a warfare context. Though they were not entirely successful in dealing with the demons who had invaded this woman, God used this incident to make them desire greater ability to work in his power to set such captives free.

* * *

A once healthy and thriving Brethren assembly in the periphery of Buenos Aires is undergoing a bitter split. Church leaders who have known and loved each other for decades are at each other's throats. Tempers flare quickly. Accusations are freely hurled at people who, until recently, have been the embodiment of godliness. After every major outburst, the leaders seem to come to their senses and break down and cry, embracing the ones who, until moments ago, were the objects of their attacks. Yet, when it's all over, the head elder has submitted his resignation and those who remain are ready to fight for the shredded mantle of leadership. Others are quietly making preparations to leave the church. A feeling of precious things slowly beginning to rot pervades the atmosphere. Something awful is happening.

Before he leaves, the head elder makes a last-ditch effort to stem the tide of destruction. He calls for a day of prayer and fasting at a retreat center two hundred miles away. As the warring factions gather for prayer and Bible study, God begins to teach them about spiritual warfare, about forces of wickedness, about rulers of geographical darkness. Slowly, the biblical truth begins to emerge that the struggle is not against flesh and blood but against those principalities who hide their presence behind misguided human beings and mask their designs under the guise of irreconcilable differences. At the end of the day there is true reconciliation between the elders. They choose to come under the mighty hand of God, and in doing so they bring the church with them. They pledge to use the spiritual authority delegated to them by the Lord Jesus himself "against all power of the enemy" (Lk 9:1), and to put a specific section of town under that spiritual authority. They challenge the principalities and powers in charge of the darkness over that region, and pledge to resist the devil until he flees.

Shortly after returning to their hometown, they encounter a new convert in their church. She had been a leader in a spiritist center in the section of town these elders have placed under Jesus' authority. She confesses that thirteen of these centers had made a pact to break up their church. They had been "praying" to Satan and his demons for strife among the Christian leaders! What these Brethren elders were unable to understand at first is now something in which they are becoming experts overnight: *spiritual warfare!* Immediately they organize a counteroffensive and, in a short time, see a large contingent of people living in the area placed under spiritual authority make a public commitment to Christ. In less than a year, an interdenominational crusade in their town produces tens of thousands of decisions of faith.

* * *

These two incidents illustrate a phenomenon that in the last ten years has become part of the daily life of a large segment of the church in Argentina: *spiritual warfare.* Direct confrontation with demonic princes and rulers. Whether it is Carlos Annacondia, a lay evangelist, leading a united crusade; or Omar Cabrera, expanding his multi-location congregation of more than sixty-five thousand; or Samuel Libert, a leading Baptist pastor, boldly preaching the gospel, there is always a common track: war against Satan and his deputies. This means intercessory prayer for those in spiritual darkness accompanied by the serving of eviction notices to the rulers of that darkness. The methodology varies. Some publicly confront the demonic forces; others do so in strict privacy, availing themselves of the weapons of prayer and fasting prior to the outreach. Still others do it through strong reliance on the written Word. But the outcome is always the same: the strong man is bound and his goods, the souls he has kept captive, are set free.

If there is one dominant element in the contemporary theology and methodology of evangelism in Argentina, it is spiritual warfare. It is an awareness that the struggle is not against a political or social system. Nor is it focused on those who are captives but, rather, against the jailkeepers, against the rulers, those in authority in the spiritual realm. The church in Argentina has learned to deal with the victimizer rather than just with the victims. In so doing, it seems to have gotten to the root of the problem. And the results are impressive.

HISTORY

Since its inception, the church in Argentina has produced extraordinary preachers and international leaders such as Luis Bush, Samuel Libert, Alberto Mottessi, Carmelo Terranova, Luis Palau, and Juan Carlos Ortiz, who have become a gift to the church at large. The first pioneers of the church in Argentina, regardless of their denominational affiliations, left an indelible commitment to sound doctrine and to the Scriptures. Every major denomination established a Bible Institute or seminary at the earliest stage of its life.

Furthermore, the spiritual fiber of the church was kept clean and pure by the fire of opposition, many times bordering on persecution. Pioneers like Pablo Besson, Erling Andresen, Carlos Rogers, and many others made absolutely clear that the gospel they preached, many times at the risk of losing their lives, was a reflection of the gospel they lived. This they passed on to the first generation of Argentine leaders.

But in spite of all this, the Argentine church never experienced great growth. Except for an evangelistic explosion in the mid-fifties when Tommy Hicks shook up Buenos Aires, the church never saw growth that was in proportion to the quality of its roots. The average congregation was smaller than one hundred members.

OMAR CABRERA

A corner was turned when Omar Cabrera began a new approach to evangelism and church-planting in Argentina. Rather than simply praying before his evangelistic meetings, as all evangelists and pastors do, he began to employ a direct approach to breaking the power of territorial spirits. His method is first to choose a town or city in which he feels the Lord wants him to establish a congregation. He then closets himself in a hotel room for several days to pray and fast, with his wife in an adjoining room looking after his needs.

It usually takes the first two or three days to allow the Holy Spirit to cleanse him, to help him disassociate himself, and to identify with Jesus. He feels he "leaves the world" and is in another realm where the spiritual warfare takes place. The attacks of the enemy at times become fierce. He has even seen some spirits in physical form. His objective is to learn their names and break their power over the city. It usually takes five to eight days, but sometimes more. Once he spent 45 days in conflict. But when he finishes, people in his meetings frequently are saved and healed even before he preaches or prays for them.[1]

At some point while he is resisting the spirits in prayer, the Lord shows him that the enemy's power has been broken. When this happens, Cabrera emerges from his prayer and fasting to announce that the time has come to begin the preaching services.

This approach has resulted in thousands coming to Christ in every meeting. Cabrera incorporates them into his Vision of the Future Church, a decentralized church that is more like a denomination, now numbering over sixty-five thousand members and meeting in more than fifty locations.

CARLOS ANNACONDIA

In 1983, several years after Cabrera had started using his approach, a lay evangelist named Carlos Annacondia was invited by veteran pastor Alberto Scataglini to the city of La Plata to hold a crusade. The church was prepared for about two hundred new converts, which would have meant a 50 percent increase. The response was such, however, that Annacondia continued to boldly preach the Word together with heavy reliance on spiritual warfare for three months, after which over forty thousand had made public professions of faith. This was beyond imagination! In fact, most people did not believe the figures at first.

After La Plata, Annacondia held a campaign in Mar del Plata that saw close to ninety thousand public decisions. From there he moved to San Justo, where seventy thousand decisions were recorded. City after city was shaken to its spiritual foundations by his aggressive preaching and spiritual warfare. Even the intellectual capital of Argentina, Cordoba, where many predicted he would fail, saw more than fifty thousand decisions recorded.

Annacondia's approach combines familiar methods such as interceding fervently before the meetings start and preaching the Word enthusiastically during the meetings with several unique features. Since he sees the context of his preaching to be the warfare between the kingdoms, Annacondia begins his work in a city by teaching the pastors how to engage in warfare prayer. "The night before the beginning of a crusade, all workers participate in a prayer meeting so intense that it reminds one of Joshua and the people marching around Jericho."[2] His public approach, then, focuses on four "times" of prayer.

> First he preaches to the unsaved and ends with a rich time of prayer for and with the new converts. People go away with the certainty that they have spoken to God. After a musical break comes a time of spiritual warfare prayer in which Carlos prays for those who are demonized. As he leads in prayer, hundreds, sometimes up to one thousand, fall to the ground under demonic oppression. They are carried by co-workers to a huge tent behind his platform—called "The Intensive Care Unit"—where they are ministered to in prayer for several hours until deliverance comes. After another break, he prays for the sick. Finally, he prays for everybody who wants to be filled with the Holy Spirit by laying hands on them. I have estimated that of the two hours that Annacondia spends on the platform ministering, over one hour is actually spent in prayer. In addition, under the platform he has a "prayer brigade" of approximately fifty people who, for the duration of the meeting (sometimes up to five hours), are in prayer.[3]

In addition to the emphasis on warfare prayer, during the meetings Annacondia from time to time openly challenges the territorial spirits. His aim is to break their power to interfere in the understanding and receiving of the message he seeks to deliver.

These methods have found their way into the local church with great success. The Pentecostal and charismatic churches have adopted them almost unchanged. And even the more conservative churches have done so in varying degrees. But one element is common to all: they are at war with a common enemy, Satan, and against him they come with divinely powerful weapons.

One result has been the emerging of large congregations. In addition, many cities have come under the spiritual authority of Jesus Christ as interdenominational ministerial associations have been formed. These associations have provided a vehicle for the Holy Spirit to move freely in cities.

ANALYZING THE FACTORS

As we would expect, there are a number of factors contributing to the incredible work God is doing in Argentina today. Many of them will be obvious from what has already been said. Some have not yet been mentioned. I have found four factors to be prominent in the above-described approach. We have tried to facilitate the preponderance factors in our attempts to bring cities to Christ.

1. Unity. Usually a spiritual unity begins in a context of functional unity, where joined activities allow previously unconnected parties to work together in a forum that permits them to gradually know and trust each other better.

At the very inception of God's visitation in Argentina, two key organizations emerged that have provided a context for functional unity. One is ACIERA, the national association of evangelical churches that brings together a prominent section of the Bible-believing churches. The other is CEP, the national Pentecostal evangelical fellowship.

In the early 1980s, *The 700 Club* also provided a channel for functional unity by opening offices in key cities and connecting the fruits of its programs to local churches. In many towns, the offices of *The 700 Club* became the forerunners of the ministerial associations.

Today in many major cities there is an interdenominational ministerial association that promotes unity. Trying to explain the reason for such precious unity, one of the pastors has said: "When the harvest is plentiful, it grows taller than the fences. And then it is impossible to know where one lot begins and the other ends. The harvest points to the Lord of the Harvest. He owns the fields."

2. Bridges. The atmosphere of unity has enabled programs and events that build bridges between denominations to take place. Perhaps the most visible one is the interdenominational newspaper *El Puente*. This paper has provided, since early 1985, a forum in which people from different backgrounds can meet, learn about each other, and then return to where they came from with a more global perspective. In recent years, similar publications have appeared, strengthening interdenominational communications.

Another unifying force in the late seventies and early eighties was M.E.I. (*Misión Evangélica Iberoamericana*). Founded by a group of young people, this agency organized key interdenominational pastors' retreats. These retreats provided a foundation for other activities to build on, such as the C.G.I. congress with Dr. David Yonggi Cho, organized by our own organization, Harvest Evangelism, in 1987. That conference saw seventy-five hundred pastors and leaders from all over gather together in Buenos Aires.

Still another significant organization is *Misiones Mundiales*, Argentina's leading national missionary agency. Under the leadership of Federico Bertuzzi it is beginning to mobilize the Argentine church to send missionaries overseas.

3. Soil preparation. Very important to the whole movement is the fact that the *soil has been prepared by the Holy Spirit.* Argentines are a very proud people. Pride is the great stumbling block as far as receiving the gospel is concerned. God dealt Argentina some severe blows as he prepared the soil for this visitation of the Holy Spirit. He did this through the shattering of three false hopes: political, economic, and military. First the political hope disappeared when Juan Perón—a very popular leader—died in 1973, and his third wife, Isabel Perón, at the time the nation's vice-president, was unable to fulfill his promises, promises that at that time had captivated the vast majority of the people. Then the economic hope was shattered when the military dictatorship that deposed Mrs. Perón experimented with the economy and, through mismanagement and corruption, created an unbearable external debt. And finally, military hope was lost when the same dictators, in order to divert attention from the economic mess they had created, invaded the Falkland Islands ("Las Malvinas" for the Argentines) and were defeated by the British forces. It was at this point that a great segment of the population, tired of the past, opened themselves to something new.

4. Spiritual warfare. It is at this juncture that God raised people like Carlos Annacondia, Alberto Scataglini, Eduardo Lorenzo, Omar Cellier, Norberto Carlini, and many others to bring to the forefront the dimensions of spiritual warfare. Omar Cabrera, who had been quietly practicing spiritual warfare, was slowly brought into the mainstream of the church. Little by little, using the authority delegated to them by the Lord Jesus himself, the church began to challenge the principalities and powers over Argentina. As the strong man was bound, his captives were set free. As the churches grew in their understanding of spiritual warfare, one aspect that became clear was that of territorial powers.

In March of 1984 a group of pastors and leaders from the

San Nicolas/Rosario area gathered at Harvest Evangelism's Retreat Center in Villa Constitución. Spiritual warfare was the subject. The gathering was prompted by the realization that close to 109 towns within 100 miles of the Training Center had no Christian witness. Preliminary studies had singled out the town of Arroyo Seco as what appeared to be the "seat of Satan" for that region. Years before, a well-known warlock by the name of Mr. Meregildo operated out of that town. He was so famous and his cures so dramatic that people from overseas would trek to Arroyo Seco. Before dying, he passed on his powers to twelve disciples. Twice a church was established in Arroyo Seco and twice it closed down in the face of severe spiritual opposition.

After several days of Bible study and prayer, the pastors and leaders came together in one accord and placed the entire area under spiritual authority. A few of them traveled to Arroyo Seco. Positioning themselves across the street from the head-quarters of Mr. Meregildo's followers, they served an eviction notice on the forces of evil. They announced to them that they were defeated and that Jesus Christ would attract many to himself now that the church was united and pledged to proclaim him.

Less than three years later, eighty-two of those towns had evangelical churches in them. An unverified report indicated that as of this writing (1994), all of them, including Arroyo Seco, may have a church or at least a Christian witness.

Another case in point is the city of Adrogué. Pastor Eduardo Lorenzo is the leader of the Baptist church, until recently the only church, in this progressive, upper-middle-class suburb of Buenos Aires. Lorenzo noticed that very few members of his congregation were actually from Adrogué. The majority came from other towns. At first they reasoned this away by seeing themselves as prophets without honor in their own homeland. Then, in 1985, the church sponsored a spiritual warfare seminar led by Dr. Ed Murphy. Shortly after that, Dr. John White visited the church and taught on the same subject. Not long after that, a new convert created a big disorder in one of the meetings as demons manifested themselves through her. As Lorenzo ministered to her over a period of several months, it was revealed that this particular woman was under the direct influence of the chief prince in charge of the darkness around Adrogué. As Lorenzo exercised spiritual authority, this prince revealed his current war plans and how successfully he had kept Adrogué under his spell. Lorenzo immediately began to teach spiritual warfare to the church and led them in a week-long prayer with fasting. On Friday of that week, the church came together and took authority over the chief demon. They immediately felt something break in the spiritual realm. In the course of a later confrontation, Lorenzo reports, the demonic prince himself confessed that he was no longer free to operate. From that time on, 40 percent of all new converts came from Adrogué. The church has grown to 950 members from an initial membership of 200. Now there is another evangelical church in town, and an ever-increasing number of businessmen and influential people are coming to Christ. The center of power has switched to the church as a result of applying spiritual warfare principles.

The challenging and binding of these territorial powers is at the heart of what is going on in Argentina today. Whether it is Omar Cabrera fasting and fighting prior to opening up a new city, or Guillermo Prein establishing a dynamic congregation where through the years others had failed before, or Hector Giménez taking for Christ the Buenos Aires downtown area, where he pastors a church of over 100,000 members, the pattern is the same: territorial powers are identified, then challenged, and eventually defeated as thousands of captives turn from the dominion of Satan to God.

PLAN RESISTENCIA

It is in this context that the Plan Resistencia was shaped. Plan Resistencia represents a unique attempt to evangelize an entire city. In the early church we see cities as the focal points of evangelism. The Great Commission begins with a city, Jerusalem (Acts 1:8), and all through the New Testament we see a catalogue of cities being totally evangelized: Samaria, Antioch, Ephesus. So much so that in Acts 19:10 we are told that "all who lived in Asia (Minor) heard the word of the Lord, both Jews and gentiles". The area referred to here encompasses scores of metropolises, many of which had populations in the hundreds of thousands. According to Acts 19:10 *everyone* in those metropolises heard the word of the Lord.

Plan Resistencia was an attempt to rediscover the dynamics of such an accomplishment. A thorough search of the Scriptures revealed the following principles as central to the Holy Spirit's strategy in the New Testament: the unity of the church, compassion for the lost, a commitment to reaching the lost now, and prayer as a key ingredient of the evangelistic strategy. With these principles in mind, some pastors in Resistencia set out to reach their city for Christ through a strategy involving, initially, a three-year plan worked out in cooperation with Harvest Evangelism.

Resistencia is a key city in northeastern Argentina, with a population of almost 400,000 people. In 1989 there were approximately fifty-three hundred believers scattered in seventy congregations. It was reported that sixty-eight of those seventy congregations were the result of splits. The city was heavily influenced by the cult of San La Muerte (Spanish for St. Death). San La Muerte is a demonic creature similar to the goddess Artemis in Acts 19. Like Ephesus, Resistencia's daily life, government, and trade were greatly shaped by this demonic cult.

Our team was invited by a small group of pastors who had been working together for some time. They were initially brought together by relief work on behalf of the thousands affected by a devastating flood. Since then they have continued to fellowship and to carry out some projects together. As they cooperated on such projects, they began to discuss the possibility of a joint effort to reach their city and invited us to help them develop a strategy.

The first issue to deal with was unity. With so many of the churches of Resistencia having been born out of splits, it seemed unlikely that the city's churches could be brought together for any purpose. According to Jesus' prayer in John 17:21, unity is a central concern of God.

With their eyes focused on planning a city-wide evangelistic effort, the original small group of pastors began to meet regularly for prayer. At one of these meetings one of the pastors suddenly turned to another and said, "I sense before the Lord that I must tell you that I love you as a brother and fellow servant. I have sinned in never telling you that, even though we have both been in the city for many years. Please forgive me." He was at once in tears, kneeling before that pastor. One repentant act led to another, and soon the men were washing each other's feet. Then someone suggested that they partake of the Lord's Supper together, something seldom done outside of the local church, and hardly ever among pastors from different denominations. The whole experience climaxed to the point that the men even took an offering for one among them who was going through severe economic strain. The presence of the Lord fell upon that "upper room" that day. The stronghold of disunity was dealt a severe blow. From that point on, the congregations met in united meetings on several occasions, and it was not uncommon for the Lord's Table to be observed as a part of a "liturgy of unity."

Another major stronghold was apathy toward the fulfillment of the Great Commission in Resistencia. The church was so small and so weak that many people had simply given up on it. In the pastors' discussions, however, God drew their attention to 2 Peter 3:9 to drive home the biblical truth that he wishes none to perish but all to come to repentance. From that point on, this truth was discussed, preached, shared in small meetings, shared in large meetings, voiced continually in prayer, promoted over radio and television, and, in fact, by all means available until the stronghold of apathy was shattered. The clearest indication that the apathy was shattered was when the believers began to refer to the unsaved as "people who have not heard the gospel *yet*." In that word *yet* there was embryonic faith. The believers were beginning to demonstrate a change in their thinking from hopelessness to the confidence that "it is only a matter of time before the entire population hears the gospel." They had become very much like an expectant mother in the early months of pregnancy—though as yet unable to see the "baby," they knew it was surely coming.

However, there was still one more major obstacle to overcome—the stronghold of ignorance. And this was the most difficult to identify and deal with. As in many parts of the world, the churches in Resistencia suffered from ignorance regarding some of Satan's most sophisticated schemes—the devices he was using against their churches. Though Paul could assert that he was "not ignorant of [Satan's] schemes" (2 Cor 2:11), the enemy had been able to keep the church in Resistencia captive without their understanding either that he was doing this or how he was doing it.

Light was shed on this subject when Peter and Doris Wagner and later Cindy Jacobs were invited to conduct training sessions for the pastors on spiritual warfare. It was not difficult for the pastors to understand the material being taught once the parallels were pointed out between Resistencia's spiritual climate and that of Ephesus in the Book of Acts (Acts 19). Spiritual mapping was also introduced. This is a strategy, similar to that engaged in by the spies sent by Joshua into the Promised Land (Nm 13; Dt 1:19-45), in which, following the guidance of the Holy Spirit, the enemy's strongholds and those characteristics of the city usable by God are identified and mapped.[4] By this means, Victor Lorenzo, one of our team members, was able to discover the influence of Satan on the city through the cult of San La Muerte.

Among other things, Victor was able to identify three

murals in Resistencia's main plaza honoring San La Muerte and two other major principalities. These murals were there ostensibly to present a historic perspective on the city since its founding. This they did. But they also apparently established in the spiritual realm the rights of these principalities to their domination of the city. In retrospect, it seems incredible that prior to the introduction of spiritual warfare and spiritual mapping, no one had identified those murals for what they were: a pictorial guide to Satan's schemes against the city and the church!

Pastors, leaders, and intercessors—the spiritual authorities in the city—were trained in how to deal with the situation in a seminar led by Cindy Jacobs and Doris Wagner. During the seminar, then, an invitation was extended to as many of these leaders as would agree to risk it to convene on Sunday morning at the main plaza to declare the Lordship of Jesus over the city and to take a firm stand against the satanic deputies over the city. A group of about forty-five people showed up to do just that. For several hours they did battle, relying on praise and warfare prayer against San La Muerte and the other powers, until all of a sudden they felt a spiritual breakthrough and knew that victory had been obtained. They then closed the meeting with praise and worship to God.

Prior to the seminar the pastors had motivated, trained, and mobilized the believers to establish places of prayer in homes all over the city. Six hundred thirty-five of these, called "Lighthouses," were established in an equal number of neighborhoods in a fashion similar to the one outlined by Paul in 1 Timothy 2:1-8. Each one of these homes displayed a large sign in one of the front windows reading, "Resistencia, it is God's time for you," and, next to it, "This is a Lighthouse of prayer." Believers began to pray for their neighbors, at first in private. Later on, they approached the neighbors to ask for their prayer requests. God surprised everyone by answering many of those requests immediately. This created a series of "spiritual IOUs" all over the city. Many unbelievers asked:

"What must I do now that God has answered my request?" They were told, "Wait until we tell you." All of this was building up to a day in July of 1990 when the entire city was visited door-to-door. Every home in Resistencia received a package of good news and prayers were offered on behalf of the needs of the people. In addition, everyone was invited to a public service that night, especially unbelievers whose prayer requests had been answered. So many people showed up at the basketball stadium that a large multitude had to be turned away. It seemed that the plan's theme, "Resistencia, it's God's time for you," had been embraced by the entire city.

This was followed by three evangelistic waves. The first consisted simply of twenty lighthouses joining forces to sponsor a neighborhood crusade. Buoyed by the success of that venture, first thirty-four and later ten more simultaneous crusades were conducted all over town with the Lighthouses feeding the people. The third and climaxing wave was a citywide crusade where thousands made public decisions for Christ.

When this evangelistic phase was over, the pastors decided to apply a direct blow to the disunity and mistrust that had characterized their relations in the past. Rather than baptizing the new converts in the privacy of their churches, they decided to have a public united baptism. They rented a covered stadium and placed eight portable swimming pools on the playing field. The swimming pools were arranged in the form of a cross. Those who were already members of the churches sat on the bleachers, while the new converts stood by the portable swimming pools next to the pastors of Resistencia. At the appropriate time, the chairman of the ministerial association led the new converts in a prayer of allegiance to Jesus Christ. Following that, the new converts entered the portable swimming pools to be baptized by the pastors into the only church in town, the Church of Jesus Christ in Resistencia.

A few months later, a census of the church was taken. It was established that the church in Resistencia had grown 102 percent. This is a phenomenal rate of growth for a church that was spiritually anemic. The entire population heard the gospel at least once. Every home was prayed for and visited with a gospel message. The strongholds of disunity, apathy, and especially spiritual ignorance had suffered severe damage. All of this, then, has resulted in a radical change in the spiritual atmosphere of the city. Today (1994), three years after these intensive "warfare evangelism" activities, the church continues to struggle with the forces of evil. But now, rather than attacking them at a surface level, the balance of power seems to have changed in the heavenlies over the city. Unconfirmed reports put the growth of the church two years after the end of "Plan Resistencia" (1993) at approximately 500 percent. Even though this has not been confirmed yet, if only one-fourth of it is correct, Resistencia will stand out as a superb example of modern city-reaching through warfare evangelism.

ANALYSIS OF PLAN RESISTENCIA

A number of key elements contributed to all of this. Much of what went on involved the employment of time-tested evangelistic methodology. However, one element entirely new to evangelistic methodology was the introduction of spiritual warfare as the context in which those methods were implemented. The training sessions in spiritual warfare, culminating in the raid on the principalities in the city's main plaza, were key elements in the breaking of the enemy's grip on the people of Resistencia. It appears that by the time the witnessing phase of the three-year plan was entered into, then, Satan's ability to blind the people had been dealt a severe blow.

It is interesting to note that close to two-thirds of the new converts came to the Lord even before the specifically evangelistic part of the outreach was started. Most of the conversions were the result of prayer evangelism emanating from the 635 Lighthouses of prayer. Personally, I believe that the awareness of how Satan had kept the city blinded to the gospel and the united response on the part of the pastors and intercessors, especially when they chose to resist San La Muerte and his forces of evil in the public plaza, played key roles in the outcome.

The challenge to San La Muerte and the other principalities after proper preparation was a tangible expression of at least the following. It involved:

1. A clear discernment of one of Satan's major schemes against the church in the city.
2. A positioning of the church in the city to resist the forces of evil keeping the people blinded to the gospel.
3. An intentional action on the part of the church to engage "all the forces of wickedness in the heavenly places" over the city.
4. A conscientious decision on the part of the church to resist those forces of evil beginning with engaging in intercessory prayer for all the saints and for those taking the gospel to the unsaved in the fashion described in Ephesians 6:18-20.
5. A decision to act boldly, to pray boldly, and to preach boldly in the context described by Paul to the church in Ephesus (Acts 6:18-20).

Even though these steps deal with the enemy, the focus of the church was not on the devil, but rather on the Lord Jesus, his Word, the ministry of the Holy Spirit, and the fulfillment of the Great Commission in the context of spiritual warfare. It is in this context that the church was able to expose the enemy and defeat him, to paraphrase Revelation 12:11, through the blood of the Lamb, a more biblically centered testimony, and a total commitment at the expense of their own lives.

STILL LEARNING

"Plan Resistencia," our first concentrated attempt at this kind of evangelism, will probably not go down in history as the best example of this approach. We have been learning additional lessons as we apply these insights in other cities. And these lessons will undoubtedly contribute to smoother and more effective city-reaching in the future. But the Resistencia story will serve as a good example of what God can do when we approach a city through warfare evangelism, based on the insights God has been bringing to us through such pioneers as Cabrera and Annacondia. What we have seen in Resistencia is that for probably the first time in modern history, the Christians of a sizable city were empowered by God to do both the spiritual warfare and the evangelism necessary to enormously impact that city for God. The success of that venture provides us with a usable prototype to be imitated and improved upon by other Christians in other cities who want to see the Holy Spirit work effectively in their contexts on a citywide basis.

We at Harvest Evangelism are now employing the principles embodied in Plan Resistencia in several cities on three continents. As those strategies are carried out, the principles are being refined and our insights sharpened. What is already clear, though, is that the wedding of spiritual principles on the human level with discernment of what goes on at the cosmic level is taking us into a new era in evangelistic outreach. At the human level, it is clear that such factors as unity, repentance, and aggressive prayer and evangelism need to be present. On the cosmic level, the breaking of satanic bondage through strongholds held by territorial spirits is crucial. Dealing with ignorance and apathy on the part of God's people will figure importantly in whatever strategies are proposed. May this chapter and this volume be used by God to increase the understanding and dedication that warfare evangelism requires.

Notes

TWO
Spiritual Power: Principles and Observations

1. C. Peter Wagner, ed., *Engaging the Enemy* (Ventura, Calif.: Regal, 1991), 47-48.
2. Wagner, 31-32.

THREE
Spiritual Warfare Pitfalls

1. I call this reality the spiritual warfare dimensions of a biblical worldview (see Ed Murphy, *The Handbook for Spiritual Warfare*, and *Spiritual Warfare* tape series and syllabus).
2. For an exhaustive study of this multidimensional sin war and a beginning definitive textbook on spiritual warfare see Ed Murphy, *The Handbook for Spiritual Warfare* (Nashville: Thomas Nelson, 1993).
3. See "Demonization and Mental Health Issues" in Murphy, 476-98.

FOUR
Dealing with Demonization

1. C. Fred Dickason, *Demon Possession and the Christian* (Chicago: Moody, 1987), 175.
2. Mark Bubeck, *The Adversary* (Chicago: Moody, 1975); Kurt Koch and Alfred Lechler, *Occult Bondage and Deliverance* (Grand Rapids, Mich.: Kregel, 1978); Ed Murphy, *Handbook of Spiritual Warfare* (Nashville: Nelson, 1992); Merrill Unger, *What Demons Can Do to Saints* (Chicago: Moody, 1977); Tom White, *The Believer's Guide to Spiritual Warfare* (Ann Arbor, Mich.: Servant, 1990).
3. Dickason, 175-76.
4. Unger, 51-52.

5. Rita Cabezas, *Des Enmascarado* (published privately in Costa Rica, reference here taken from unpublished English translation, 1988).
6. See *Deep Wounds, Deep Healing,* by Charles H. Kraft (Ann Arbor, Mich.: Servant, 1993).

FIVE
Twenty-One Questions

1. Everett Rogers, *Diffusion of Innovations* (New York: Free Press, 1983). I have adapted Rogers' terms slightly so that his Early Majority and Late Majority have become my Middle Adopters and Late Adopters.
2. Francis Frangipane, "Our Authority in Christ," *Charisma,* July 1993, 40.
3. Tom White, *Breaking Strongholds* (Ann Arbor, Mich.: Servant, 1993), 156.
4. Wayne Grudem, "Miracles Today," *The Kingdom, The Power and the Glory,* Gary Greig and Kevin Springer, eds. (Ventura, Calif.: Regal, 1993), 77.
5. John Dawson, *Taking Our Cities for God* (Lake Mary, Fla.: Creation, 1989), 137.
6. Grudem, 75.
7. Grudem, 75-76.
8. White, *The Believer's Guide to Spiritual Warfare,* 34.
9. Walter Wink, *Naming the Powers* (Philadelphia: Fortress, 1984), 9-10.
10. C. Peter Wagner, *Warfare Prayer* (Ventura, Calif.: Regal, 1992), 32.
11. Dawson, 19.
12. Clinton E. Arnold, *Powers of Darkness* (Downers Grove, Ill.: InterVarsity Press, 1992), 158.
13. See Ramsay MacMullen, *Christianizing the Roman Empire, A.D. 100-400* (New Haven, Conn.: Yale University Press, 1984), 26.
14. Paul Reid, *A New Easter Rising* (Leigh Lanes, Northern Ireland: Logikos, 1993), 60.

SIX
A Biblical Perspective

1. J.A. MacMillan, "The Authority of the Believer," reprinted from an issue of *The Alliance Weekly,* date unknown.

SEVEN
How Satan Works at the Cosmic Level

1. F.F. Bruce, *The Epistle to the Hebrews* (Grand Rapids, Mich.: Eerdmans, 1964), 32-33.
2. Walter Wink, *Unmasking the Powers* (Philadelphia: Fortress, 1986), 90-91.

3.Wink, *Unmasking the Powers,* 50-52.

4. Hendrik Berkhof, *Christ and the Powers* (Scotsdale, Pa.: Herald, 1977), 63.

5. *Zondervan Pictorial Encyclopedia* (Grand Rapids, Mich.: Zondervan, 1975), vol. 1, 431-32.

6. Berkhof, 14-16.

7. F.F. Bruce, *Commentary on the Epistle to the Colossians* (Grand Rapids, Mich.: Eerdmans, 1965), 198.

8. See Wink, *Naming the Powers* for an extensive analysis of these terms.

9. Heinrich Schlier, *Principalities and Powers in the New Testament* (New York: Herder & Herder, 1962), 14-15.

10. Rob Van der Hart, *The Theology of Angels and Devils* (Notre Dame: Fides, 1972), 87.

11. Dawson, 79.

12. Wink, *Unmasking the Powers,* 54.

13. Wink, *Naming the Powers,* 54.

14. McCandlish Phillips, *The Spirit World* (Wheaton, Ill.: Victor, 1970), 21-24.

15. Richmond Chiundiza, "High-Level Powers in Zimbabwe," in Wagner, *Engaging the Enemy,* 123.

16. Francis Frangipane, *The Three Battlegrounds* (Marion, Ill.: River of Life Ministries, 1989), 21.

17. From unpublished notes of Cindy Jacobs sent to the author in November 1990.

18. Philip Steyne, *Gods of Power* (Houston: Touch, 1989), 17, 46.

19. C. Peter Wagner, "Territorial Spirits," in C. Peter Wagner and F. Douglas Pennoyer, eds., *Wrestling with Dark Angels* (Ventura, Calif.: Regal, 1990), 76.

20. Phillips, 27.

21. Wagner, *Warfare Prayer,* 79.

22. Dianne Core, "We Are in the Middle of Spiritual Warfare," *The New Federalist,* October 1989, 15.

23. From a workshop on occult crime put on by the Ontario, California, Police Department in 1990.

24. From unpublished notes sent to the author by Hector Torres in November 1990.

25. Robert H. Glover, *The Bible Basis of Missions* (Chicago: Moody, 1946), 180.

26. Jonothan Goforth, *By My Spirit* (New York: Harper & Brothers, 1930), 184-85.

27. Glover, 181.

28. Paul Yonggi Cho, "City Taking in Korea" in Wagner, *Engaging the Enemy,* 117-18.

29. Berkhof, 47.

30. From an oral presentation by Dick Eastman to the Spiritual Warfare Network consultation in 1991 and to be mentioned in his upcoming book, *The Jericho Hour,* to be published in 1994.

31. B.J. Willhite, "Dangers and Pitfalls of Spiritual Warfare," an unpublished paper for the Spiritual Warfare Network consultation, November 30, 1990, 4-5.

32. Willhite, 5.
33. Berkhof, 39, 43.
34. Chiundiza, 126.
35. Schlier, 61-62.
36. Wink, *Unmasking the Powers,* 64-65.
37. C.S. Lewis, *The Lion, the Witch, and the Wardrobe* (New York: Collier, 1950).

EIGHT
Advancing God's Kingdom

1. Jesse Penn-Lewis, *War on the Saints* (New York: Thomas E. Lowe, 1987), appendix.
2. Frank Boshold, *Blumhardt's Battle: A Conflict with Satan* (New York: Thomas E. Lowe, 1970), 7.
3. Charles Finney, *Charles G. Finney, An Autobiography* (Old Tappan, N.J.: Revell, 1908), 141.
4. Finney, 99.
5. Norman Grubb, *Rees Howells, Intercessor* (Ft. Washington, Pa.: Christian Literature Crusade, 1970), 246.
6. Grubb, 250.
7. Grubb, 252.

ELEVEN
Argentina—Evangelizing in a Context of Spiritual Warfare

1. Wagner, *Engaging the Enemy*, 45.
2. Edgardo Silvoso, his chapter in Wagner's *Engaging the Enemy*, 114.
3. Silvoso in Wagner, *Engaging the Enemy*, 112.
4. See C. Peter Wagner, *Breaking Strongholds in Your City* (Ventura, Calif.: Regal, 1993).

Bibliography

Anderson. Neil. *The Bondage Breaker*. Eugene, Ore.: Harvest House, 1990.

Anderson. Neil. *Victory Over the Darkness*. Ventura, Calif: Regal, 1990.

Arnold, Clinton E. *Ephesians: Power and Magic*. Cambridge: Cambridge Univ., 1989.

Arnold, Clinton E. *Powers of Darkness: Principalities and Powers in Paul's Letters*. Downers Grove, Ill.: InterVarsity Press, 1992.

Basham, Don. *Can a Christian Have a Demon?* Monroeville, Pa.: Whitaker, 1971.

Basham, Don. *Deliver Us from Evil*. Old Tappan, N.J.: Revell, 1972.

Berkhof, Hendrik. *Christ and the Powers*. Scotsdale, Pa.: Herald, 1977.

Bernal, Dick. *Curses*. Shippensburg, Pa.: Companion, 1991.

Birch, George A. *The Deliverance Ministry*. Cathedral City, Calif.: Horizon, 1988.

Blue, Ken. *Authority to Heal*. Downers Grove, Ill.: InterVarsity Press, 1987.

Boshold, Frank. *Blumhardt's Battle: A Conflict with Satan*. New York: Thomas E. Lowe, 1970.

Bridge, Donald. *Signs and Wonders Today*. Downers Grove, Ill.: InterVarsity Press, 1985.

Bruce, F.F. *Commentary on the Epistle to the Colossians*. Grand Rapids, Mich.: Eerdmans, 1965.

Bruce, F.F. *The Epistle to the Hebrews*. Grand Rapids, Mich.: Eerdmans, 1964.

Bubeck, Mark. *The Adversary*. Chicago: Moody, 1975.

Bubeck, Mark. *Overcoming the Adversary*. Chicago: Moody, 1984.

Bubeck, Mark. *The Satanic Revival*. San Bernardino, Calif.: Here's Life, 1991.

Cabezas, Rita. *Des Enmascarado*. Published privately in Costa Rica. Reference here taken from unpublished English translation.

Caird, G.B. *Principalities and Powers*. Oxford: Clarendon, 1956.

Carty, Jay. *Counterattack*. Portland, Ore.: Multnomah, 1988.

Chandler, Russell. *Understanding the New Age*. Dallas: Word, 1988.

Christensen, Evelyn. *Battling the Prince of Darkness*. Ventura, Calif.: Victor, 1990.

Core, Dianne. "We Are in the Middle of Spiritual Warfare," *The New Federalist* October (1989): 15.

Dawson, John. *Healing America's Wounds.* Ventura, Calif.: Regal, 1994.

Dawson, John. *Taking Our Cities for God.* Lake Mary, Fla.: Creation House, 1990.

Deere, Jack. *Surprised by the Power of the Spirit.* Grand Rapids, Mich.: Zondervan, 1993.

Dickason, C. Fred. *Demon Possession and the Christian.* Chicago: Moody, 1987.

Duewel, Wesley. *Mighty Prevailing Prayer.* Grand Rapids, Mich.: Francis Asbury Press, 1990.

Finney, Charles. *Charles G. Finney, An Autobiography.* Old Tappan, N.J.: Revell, 1908.

Frangipane, Francis. *The House of the Lord.* Lake Mary, Fla.: Creation House, 1991.

Frangipane, Francis. *The Three Battlegrounds.* Marion, Ill.: River of Life Ministries, 1989.

Friesen, James. *Uncovering the Mystery of MPD.* San Bernardino, Calif.: Here's Life, 1991.

Garrett, Susan R. *The Demise of the Devil.* Minneapolis: Fortress, 1989.

Garrison, Mary. *How to Conduct Spiritual Warfare.* Hudson, Fla.: Box 3066, 1980.

Gibson, Noel and Phyl. *Evicting Demonic Squatters and Breaking Bondages.* Drummoyne, NSW, Australia: Freedom in Christ Ministries, 1987.

Glover, Robert H. *The Bible Basis of Missions.* Chicago: Moody, 1946.

Goforth, Jonathan. *By My Spirit.* New York: Harper & Brothers, 1930.

Good News Bible: The Bible in Today's English Version. Nashville: Nelson, 1976.

Goodman, Felicitas D. *How About Demons?* Bloomington, Ind.: Indiana Univ., 1988.

Green, Michael. *I Believe in Satan's Downfall.* Grand Rapids, Mich.: Eerdmans, 1981.

Greenwald, Gary L. *Seductions Exposed.* Santa Ana, Calif.: Eagle's Nest, 1988.

Grieg, Gary S. and Kevin N. Springer, eds. *The Kingdom and the Power.* Ventura, Calif.: Regal, 1993.

Groothuis, Douglas R. *Confronting the New Age Movement.* Downers Grove, Ill.: InterVarsity Press, 1988.

Groothuis, Douglas R. *Unmasking the New Age.* Downers Grove, Ill.: InterVarsity Press, 1986.

Grubb, Norman. *Rees Howells, Intercessor.* Ft. Washington, Pa.: Christian Literature Crusade, 1970.

Hammond, Frank and Ida Mae. *Demons & Deliverance in the Ministry of Jesus.* Plainview, Tex.: The Children's Bread Ministries, 1991.

Hammond, Frank and Ida Mae. *Pigs in the Parlor*. Kirkwood, Mo.: Impact, 1973.

Harper, Michael. *Spiritual Warfare*. Ann Arbor: Servant, 1984.

Kallas, James. *Jesus and the Power of Satan*. Philadelphia: Westminster, 1968.

Kallas, James. *The Satanward View*. Philadelphia: Westminster, 1966.

Kinnaman, Gary D. *Overcoming the Dominion of Darkness*. Old Tappan, N.J.: Revell, 1990.

Kinsley, David. *Hindu Goddesses: Visions of the Divine Feminine in the Hindu Religious Tradition*. Berkeley: Univ. of California Press, 1986.

Koch, Kurt. *Between Christ and Satan*. Grand Rapids, Mich.: Kregel, 1962, 1971.

Koch, Kurt. *Demonology Past and Present*. Grand Rapids, Mich.: Kregel, 1973.

Koch, Kurt. *Occult ABC*. Grand Rapids, Mich.: Kregel, 1986.

Koch, Kurt and Alfred Lechler. *Occult Bondage and Deliverance*. Grand Rapids, Mich.: Kregel, 1978.

Kraft, Charles H. *Christianity with Power*. Ann Arbor, Mich.: Servant, 1989.

Kraft, Charles H. *Deep Wounds, Deep Healing*. Ann Arbor: Servant, 1993.

Kraft, Charles H. *Defeating Dark Angels*. Ann Arbor: Servant, 1992.

Larson, Bob. *Satanism*. Nashville: Nelson, 1989.

Lewis, C.S. *The Lion, the Witch and the Wardrobe*. New York: Collier, 1950.

Linn, Dennis and Matthew Linn. *Deliverance Prayer*. New York: Paulist, 1981.

Linn, Dennis and Matthew Linn. *Healing Life's Hurts*. New York: Paulist, 1979.

MacMillan, J.A. "The Authority of the Believer," reprinted from an issue of *The Alliance Weekly*, date unknown.

MacMullen, Ramsay. *Christianizing the Roman Empire*. New Haven: Yale, 1984.

MacNutt, Francis. *Healing*. Notre Dame, Ind.: Ave Maria, 1974.

MacNutt, Francis and Judith. *Praying for Your Unborn Child*. New York: Doubleday, 1988.

McAll, Kenneth. *Healing the Family Tree*. London: Sheldon Press, 1982.

Mallone, George. *Arming for Spiritual Warfare*. Downers Grove, Ill.: InterVarsity Press, 1991.

Montgomery, John W., ed. *Demon Possession*. Minneapolis: Bethany, 1976.

Murphy, Ed. "From My Experience: My Daughter Demonized?" in *Equipping the Saints*. Vol. 4, No.1, Winter 1990, 27-29.

Murphy, Ed. *The Handbook of Spiritual Warfare*. Nashville: Nelson, 1992.

Murphy, Ed. *Spiritual Warfare* tape series and syllabus. Nashville: Nelson, 1991.

Murphy, Ed. *We Are at War.* Nashville: Nelson, 1992.

Nevius, John R. *Demon Possession.* Grand Rapids, Mich.: Kregel, 1894, 1968.

New International Version of the Holy Bible. Grand Rapids, Mich.: Zondervan, 1978.

New King James Bible. Nashville: Nelson, 1982.

Otis, George, Jr. *The Last of the Giants.* Tarrytown, N.Y.: Chosen, 1991.

Payne, Leanne. *The Healing Presence.* Westchester, Ill.: Crossway, 1989.

Peck, M. Scott. *People of the Lie.* New York: Simon & Schuster, 1983.

Penn-Lewis, Jesse. *War on the Saints.* New York: Thomas E. Lowe, 1973.

Peretti, Frank. *Piercing the Darkness.* Westchester, Ill.: Crossway, 1989.

Peretti, Frank. *This Present Darkness.* Westchester, Ill.: Crossway, 1986.

Phillips, McCandlish. *The Spirit World.* Wheaton, Ill.: Victor, 1970.

Powell, Graham and Shirley. *Christian Set Yourself Free.* Westbridge, S.C.: Center Mountain Ministries, 1983.

Pullinger, Jackie. *Chasing the Dragon.* Ann Arbor, Mich.: Servant, 1980.

Pullinger, Jackie. *Crack in the Wall.* London: Hodder and Stoughton, 1989.

Reddin, Opal, ed. *Power Encounter.* Springfield, Mo.: Central Bible College, 1989.

Rockstad, Ernest. *Demon Activity and the Christian.* Andover, Kans.: Faith & Life, n.d.

Rockstad, Ernest. *Triumph in the Demons Crisis.* Cassette series. Andover, Kans.: Faith & Life, 1976.

Sandford, John and Mark Sandford. *A Comprehensive Guide to Deliverance and Inner Healing.* Grand Rapids, Mich.: Chosen, 1992.

Sandford, John and Paula. *Healing the Wounded Spirit.* Tulsa: Victory, 1985.

Sandford, John and Paula. *The Transformation of the Inner Man.* South Plainfield, N.J.: Bridge, 1982.

Scanlan, Michael and Randall J. Cirner. *Deliverance from Evil Spirits.* Ann Arbor, Mich.: Servant, 1980.

Schlier, Heinrich. *Principalities and Powers in the New Testament.* Freiburg: Herder, 1961.

Schoenberger, Carl. "Akihito and Final Ritual of Passage." *Los Angeles Times,* November 23, 1990, Vol. 109, A4.

Seamands, David. *Healing for Damaged Emotions.* Wheaton, Ill.: Victor, 1981.

Seamands, David. *Healing Grace.* Wheaton: Victor, 1988.

Seamands, David. *Healing of Memories.* Wheaton: Victor, 1985.

Seamands, David. *Putting Away Childish Things.* Wheaton, Ill.: Victor, 1982.

Shaw, James D. and Tom C. McKenney. *The Deadly Deception.* Lafayette, La.: Huntington, 1988.

Sherman, Dean. *Spiritual Warfare for Every Christian.* Seattle: Frontline, 1990.

Sherrer, Quin and Ruthanne Garlock. *A Woman's Guide to Spiritual Warfare.* Ann Arbor, Mich.: Servant, 1991.

Shuster, Marguerite. *Power, Pathology, Paradox.* Grand Rapids, Mich.: Zondervan, 1987.

Spiro, Melford. *Burmese Supernaturalism.* Philadelphia: Institute for the Study of Human Issues, 1978.

Springer, Kevin, ed. *Power Encounters among Christians in the Western World.* San Francisco: Harper, 1988.

Steyne, Philip. *Gods of Power.* Houston: Touch, 1989.

Subritzky, Bill. *Demons Defeated.* Chichester, England: Sovereign World, 1985.

Sumrall, Lester. *Demons: The Answer Book.* Nashville: Nelson, 1979.

Tambiah, S.J. *Buddhism and the Spirit Cults in Northeast Thailand.* New York: Cambridge Univ. Press, 1970.

Tenney, Merril C., ed. *Zondervan Pictorial Encyclopedia.* Grand Rapids, Mich.: Zondervan, 1975.

Unger, Merrill. *Biblical Demonology.* Chicago: Scripture Press, 1952.

Unger, Merrill. *Demons in the World Today.* Wheaton, Ill.: Tyndale, 1971.

Unger, Merrill. *What Demons Can Do to Saints.* Chicago: Moody, 1977.

Van der Hart, Rob. *The Theology of Angels and Devils.* Notre Dame: Fides, 1972.

Wagner, C. Peter. *Breaking Strongholds in Your City.* Ventura, Calif.: Regal, 1993.

Wagner, C. Peter. *Churches That Pray.* Ventura, Calif.: Regal, 1993.

Wagner, C. Peter.ed. *Engaging the Enemy.* Ventura, Calif: Regal, 1991.

Wagner, C. Peter. *How to Have a Healing Ministry in Any Church.* Ventura, Calif.: Regal, 1988.

Wagner, C. Peter. *Prayer Shield.* Ventura, Calif.: Regal, 1992.

Wagner, C. Peter. ed. *Territorial Spirits.* Chichester, England: Sovereign World, 1991.

Wagner, C. Peter. *The Third Wave of the Holy Spirit.* Ann Arbor, Mich.: Servant, 1988.

Wagner, C. Peter and F. Douglas Pennoyer, eds. *Wrestling with Dark Angels.* Ventura, Calif.: Regal, 1990.

Wagner, Elizabeth. *Tearing Down Strongholds: Prayer for Buddhists.* Kowloon Hong Kong: Christian Literature Crusade, 1988.

Warner, Timothy M. *Spiritual Warfare.* Wheaton, Ill.: Crossway, 1991.

White, John. *When the Spirit Comes in Power: Signs and Wonders among God's People.* Downers Grove, Ill.: InterVarsity Press, 1988.

White, Thomas B. *The Believer's Guide to Spiritual Warfare.* Ann Arbor, Mich.: Servant, 1990.

White, Thomas B. *Breaking Strongholds: How Spiritual Warfare Sets Captives Free.* Ann Arbor, Mich.: Servant, 1993.

Willhite, B.J. "Dangers and Pitfalls of Spiritual Warfare." Paper for Spiritual Warfare Network, 1990.

Williams, Don. *Signs and Wonders, and the Kingdom of God.* Ann Arbor, Mich.: Servant, 1989.

Wimber, John. *Power Evangelism.* Second revised and expanded edition. San Francisco: Harper, 1992.

Wimber, John. *Power Healing.* San Francisco: Harper & Row, 1987.

Wink, Walter. *Engaging the Powers.* Minneapolis: Fortress, 1992.

Wink, Walter. *Naming the Powers.* Philadelphia: Fortress, 1984.

Wink, Walter. *Unmasking the Powers.* Philadelphia: Fortress, 1986.

Index